My dearest Michelle,
Looking forward to
spending this exciting
year together.
    All my love,
      John xxxx

Gorky's Tolstoy and Other Reminiscences

Gorky's
Tolstoy
& Other
Reminiscences

Key Writings by and about
Maxim Gorky

Translated, Edited, and Introduced by
Donald Fanger

Yale University Press · New Haven & London

Published with assistance from the
Louis Stern Memorial Fund.

Printed in the United States of America.

Library of Congress Cataloging-in-Publication Data

Gorky, Maksim, 1868–1936.
Gorky's Tolstoy and other reminiscences : key writings by
and about Maxim Gorky / Maxim Gorky ; translated, edited,
and introduced by Donald Fanger.
p. cm.
Includes bibliographical references.
ISBN 978-0-300-11166-8 (cloth : alk. paper)
1. Gorky, Maksim, 1868–1936. 2. Authors, Russian—20th
century—Biography. 3. Tolstoy, Leo, graf, 1828–1910.
I. Fanger, Donald. II. Title.
PG3465.A3F36 2007
891.78'309—dc22   2007028887

A catalogue record for this book is available
from the British Library.

The paper in this book meets the guidelines for permanence
and durability of the Committee on Production Guidelines for
Book Longevity of the Council on Library Resources.

10 9 8 7 6 5 4 3 2 1

To D. G., H. B., S. F., and the rest—gratefully.

My thoughts and feelings will never arrive at a common denominator.
—*Gorky to F. D. Batiushkov (1898)*

Like a mouse in a trap, a man's thought thrashes about in search of freedom, in search of answers to the social and cosmic conundrums of existence, and both are equally demanding and important. One needs to have a very clear feeling of all the consistency—and at the same time of all the contradictions—of these thrashings-about of captive thought.

Whatever a person speaks about, he is teaching; the rejection of sermonizing and didacticism is also a kind of sermonizing and didacticism; those who most artfully conceal their didacticism are considered the best writers.

But behind everything that gets said there is something that remains unsaid, either from muteness of the soul, or from lack of strength to express the inexpressible, sometimes out of modesty (which must be called false), often out of pity for people, not infrequently out of contempt for them, and (much more seldom) out of a praiseworthy desire to hide the sores and wounds of one's own soul.
—*Gorky to the critic Kornei Chukovsky (1919)*

He is very lonely—he, who is hardly ever to be seen alone! I have the impression that, if only we could have contrived to be alone together (with the language barrier somehow set aside), he might well have clasped me to him and sobbed, without speaking, for a long time.
—*Romain Rolland on his visit to Gorky in July 1935*

He was unique and distinctive in everything he did. Everyone got used to the fact that he couldn't be fitted into any framework.
—*E. D. Kuskova (1936)*

Contents

Preface

This is a book of translations.

It is meant for those interested or interestable in Tolstoy, Chekhov, and a number of other Russian writers, as well as those interested in the art of the memoir, the literature and politics of the early twentieth century, and the richly enigmatic figure of Maxim Gorky, a giant on the cultural scene for the forty years preceding his death in 1936.

The book originated as a simple attempt to bring back into print one of Gorky's greatest writings—his reminiscences of Tolstoy, by common consent the best thing ever written about Tolstoy the man. Leonard Woolf and S. S. Koteliansky had published a translation soon after the initial Russian text appeared, and it remained in print for many decades.* In later editions they added Gorky's memoirs of Chekhov and Leonid Andreyev, as I have done here, for the memoirs in question are very much of a piece. They did not, however, provide any introductions, nor did they explain any of the many names and places and citations that no foreign reader (or many Russians, for that matter) could be expected to recognize.

But that was more than eighty years ago, and over the past eight decades it became clear not only that Gorky's first translators had been working from texts that were incomplete, but that rich contextual material, unavailable to them, had seen the light inside and outside Soviet Russia. The present edition corrects the former and incorporates much of the latter, I believe for the first time in English.

Thus the reader will find some supplementary variants of the Tolstoy memoir, as well as a vivid memoir Gorky wrote of the man who figures so constantly (though without much in the way of identification) in its implicit drama, and then makes a crucial reappearance near the end of the Chekhov memoir—L. A. Sulerzhitsky.

* Maxim Gorky, *Reminiscences of Leo Nicolayevitch Tolstoi.* Authorized translation from the Russian by S. S. Koteliansky and Leonard Woolf (Richmond [Eng.]: L. & V. Woolf at the Hogarth Press, 1920).

Finally, I have added Gorky's shorter but quite remarkable memoir of the poet Alexander Blok.

That was going to be the book. It is now the first section of the book.

The book grew because these memoirs prepared a new stage in Gorky's writing in which, though long since internationally famous, he claimed to be learning for the first time how to write. That stage came to be represented by a volume published in 1924 and significantly entitled *Fragments From My Diary. Reminiscences.* The Blok memoir comes from it—as do a handful of specimen sketches that show Gorky turning his memoirist's attention to some of his nonfamous countrymen. (His original title for the volume was *A Book About Russian People.*) This section, like the first, shows him writing (in Viktor Shklovsky's phrase) as a civilian; there are no dogmas—or even "beliefs"—in or around any of these pieces.

The result is that both sections are gripping writing, on the borderline between nonfiction sketches and literary writing at its subtlest. At the same time, they are full of self-revelation (overt and inadvertent), so that in the end the reader comes to infer a great deal about this notoriously reticent man.

The final result is that both sections present what will be to many a surprising and unfamiliar Gorky.

The third and last section seeks to do the same by citing the words of others. Here I have included the poet Khodasevich's great memoir of Gorky, which for depth of insight and brilliance of presentation does for Gorky what Gorky did for Tolstoy. Included as well are three key items for understanding Gorky—Boris Eikhenbaum's brief but seminal account of his uniqueness among Russian writers, Evgeny Zamiatin's obituary memoir (which is as good an introduction as one could wish for to the man and the career), and Georgy Adamovich's extraordinary and judiciously ambivalent look at the place Gorky finally made for himself in the hearts and minds of many Russians.

Other commentaries, and other memoirs and sketches—not to mention specimens of the fiction—might have been included. But all the items presented here can, I believe, fairly be called essential to understanding a figure who, as the clichés are stripped away from him, becomes ever more enigmatic as man, as writer, and as historical phenomenon.

The reader will find, I think, that the sections illuminate each other, being interconnected in myriad ways and constituting a kind of do-it-yourself kit for constructing a partial but coherent model of a major figure in the history of the twentieth century. They can be read in any order.

Acknowledgments

Every book is a solitary labor, but no book is the work of a single individual. Many have helped this one along, contributing insights, advice and encouragement, and I thank them all—most particularly Leonie Gordon, Chester Aaron, Daniel Aaron, Hugh McLean, Caryl Emerson, Jurij Striedter, Georges Nivat, Harry Shukman, Vladimir Gitin, Georgii Levinton, Marietta Chudakova, Laurence Senelick, Robert Scanlan, Barry and Gretchen Mazur, and the late, much-missed Edward J. Brown.

Thanks also to the *Times Literary Supplement*, in whose issue of July 18, 1997, a portion of the Introduction first appeared.

Transliteration, Annotation, and Russian Names

Because this book is addressed to readers without knowledge of Russian, the text generally presents Russian names and terms in their most phonetically accessible and/or most familiar guise. Documentation is a different matter, since its aim is to allow unambiguous reconstruction of the Cyrillic original; for that purpose the international scholarly system of transliteration, barbarous as it looks to a nonspecialist, is clearly preferable. So, for example, "Gorky" in the text becomes "Gor'kij" in the endnotes, "Khodasevich" becomes "Xodasevič," etc.

A similar double standard underlies the distinction between footnotes and endnotes, and for similar reasons. No reader should have to hunt through the back of the book in pursuit of clarifications or explanations; they belong naturally underneath the lines they are meant to clarify or explain. By the same token, bibliographical references need to be given, but not in a way that needlessly interrupts the reading of any text; hence they are to be found in the endnotes at the back of the book.

I have tried to be consistent in observing these distinctions.

As for Russian names: All consist of a given name, a patronymic (an obligatory middle name, fashioned from the father's given name), and a surname; for example, Lev Nikolayevich [= son of Nikolai] Tolstoy. Acquaintances would refer to him as "Lev Nikolayevich" (as Gorky does in his memoir, sometimes simply by the initials "L. N."), while his wife might address him using a diminutive of his given name—"Lyovochka" or "Lyovushka."

The case of Gorky is more complex. He was born Alexei Maximovich Peshkov, but from the age of twenty-four on he published under the pseudonym of "Gorky"; in the beginning it was simply "M. Gorky," but soon the initial expanded to "Maxim." Only in print, however: all his life he remained "Alexei Maximovich" to friends, acquaintances, and correspondents. The man had a name and patronymic, as all Russians did; the pseudonym, on the other hand, understandably enough lacked a patronymic. But "Gorky" so far became the man that the Institute of World Literature of the Academy of Sciences was officially (if confusingly) named the A. M. Gorky Institute of World Literature, as if there had ever been an individual by that name!

Gorky's Tolstoy and Other Reminiscences

Introduction

The Singularity of M. Gorky

... une grande vie, difficile et hors série ...

—N. BERBEROVA

" 'Man!'—it has a proud ring!"

Who today could repeat Maxim Gorky's most famous line without embarrassment? The temptation is strong to lump him with his coevals Wells and Galsworthy as a writer whose popularity was once immense but whose moment is long past; whose esthetic and political vocabularies have dated disastrously; a figure not simply too productive but too familiar, too much praised by the wrong people, too compromised. More dead than alive.

His singularity, for all that, remains absolute. It brought him an unprecedented celebrity, first in Russia, then throughout the world, which he retained through four violently dramatic decades up to his death in 1936; and it was freighted with large-scale significance of the most varied kinds, political and cultural quite as much as literary.

That singularity is still waiting to be addressed comprehensively; even the major components have yet to receive dispassionate and detailed consideration. We have nothing approaching a full-scale study of his artistic work, in English or in Russian: the best critics have tended to deal with it briefly and/or spottily. Nor is there any serious consensus on the Gorky canon; it would be hard to point to an adequate, let alone exemplary, collection. Though Thomas Mann and Marina Tsvetayeva thought him worthy of the Nobel Prize, we—and in this I include Russians, freed now from obligatory obeisances and suppressions—are still far from being able to see the most famous Russian writer of his time either steadily or whole.

Part of the reason lies in the peculiar phenomenology implicit in the name Gorky, which can refer to the private man who chose it as a pseudonym, to the author who is to be found only in the writing, or to the legend

1

that arose from the conjunction of the two and took on, almost with Gorky's first publication, a life and influence of its own.

Born Alexei Maximovich Peshkov in 1868, "M. Gorky" (the name means "bitter," though bitterness was never one of his qualities) burst on the Russian literary scene in the mid-1890s, representing—in both senses of the word—a new stratum of society as well as a set of new literary attitudes. Here was a writer who had actually emerged from "the people," who wrote of and for them with none of that pious sympathy for suffering traditional among the intelligentsia*; a hater of the very Russian peasant whom Turgenev, Tolstoy, and Dostoyevsky had sanctified; a Nietzschean autodidact, energetic, rebellious, impossible to pigeonhole.

His escaping all the traditional categories and identifications was evident from the beginning, when, as one scholar notes, he "put contemporaries in a difficult situation: he deprived them of the indices they were accustomed to use in judging any new literary phenomenon." At that time journals were strictly classified according to "tendency," and publishing in the journals of one camp automatically closed off the others to a writer. The young Gorky "was virtually the only one among beginning writers who in a short space of time managed to be published in the journals of three different parties, each of them antagonistic to the others"—and no

---

* In *My Universities,* the last volume of his autobiographical trilogy, Gorky writes of the students he met as a young man in Kazan:

> When they talked about the people, I felt—with amazement and self-mistrust—that here was a subject on which I couldn't think as they did. For them the people was the embodiment of wisdom, spiritual beauty, and goodheartedness, an entity almost godlike and homogeneous, a receptacle for the principles of the excellent, the just, the majestic. I didn't know such a people. I had seen carpenters, longshoremen, bricklayers; I had known Yakov and Osip and Grigory—and here were [these students] talking about "the people" as some homogeneous whole, and regarding themselves as being far beneath it and dependent on its will. While to me it seemed that it was precisely these students who were the incarnation of beauty and strength of mind, that it was in them that a kind and humane will to live was concentrated and burned—a will to the free building of a new life in the light of new canons of love for humanity.

(M. Gor'kij, *Polnoe sobranie sočinenij,* vol. 16 [Moscow: "Nauka," 1973], 35.)

The best example of how firmly he held to this view is his great autobiographical trilogy. Mirsky calls it "one of the strangest autobiographies ever written" because "it is about everybody but himself."[13] This deliberate blur at the center of Gorky's autobiography seems doomed to have its counterpart at the center of any biographical account of him.

Still, the contours are becoming clearer in light of materials published in Russia in the past decade and a half. Free of the distortions and suppressions that were mandatory under the Soviet regime, what they show is a highly fallible individual. "Gorky is an icon today," Kornei Chukovsky confided to his diary, "precisely because he is not psychological, because he is uncomplicated, elementary."[14] Elsewhere he calls him "a simpleton." Tynianov said of him: "Gorky is a weak-willed man who bends to the influence of others, but a lovely man and a poetic, magnificent artist (in life, too)."[15]

And Marietta Chudakova, a leading historian of twentieth-century Russian literature, finds him to have been "scarcely aware of what constituted the main strength of his talent"—and his publications, as a result, to be "as disorderly as was his adolescent reading."[16]

V. F. Sokolov, voicing the attitude toward Gorky of a considerable number of his fellow writers and artists, wrote in 1919: "This well-known Russian writer is the most puzzling and enigmatic figure when seen against the background of Soviet Russia. Apparently a Bolshevik. And at the same time their adversary. Their defender and friend. And at the same time one of those who do not accept Bolshevism, who are alien and distanced from it [čužd emu i dalek]." He quotes Gorky: "The misfortune of the Soviet Russian regime is that 95 per cent of Communists are dishonest people, far from communism, inclined to fraud and bribes. . . . And all the same one must work with the Soviet government. . . . That is my opinion." Sokolov comments: "He does not answer and has not answered the fundamental question. How is it possible to go hand in hand with people whose lack of decency [nečistoplotnost'] is clear to him. . . . Maxim Gorky considers himself not to be a Bolshevik, not to be with them. But the Russian intelligentsia considers him a Bolshevik and neither understands nor accepts his duplicity [*dvojstvennost'*]."[17]

When Gorky moved abroad in 1921, ostensibly to take care of his health but in good part because Lenin had wearied of the writer's intercessions on behalf of persecuted intellectuals,* he was at pains not to be identified either with the Soviet regime or with the émigré community. In part this reflected genuine indecision, but it also reflected his insistence on maintaining a status literally unique: neither an emigrant nor in Europe on business, not a tourist and not anyone's guest, he was there simply as Maxim Gorky.[18]

In the Soviet era no one dared to ask how he supported himself, his son Maxim and Maxim's family, his secretary/mistress, and the rest of the dozen or so regular members of his household, not to mention the constant guests at the villa he rented in Sorrento on the Bay of Naples. The living was not luxurious, but it was comfortable. Part of his revenues came from royalties, but in the late twenties these were not what they once had been; another part, it now turns out, were channeled to him by the Commissariat of Enlightenment (Narkompros) as a sort of allowance. (It is not clear whether, in his general indifference to money, he was aware of this.)

So it was that when he succumbed to the Soviet government's blandishments and returned—in 1928, on the occasion of his sixtieth birthday, for a long visit, followed by others until he settled in Moscow for good in 1933—he did so for a variety of reasons, all of them having to do, one way or another, with preserving his singularity as an apparently sovereign presence on the cultural scene. He would be going home, where his readers were and where he would be welcomed as a living classic. And he clearly

---

* Lenin is quoted as saying to an associate at the time: "[Gorky] has delicate nerves; he's an artist after all. . . . It's better if he leaves, gets medical treatment, rests, and looks at all this from a distance. Meanwhile we'll sweep our streets clean and then say: 'Things in Russia are a little more seemly now; we can invite our artist back to see.'" Vitalij Šentalinskij, *Raby svobody. V literaturnyx arxivax KGB* (Moscow: Parus, 1995), 315. An English version of this book, translated from a French version, was published as Vitaly Shentalinsky, *Arrested Voices: Resurrecting the Disappeared Writers of the Soviet Regime,* John Crowfoot, trans. (New York: Martin Kessler, Free Press, 1993).

had hopes of influencing domestic policy, softening it, through his relations with Stalin and through a developing friendship with the chief of
Stalin's secret police, Genrikh Yagoda.

He was treated like a potentate, given the art-nouveau mansion of the
prerevolutionary millionaire Ryabushinsky to live in, along with the estate
outside Moscow where Lenin had died, and another in the Crimea. There
are reasons to believe that he may also have been given an unlimited government bank account around that time. In 1932 his native city of Nizhnii
Novgorod was renamed Gorky in his honor, along with the Moscow Art
Theater, the Academy of Sciences Institute of World Literature, the main
thoroughfare of central Moscow (Tverskaia ulitsa), and scores of schools
and factories. Inside the country his renown, officially promoted (and hence
not to be questioned), was second only to Stalin's.

That renown does not seem to have translated into effective or lasting
influence on policy, save in the area of Soviet literature, where Gorky's lifelong preference for the hope-filled "truth" of tomorrow over the dispiriting
truth of the actual became, under the name of Socialist Realism, the guid-
ing dogma incumbent on all writers for the next half-century.*

Once that had been put in place at the First Congress of Soviet Writers in 1934, Gorky's usefulness to Stalin was at an end, and he was increasingly isolated from friends and colleagues. His spirits and his health
deteriorated. In his final two weeks, specially printed copies of the newspapers, from which the daily bulletins about his health had been removed,
were delivered to his residence. One of the last notes he dictated reads:
"End of novel End of hero End of author." He died on June 18, 1936.

---

* Explaining to a former comrade-in-arms his decision to return in 1928, he had declared: "The point is that I most sincerely and unshakably hate the truth that is 99 percent
an abomination [*merzost'*] and a lie. You are probably aware that when I was in Russia I
spoke out, in public, in print, and in comradely conversations, against 'self-criticism,'
against the deafening and blinding of people with the dust of everyday life. I naturally had
no success. But that does not dampen my ardor, for I know that to the 150 million–strong
Russian people that truth is harmful, and that people need a different truth, one which
would not depress but rouse their working and creative energy." (E. D. Kuskova, "Tragedija
Maksima Gor'kogo," *Novyj Žurnal*, kn. 38 [1954]: 241–42.)

A whole volume of documents, entitled "Around Gorky's Death," was published in 2001, full of gripping documentary detail but inconclusive in the face of the question: Did Stalin have him killed?[19] The arguments pro and con are circumstantial, but clear evidence is lacking—probably forever.

The other question about these painful last years, large and similarly unanswered, concerns the state of Gorky's awareness of the real state of affairs, both in the country and in his own situation. Did he really believe that the inmates in the forced labor camps he celebrated were in fact being happily rehabilitated? How much, in general, did he let himself see—or, once he'd seen it, keep in mind? His capacity for not seeing what he chose not to see was formidable, and is well attested.

How deep this talent for denial may have gone is a matter for speculation. It is at least possible that his inner life, in his final years if not before as well, was stunted, perhaps to the point of atrophy. Certainly the phenomenon would not have been confined to him. One is accustomed to speak of repression in the Soviet Union as an external thing, but indications are plentiful that the internal variety was a widespread if not epidemic response to the conditions of life in the Stalinist period.

Perhaps this was what led the astute Yuri Tynianov to call Gorky "an enchanting man—and a terrifying one [*čelovek čarujuščij i—strašnyj*]."[20]

The Gorky who was so concerned not to "spoil the biography" did spoil it in the end. He did so, as one old friend wrote, by outliving himself—both as writer and man.[21] The story of his final years is the story of his reduction to life size, and it matches symmetrically—in drama and significance—the story of his emergence four decades earlier. It is in fact the unraveling (*dénouement*) of what had been knitted up four decades earlier: he loses the singularity he had assumed then—and takes on representativeness.*

It is the pattern of tragedy.

* Cf. the conclusion of Vitaly Shentalinsky's revisionist portrait of Gorky, drawn from the archives of the KGB: "But how are we to separate the death mask from the living face, discern the man, and grasp what happened to him—which is to say, to us all?" (*Raby svobody. V literaturnyx arxivax KGB* [Moscow: Parus, 1995], 365.)

The post-Soviet drop in Gorky's fortunes reflects this. The first scholar to go through the Gorky material in the files of the secret police finds much in his behavior to condemn. Yet he concludes: "Gorky's constant waverings between the desire to preserve his spiritual independence and the fear of falling behind the locomotive of revolution, between the traditions of European humanism, which he idolized, and the barbaric and bloody creation of a new and unprecedented world—these are the contradictions that run through his whole life and constitute his tragedy."[22]

Not all were prepared to offer the sympathy that a tragic view demands. The renamings which Stalin had ordered in 1932 on the assumption that Gorky must harbor some version of his own megalomania were promptly undone. The city of Gorky, ironically most familiar to non-Russians as the place to which the Brezhnev regime exiled the dissident Sakharov, became Nizhnii Novgorod once more. The Moscow Art Theater dropped Gorky from its name. The logo of the *Literary Gazette,* which had long featured the profiles of Pushkin and Gorky, for a time featured that of Pushkin alone.* Publications appeared with titles like "Gorky Without Greasepaint," "The Tragedy of Gorky," "A Bad Taste in the Mouth from Gorky." Gorky's celebration of the GULAG was detailed and attacked as a disgrace. His articles of the thirties, beginning with the one entitled "If The Enemy Does Not Surrender He Will Be Destroyed," received frequent condemnation. The "great humanist's" unsettling capacity for hatred came in for sustained analysis. His correspondence with Stalin, Yagoda, and other Soviet leaders was published. Arguments were made in mitigation, but condemnation prevailed. Most recently there have been signs of attempts at a fresh view, more

---

* Gorky's profile had first appeared on the centenary of his birth in 1968. Its unannounced dropping in 1990 occasioned lively debate, and in 2004 he was restored to the logo. The editor, Yuri Poliakov, explained the restoration at the time by pointing out that Pushkin had been part of the first *Literary Gazette,* which came out in 1830, and that Gorky had been put there beside him because the paper had been started up again in 1929 at Gorky's initiative "to carry out the principle of the free competition of various groups and tendencies." This program—and the very name, emphasizing connection with prerevolutionary traditions—was a clear challenge to the fanatics of the time.

nuanced and dispassionate, of the man, his life, his career, and his politics. The time may be coming—though it hardly seems imminent—when it will be possible to see Gorky steadily and see him more or less whole.

Meanwhile, what seems likely—as the current flood of revisionist attention suggests—is that the time has come for resolving the Gorky phenomenon back into its constituent parts, which is to say, for sundering the writer from the public figure and biographee (fascinating as the latter two are). If so, Gorky will prove yet again to have a fate like no other—for the process includes the possibility of being discovered for the first time, three-quarters of a century after his death, as a modern writer.

PART ONE

Gorky: Memoirs

1

Lev Tolstoy

Since their first publication in 1919, Gorky's reminiscences of Tolstoy have attracted superlatives. In a letter to the author, the critic Kornei Chukovsky praised them as "the fairest and truest of all the things that have been written about [Tolstoy]," adding parenthetically: "And I have now read a whole bookcase full."[1] The great theoretician and historian of Russian literature Boris Eikhenbaum—himself a brilliant analyst of Tolstoy's writings—concurred, stressing the importance of Gorky's integral image of Tolstoy, his rejection of the common tendency to approach Tolstoy in Tolstoy's own terms (the pre-crisis artist, the post-crisis saint). His conclusion: "Gorky liberates Tolstoy from 'Tolstoyanism' and makes him a truly powerful, gigantic, terrifyingly Russian figure."[2] Yet another leading Russian scholar, Lidia Ginzburg, points to new grounds for appreciation when she finds Gorky's reminiscences of Tolstoy to be "among the best things Gorky ever wrote," as well as "the best thing ever written about Tolstoy as an individual."[3]

To all these emphases Alfred Kazin adds still other, more universal ones, ranking Gorky's reminiscences as "surely among the most beautiful things ever written by one human being on the character of another," and calling attention to the double portraiture that provides so much of the force and tension of the work: "A masterpiece, set down in scattered notes that Gorky himself evidently did not mind losing at one time, so much had he revealed of himself in grappling with the fascinating mystery that was Tolstoy."[4]

They were, unquestionably, the two most famous writers in Russia when they met for the first time in Moscow in January 1900. Tolstoy was seventy-two, Gorky thirty-two, and what Isaiah Berlin says of Tolstoy at thirty-two—that, though famous by then as a writer, he gave the impression of having "wandered [into literature] from another, less intellectual . . . and more primitive world"— could with equal justice be said of Gorky at the same age.[5] The previous year Chekhov had reported to Gorky in a letter that Tolstoy had praised him as "a re- markable writer." "You pique his curiosity," Chekhov explained, pointing to what would remain Tolstoy's dominant attitude toward his young colleague.

A few days after that first meeting, Tolstoy wrote in his diary: "Must note: Gorky was here. A very good talk. And I liked him. A real man of the people." As for Gorky, the detailed account he sent Chekhov in a letter of January 22, 1900, contains so many of the themes and perspectives that were to go into his memoir—their sincerity signaled inter alia by the awkward phrasing, the super- abundance of intensifying adverbs, and the unresolved contradictions—as to warrant extended citation:

> Well, I've been to visit Lev Nikolayevich. That was eight days ago and I
> still can't sort out my impressions. I was struck first of all by his looks:
> I had pictured him differently—taller, broader-framed. But he turned
> out to be a little old man and for some reason reminded me of the tales
> about that eccentric genius Suvorov.* But when he started speaking I
> listened in amazement. Everything he said was astonishingly simple,
> profound, and, though sometimes I thought it completely untrue, terri-
> bly good. The main thing is that it was utterly simple. All the same, he
> is, when all is said and done, a whole orchestra, though one where not
> all the trumpets play in harmony. And that too is a very good thing,

* Alexander Vasilievich Suvorov (1729-1800), Russian field marshal, distinguished participant in Russia's many wars of the late eighteenth century.

because it's very human—that is, characteristic of man in general. When you come right down to it, it's awfully stupid to call a man a genius. It's utterly incomprehensible—what is a genius? It's much simpler and clearer just to say "Lev Tolstoy"—that's both concise and utterly original, i.e., it's absolutely unlike anything else and is, moreover, somehow forceful, particularly forceful. To see Lev Nikolayevich is very important and useful, although I by no means consider him a miracle of nature. You look at him and it's terribly pleasant to feel that you are also a man, to realize that it's possible for a man to be a Lev Tolstoy. Do you understand?—you feel good for man in general. He treated me very well, but that, it goes without saying, is unimportant. What he said about my stories is also unimportant, but all of it, taken together, is somehow important—everything that was said, the way he said it, the way he sat, the way he looked at you. It was all very much of a piece, and it had a powerful beauty. I had never really believed he was an atheist, though I felt it, but now, having heard the way he speaks about Christ and having seen his eyes—too clever for a believer—I know that he is indeed an atheist, and a profound one. Don't you think so?[6]

Tolstoy, in his first letter to Gorky (February 1900), tells him:

I am very, very glad to have gotten to know you, and glad to find myself fond of you. Aksakov used to say that some people are better (he said wiser) than their books, and others worse. I liked your writing but I found you better than your writing. So there's my compliment to you; its main virtue is in its sincerity.[7]

There are indications that Gorky visited Tolstoy in Moscow in February or March, and at his estate at Yasnaya Polyana in the fall.

In April 1901 Gorky was arrested for revolutionary agitation among the students and shipyard workers in Nizhnii Novgorod. Tolstoy's intercession with the authorities led to his being released from jail and placed under house arrest—with the possibility, six months later, of visiting the Crimea for reasons of health. It was there, from mid-November of 1901 into April of 1902, that the meetings described in Gorky's memoir took place. Tolstoy was staying at Gaspra, the estate of Countess Panina; Gorky had settled in Oleiz, a scant mile away. They met frequently in these months, but never afterward.

In November 1910, when the first announcement of Tolstoy's death reached Gorky, he described his reactions in a series of letters:

> I howled, overwhelmed with despair, and wept the whole day—never before so agonizingly, so inconsolably, so much. . . . Now I wait tensely for news from Russia about him, the soul of our nation, the genius of our people. There is a great deal in that soul that I find alien and down-right inimical, but I had not realized how deeply and avidly I loved the man Tolstoy! I am outraged by the attempts that have already begun to make a "legend" out of him and found a "religion" on it—a religion of that fatalism which is so disastrous for us Russians, given how passive we are to begin with.[8]

> I howl shamelessly and uncontrollably as soon as I imagine him lying with his face to the sky, his hands folded on his chest, and those Mongo-lian cheekbones that will no longer frame his wide and wise smile . . . I feel myself an orphan . . . Our national genius is gone from our life.[9]

The report that Gorky was reacting to proved premature; Tolstoy in fact died a few days later, prompting the unfinished letter that was to become the second part of Gorky's memoir nine years later.

Gorky is right when he declares in his memoir that Tolstoy's interest in him was primarily "ethnographic." He was the object of the great man's curiosity more than of his affection; a certain (inconstant) benevolence, together with respect for Gorky's experience and talent, seems to have been the best that Tolstoy could muster in the way of feeling for him. The worst was condescension, and Tolstoy was not above a certain feline toying with him; neither attitude was consistent, but either or both might erupt suddenly at any time. Gorky for his part was more consistent, evincing a "respect that transcended resentment and went out in love and awe to the great writer, seeking the meaning of his human strangeness."[10] Personal feelings aside, each took a strongly negative view of the other's beliefs. On November 23, 1909, just a year before his death, Tolstoy wrote in his diary:

> Read about Gorky after dinner. And, strange to say, a negative feeling towards him with which I am struggling. I justify myself with the fact that he is, like Nietzsche, a harmful writer: a major gift and the absence of any religious convictions at all—i.e., any concern with the significance of life— and together with that a cocksureness, supported by our "educated world," which sees him as its spokesman, that further infects that world.[11]

Gorky reciprocated by angrily rejecting Tolstoy's religiosity, his pacifism, and his political positions. When each regarded the other in relation to what he thought Russia needed, each found much not simply to reject but to deplore.

Both, that is to say, nourished utopian visions.[12]

The utopian tendency was only one of the things they had in common. Both suffered from a radical aloneness, and both fought a core nihilism; Gorky was simultaneously observing and projecting when he emphasized the latter in Tolstoy. Both were anarchists by temperament and instinct. And both, easily moved to tears, were (as Gorky writes of Tolstoy) "fundamentally, in the depth[s] of [their] soul[s], indifferent to people." The play of these primal affinities and repulsions, by turns subliminal and overt, is one of the things that give Gorky's account much of its crackling energy and visceral power.

Another, of course, is the form.

Gorky approached it tentatively, and with difficulty. He began, toward the end of 1917, to tell and re-tell acquaintances about his meetings with Tolstoy. These oral presentations, praised for their vividness by many who heard them, amounted to drafts of the eventual memoir, in which Gorky would vary emphases, adding new details and eliminating others. One scholar who heard him do so recalls one such account:

> In the telling Gorky was repeatedly moved to tears, which he would hasten to wipe away as unobtrusively as he could . . . When he had finished, we were all silent for a while; at length I, a starched and buttoned-up young man at the time, couldn't help exclaiming: "Alexei Maximovich, that was so interesting! Why don't you write it down?" "I've tried to do it several times," Gorky replied, "but it didn't work out."[13]

In fact, he had made extensive notes on little scraps of paper after each of his meetings with Tolstoy, thrown them into a drawer—and then lost them for a long time. He had been rehearsing his oral accounts for over a year when a trove of these notes was rediscovered (though some—it is not clear how many—proved lost forever). "He wanted to polish them," according to a colleague, "but one time he brought them to the publisher, threw them on the table, and said, 'I can't do anything with them. Let them remain as they are.' "[14] Viktor Shklovsky, however, found "the story about Lev Tolstoy as a thing made up of various scraps of paper, lost and found," though literally true, to be misleading: "The book is composed of bits and pieces, firmly joined together. I have had occasion to see the manuscript and I know how many times those pieces were rearranged in order to achieve that solidity."[15] It was, in other words, a hybrid thing. Shklovsky calls it "an original montage of artistic reminiscences," and explains: "In a different time all these observations would have served only as material for a coherent work; they would have appeared in it transformed. But here they are printed, so to speak, naked. This is a writer's notebook, but one presented—and legitimately—as a finished work of art."[16] Gorky had hit on a way to formalize the work while retaining the immediacy of the notes that constituted it, along with their open-endedness.*

The result is a kind of sustained poem in prose, built, as all poetry is, on un-commented juxtaposition, on recurrent (and often clashing) patterns of motif (the "little old" protagonist, "thin," "gray," and ordinary, and the "exceptional" man, the "great artist," "sage," "wizard," "sorcerer," "trickster," and "god"), the whole studded with metaphors and suffused with intense feeling, both shown and implied. It also displays patterns of relationship among the centrally recurring characters—Tolstoy, Gorky, Chekhov, and Sulerzhitsky—which not only bring them to richer life in the documentary sense, but allow a reader to experience the whole as a kind of short novel in embryo.[17] This double effect is enhanced when one reads Gorky's companion memoirs of Chekhov and Sulerzhitsky (translated below) alongside the central document. They are the characters, together with Gorky himself, who bring Tolstoy out of that aloneness which Gorky sees as his deepest trait. (Tolstoy's diary contains ample confirmation of the memoirist's intuition; for example, "Among all these people I am alone, utterly lonely and alone. And the awareness of this loneliness and the need to associate with all these people and the impossibility of doing so are enough to drive me out of my mind.")[18]

And then there is the matter of Gorky's extraordinary self-revelation in this remarkable document—but that is a matter best left for each reader to grasp and construe for him- or herself.[19]

◄•►

* "Reminiscences of Lev Nikolayevich Tolstoy" was published in 1921, republished without change in 1922, and then in fuller form as *M. Gor'kij, Vospominanija* (Berlin, 1923). Further additions were made in 1927 for Gorky's collected works; it is from this last version that the present translation has been made.

M. Gorky: "Lev Tolstoy"

This little book has been assembled from the fragmentary notes I made when I was living in Oleiz and Lev Nikolayevich [Tolstoy] was staying in Gaspra, at first seriously ill and then recuperating from his illness.* I thought these notes, casually jotted down on different scraps of paper, had been lost, but recently I found a number of them. I have appended an unfinished letter written in response to the news of Lev Nikolayevich's "flight" from Yasnaya Polyana and subsequent death. I print the letter just as I wrote it at the time; not a word has been changed. Nor have I tried to finish it; there are reasons which make that quite impossible.

—M. Gorky

NOTES

I

The thought that clearly and most constantly gnaws at his heart is the thought of God. Sometimes it seems to be not even a thought, but rather an intense resistance to something he feels to be stronger than himself. He speaks of it less than he would like to, but it is always on his mind. This is hardly a sign of age, or a presentiment of death. No, I think it comes from simple human pride. Also a little from resentment, because, being Lev Tolstoy, he finds it insulting to have to subordinate his will to some streptococcus. If he were a scientist he would, of course, construct hypotheses of genius and make great discoveries.

II

He has amazing hands—ugly, knotted with swollen veins, and yet full of special expressiveness and creative force. Leonardo da Vinci probably had

* Gaspra was the estate of Countess S. V. Panina on the southern seacoast of the Crimea, near Yalta; Oleiz was about a kilometer and a half from Gaspra.

hands like that. Hands like that can do anything. Sometimes when he is talking he moves his fingers, gradually contracting them into a fist which he will
fling open just as he comes out with some well-chosen and weighty word.
He is like a god, not Sabaoth or any of the Olympians, but some Russian
god who "sits on a throne of maple under a golden lime tree"—perhaps not
very majestic, but quite possibly more cunning than all the other gods.

III

He treats Sulerzhitsky* with the tenderness of a woman. Chekhov he
loves like a father—you feel the pride of a creator in this love—but what
Suler evokes in him is simply tenderness, together with an interest and delight of which the old wizard seems never to tire. There may be something
faintly ridiculous in this feeling, like an old maid's love for her parrot or
lapdog or tomcat. Suler is like a wonderfully free bird that has flown in
from some strange foreign land. A hundred people like him could change
the face and soul of any provincial city—the face would get smashed but
the soul would be filled with a passion for wild things and brilliant mischief.† To love Suler is easy—there is a certain gaiety involved—and when
I see how the women slight him it astonishes and infuriates me. All the

---

* Leopold Sulerzhitsky (or Suler, as Tolstoy liked to call him) is, along with Chekhov
and Gorky, a recurrent presence in this memoir and a key figure in the shadowy "family
drama" or novel manqué that some readers have found implied in the interactions of these
three with Tolstoy and each other. For more details on this colorful figure, see Gorky's
sketch "L. A. Sulerzhitsky" below, pp. 106–114.

† Gorky's word here—and it is one that he uses repeatedly to characterize Tolstoy—is
the untranslatable *ozorstvo*. "Mischief" is a weak approximation; "trouble-making" or
"provocation" are often involved. An *ozornik*—one who practices *ozorstvo*—can be a tease
(but a serious one), which is to say a provocateur, or a trickster (Rabelais' Panurge was an
ozornik), a simple mischief-maker or an inveterate troublemaker. The adjectival form of the
word is *ozornoj;* "wily," "impudent," "sly," "foxy," "crafty," and "subdolous" reflect aspects of its meaning but are in no case equivalents. Wherever these or related words are
used in this translation, they should be understood as referring to the more robust and in-
clusive Russian word (or its derivatives).

same, it may be that their offhandedness is a cover for wariness. Suler is unreliable. There is no telling what he'll do tomorrow—maybe throw a bomb, or maybe join a tavern choir. He has enough energy in him for three lifetimes. He has so much of the fire of life that he seems to sweat sparks, like overheated iron.

But once he got seriously angry with Suler. Leopold, with his inclination to anarchism, liked to hold forth about the freedom of the individual; he did this often, and when he did L. N. always made fun of him. I remember that Suler once got hold of a little brochure by Prince Kropotkin that fired him up so much he spent the whole day telling everyone about the wisdom of anarchism and pontificating unbearably.

L. N., irritated, said to him: "Stop, Lyovushka, we've had enough, You keep repeating one word like a parrot—'freedom, freedom'—but what does it mean? If you were to achieve freedom in your sense, the way you imagine it, what would be the result? In the philosophical sense, a bottomless void, while in life, in practice, you'd turn into a loafer and panhandler. If you were free in your sense, what would connect you with life, with people? Look at the birds. They're free, but they build nests all the same. You on the other hand wouldn't even build a nest; you'd rather satisfy your sexual desires when and as you can, like a dog. Think it over seriously and you'll see—you'll feel—that when all is said and done freedom is a vast, boundless emptiness."

Frowning angrily, he said nothing for a minute, then added, a little more softly: "Christ was free, so was Buddha, and both took on themselves the sins of the world, voluntarily embraced the captivity of earthly life. And beyond that no one has gone. No one. As for you and me—come on! We all look for freedom from our obligations to others, while it's precisely that feeling of obligation to others that makes us human. If we didn't have it we would live like wild animals . . ."

He grinned.

"Look at us, trying after all to reason out how to live better. There's not much use in it, but there's still some. Here you are, arguing with me and getting so mad that your nose turns blue, but you're not hitting me, you're not even cursing. If you really felt yourself free, you'd kill me and that would be that."

After another pause he added:

"Freedom is when everything and everyone is in agreement with me, but then I wouldn't exist because we all have the sensation of being ourselves only in conflict and contradiction."

IV

Goldenweiser was playing Chopin, which prompted the following thoughts from Lev Nikolayevich:

"Some minor little German potentate said, 'Where you want to have slaves, you should have as much music composed as possible.' That is a correct idea, a correct observation. Music blunts the mind. Catholics understand this better than anyone. Our Orthodox priests, of course, could never reconcile themselves to Mendelssohn in church. One of them in Tula assured me that Christ himself was not a Jew, although he was the son of the Jewish God and his mother was a Jew. He admitted those things, but said all the same, 'That could not be.' I asked him, 'So how do you explain it?' He shrugged and said, 'This to me is a great mystery!'"

V

"Our intelligentsia is like the Galician prince Vladimirko, who said 'most daringly' back in the twelfth century: 'There are no miracles in our time.' Six hundred years have passed, and the intelligentsia keep repeating to each other: 'There are no miracles, there are no miracles'—while the whole Russian people believes in miracles just as they did in the twelfth century."

VI

"The minority need God because they've got everything else, the majority because they've got nothing."

I would put it differently: the majority believe in God out of timidity, and only a few from fullness of soul.*

"Do you like Andersen's fairy tales?" he asked, musing. "I didn't understand them when they were published in Marko Vovchok's Russian translation, but ten years later I picked up the book again, read it through— and had such a strong feeling that Andersen must have been very lonely. Very. I don't know his life; it seems he was dissolute and traveled a lot, but that only confirms my feeling that he must have been lonely. It's precisely for that reason that he wrote for children, though it is a miscalculation to think that children are more compassionate than adults. Children pity nothing; they don't know how to pity."

VII

He advised me to read the Buddhist scripture. About Buddhism and Christ he always speaks sentimentally; and he speaks especially badly about Christ. His words show no enthusiasm, no strong emotion, his heart is not in them. I think he considers Christ naive and deserving of pity, and although he (sometimes) admires him, I doubt that he loves him. It's as though he worries that if Christ came to a Russian village the girls would laugh at him.

VIII

Today the Grand Duke Nikolai Mikhailovich was there. Seems to be an intelligent man. He behaves very modestly, speaks little. He has sympathetic eyes and a fine figure. Reserved gestures. L. N. smiled at him affectionately, speaking French and English by turns. In Russian he said:

* Gorky's note: To obviate misunderstanding I should say that I regard religious writings as purely literary, and the lives of Buddha, Christ and Mohammed as fantastic novels.

"Karamzin wrote for the Tsar, Solovyov writes at length and tediously, whereas Kliuchevsky writes for his own amusement.* He's a sly one: You read what seems to be praise, but once you think about it you see that it was really condemnation."

Someone mentioned Zabelin.†

"A very nice fellow. A kind of scrivener. An amateur junk man. Collects everything, the useful and the useless alike. He describes food as if he hadn't had a square meal in his life. But he's very, very amusing."

IX

He reminds me of those pilgrims who spend their lives criss-crossing the earth, stick in hand, traveling thousands of miles from monastery to monastery, from one set of relics to another, terribly homeless, strangers to everyone and everything. The world is not for them, nor is God. They pray to him out of habit but secretly hate him: Why, why does he drive them from one end of the earth to the other? People are stumps, roots, stones in the road—you trip over them, painfully at times. You could get along without them, but it is pleasant at times to startle a man with your unlikeness to him, to flaunt your disagreement.

X

"Frederick the Great said it very well: Every man must save himself *à sa façon*.' He also said: 'Think as you like, so long as you obey.' But when he was dying he admitted, 'I am tired of ruling slaves.' So-called great men are always terribly contradictory. That is forgiven them, as is any other folly. Although contradictoriness is not a folly: a fool can be stubborn, but

---

* Nikolai Mikhailovich Karamzin (1766–1826), Sergei Mikhailovich Solovyov (1820–1879), and Vasilii Osipovich Kliuchevsky (1841–1911) are all famous historians of Russia.

† Ivan Egorovich Zabelin (1820–1908), a historian and archaeologist.

contradictions are beyond him. Yes, Frederick was a strange man all right: among the Germans he earned the reputation of being their best ruler, and yet he couldn't stand them. He didn't even like Goethe and Wieland . . ."

XI

"Romanticism comes from the fear of looking truth in the eye," he said yesterday evening a propos of the verses of Balmont.* Suler, lisping with excitement, would not agree with him and recited some more poems with great feeling.

"Those, Lyovushka, are not poems but charlatanism, 'asinistics' as they used to say in the Middle Ages—a senseless weaving of words. Poetry is artless; when Fet wrote:

> . . . I do not know myself what I shall
> Sing, but only that a song is welling

he expressed the Russian people's true feeling about poetry. The peasant doesn't know either what he is singing—'*Okh*,' and '*oy*,' and '*ay*'—but it's a real song, coming straight from the soul, like a bird's. These new poets of yours invent everything. There are silly French things called *articles de Paris,* well, that's what your versifiers produce. Nekrasov is another whose wretched verses are invented from start to finish."

"And Béranger?" Suler asked.

"Béranger is a different matter! What do we have in common with the French? They are sensualists; the life of the spirit is not as important for them as the flesh. The main thing for a Frenchman is a woman. They are a used-up, played-out people. Doctors tell us that all consumptives are sensualists."

Suler began to argue in that plainspoken way of his, pouring out a torrent of words helter-skelter. L. N. looked at him and said with a broad smile:

---

* Konstantin Dmitrievich Balmont (1867–1942), Russian Symbolist poet, famous around the turn of the century for the sonorities of his verse.

"You're petulant today, like a girl who should be getting married but doesn't have a man . . ."

XII

Illness has left him a little more dried up; it has burnt something away in him. Internally too, it's as if he's become lighter, more transparent, on better terms with life. His eyes are even keener; his glance is piercing. He listens attentively and seems to be recalling something he had forgotten, or else waiting confidently for something new that is still unknown. In Yasnaya Polyana he struck me as a man who knew everything, who had nothing more to learn, a man whose questions had all been resolved.

XIII

If he were a fish it is clear that he would swim only in the ocean, avoiding inland seas and, most particularly, the fresh water of rivers. Here he is surrounded by small fry who swarm and dart. What he says is not interesting or needful to them, and his silence neither intimidates nor moves them. And yet, for all that, he manages his silences impressively, with great skill, like a real hermit. Although he's voluble enough on his obligatory topics, you feel that there is even more on which he keeps silent. There are some things he cannot say to anyone. He must surely have thoughts of which he is afraid.

XIV

Someone sent him an excellent version of the folktale about Christ's godson. He read it with pleasure to Suler and Chekhov, and read it marvelously. He was especially amused by the description of how demons torment landowners, and there was something in that I found unpleasant. He is not capable of insincerity, but if that was sincere it's even worse.

Later he said:

"How well the peasants put their stories together—everything is simple, few words but plenty of feeling. Real wisdom is laconic, like 'Lord have mercy.'"

But the tale is a cruel one.

XV

His interest in me is an ethnographic interest. To him I belong to a tribe he doesn't know very well—that, and no more.

XVI

I read him my story "The Bull." He laughed a lot and praised me for knowing the "tricks of the language."

"But you don't handle the words skillfully enough. All your peasants talk very cleverly. In real life their speech is stupid and awkward, it's hard to see what they're getting at. That's done on purpose; the stupidity of their words is designed to get the other man to say what's on his mind. A good peasant will never show what he's thinking right off the bat; there'd be no advantage for him in doing that. He knows that people are simple and direct with a stupid person, and that's just what he's after! If you're open with him, he sees all of your weak spots immediately. He's mistrustful; he won't share his inmost thoughts even with his wife. But in your stories everything is straightforward, and every story features a general convocation of clever people. And they all speak in aphorisms, that's not true to life either: Russian is not a language for aphorisms."

"What about proverbs and sayings?" I asked.

"That's a different matter. They weren't made up today."

"But you yourself often speak in aphorisms."

"Never! And then you touch up everything, people and nature both, but especially people. Leskov did the same thing. A preposterous writer. So ornate. People stopped reading him a long time ago. Don't let anyone influence you, don't be afraid of anyone, then you'll be fine."

XVII

In his diary, which he gave me to read, I was struck by a strange aphorism: "God is my desire."

Returning the diary today, I asked what that meant.

"An unfinished thought," he said, screwing up his eyes and looking at the page. "I must have meant God is my desire to know him . . . No, that's not it . . ." He laughed, rolled the little notebook up, and stuck it in the broad pocket of his smock. His relations with God are very uncertain; sometimes they remind me of the relations between "two bears in a single lair."

XVIII

On science:

"Science is a gold ingot prepared by an alchemist, a charlatan. You want to simplify it and make it comprehensible to the people—which means minting a great quantity of counterfeit coins. When the people come to understand the true value of these coins they will not thank us."

XIX

We were walking in the park of the Yusupov estate, and he was telling wonderful stories about the life of the Moscow aristocracy. A large peasant woman at work in a flower bed was bent over at an angle that bared her elephantine legs; her ten-pound breasts were heaving. He studied her.

"It's caryatids like her that supported all that splendor and extravagance. Not just the work of peasant men and women, and not just the institution of serfdom, but literally the blood of the people. If the gentry hadn't mated with horses like that one from time to time, it would have died off long since. You can't spend your powers the way the young men of my generation did with impunity. But once they'd sowed their wild oats, many of them married their housemaids and produced good offspring—so that here too they were saved by the muzhik's strength. It comes in handy everywhere. And it's right that one half of the aristocracy should always spend its powers on itself, and that the other half should mix its own with the thick blood of the peasants and thin it out a little. That's a useful thing."

XX

He speaks about women readily and at length, like a French novelist, but always with the crudeness of a Russian muzhkik, which in the beginning used to bother me extremely. Today in the Almond Grove he asked Chekhov:

"Were you very lecherous as a young man?"

A. P. gave an embarrassed little smile, tugged at his beard, and mumbled something, while L. N., gazing out at the sea, confessed:

"I could never get enough . . ."

He pronounced this wistfully, adding a salty peasant word at the end of the sentence, and for the first time I noticed how naturally he came out with the word, as if he didn't know another that would do as well. And when words of that kind issue from that shaggy mouth, they all sound simple and ordinary, and lose their barracks-room crudity. Our first meeting comes to mind and what he said about my stories "Varen'ka Olesova" and "Twenty-Six Men and a Girl." From the conventional point of view, what he said amounted to one long string of "indecent" words. That troubled me at the time; I was even offended: I thought he must consider me incapable of understanding any other kind of language. Now I see how foolish it was to take offence.

XXI

He was sitting on a stone bench under the cypresses, small, gray, dried-up, but all the same like a Sabaoth, a little tired and entertaining himself by whistling, trying to imitate the song of a chaffinch. The bird was singing in a dark green thicket; he was looking in its direction, screwing up his keen little eyes and, pursing his lips like a child, whistling awkwardly.

"That bird is in a frenzy. Listen how it carries on! What is it?"

I told him about the chaffinch and its characteristic jealousy.

"One song all its life and it's jealous! A man has hundreds of songs in his soul but he gets blamed if he surrenders to jealousy—is that fair?" he wondered aloud. "There are moments when a man tells a woman more than she should know about him. Once he's said it he forgets, but she remembers. Perhaps jealousy comes from a terror of being devalued, a fear of being humiliated and looking ridiculous. It's not the woman who holds you by your [. . .] who is dangerous, but the one who holds you by your soul."

When I pointed out that this seemed to contradict what he'd written in *The Kreutzer Sonata,* the radiance of a smile spread across his beard and he answered, beaming:

"I am not a chaffinch."

Strolling that evening, he suddenly said:

"Man endures earthquakes, epidemics, the horrors of disease and all sorts of emotional torment, but the most agonizing tragedy was, is, and will be the tragedy of the bedroom."

He said this with a solemn smile—his smile at times is so broad and serene, it is the smile of a man who has overcome something extremely difficult, or of a man tormented for a long time by a sharp pain that has suddenly ceased. Every thought burrows into his soul like a tick; he either tears it out on the spot, or else lets it drink its fill of blood until, when ready, it falls off imperceptibly of its own accord.

In the middle of some fascinating remarks about stoicism, he frowned abruptly, clucked disapprovingly, and said:

" 'Bedquilt,' but not 'bedquilted'; there is the noun 'bedquilt' and the verb 'to quilt,' but there is no verb 'to bedquilt . . . ' "

This clearly had nothing to do with the philosophy of the Stoics. Noticing my puzzlement, he hastened to explain, nodding at the door of the adjoining room: "In there they say 'a bedquilted coverlet'!"

Then he continued:

"As for that sentimental windbag Renan . . ."

Many times he has told me:

"You relate things well—in your own words, effectively, not bookishly."

But he almost always picks up on carelessness of speech, *sotto voce,* as if to himself:

"Close, but not quite—'absolutely' when 'perfectly' would do!"

And sometimes there are open reproaches:

"'A puny personage'—how can you put two words so different in spirit together? That's bad . . ."

His sensitivity to forms of speech can be morbidly keen. Once he said:

"I remember some writer's using 'feline' and 'beeline' in the same sentence. I was literally nauseated."

At times he would ponder:

"'Reigning' and 'raining'—what's the connection?"

And once, coming out of the park, he said:

"Just now the gardener said, 'in the end it was agreed.' That's strange, no? 'What they wound up with was a greed.' How are these phrases related? I don't like philologists, they're pedants, but they have important work to do on language. We speak using words we don't understand. For instance, how were the verbs 'scatter' and 'skitter' formed?"

He kept returning to Dostoyevsky's use of language:

"He wrote barbarously and even made it ugly on purpose—I'm sure it was on purpose, out of coyness. He liked to show off. In *The Idiot* he has a phrase: 'in his brazen pestering and advertising of the acquaintance.' I think he deliberately used the word 'advertising' because it's foreign and Western. But you can also find unforgivable lapses in him. The Idiot says: "A donkey is a good and useful person" and no one laughs, although these words would surely have elicited laughter, or at the least some comment. He says this in the presence of three sisters who love making fun of him, especially Aglaya. The book is generally considered a bad one, but the main thing that's bad in it is that Prince Myshkin is an epileptic. If he were healthy, his real innocence and purity of heart would move us deeply. But Dostoyevsky couldn't find the courage to make him a healthy man. Besides, he didn't like healthy people. He was sure that since he himself was sick the whole world must be sick . . .

He read Suler and me a variant of the fall of "Father Sergius"*—a brutal scene. Suler pursed his lips and fidgeted uneasily.

"What's wrong? Don't you like it?" L. N. asked him.

"It's too cruel—like something by Dostoyevsky. That putrid girl, and her breasts like pancakes, and all. Why couldn't he sin with a woman who was beautiful and healthy?"

"That would have been a sin with no justification. This way you can justify it by pity for a girl no one would want."

"I don't understand . . ."

"There's a lot you don't understand, Lyovushka, you're not canny . . ."

His son Andrei's wife came in and the conversation broke off. But when she and Suler had left the room, L. N. said to me:

"Leopold is the purest man I know. He's like that himself: if he did something bad it would be out of pity for someone."

XXII

The subjects he talks about most often are God, the peasant, and woman. About literature he speaks seldom and grudgingly, as if literature were something alien to him. My impression is that he regards women with implacable hostility and loves to punish them—unless they're like Kitty or Natasha Rostova; i.e., if they're not limited enough to suit him. Is this the hostility of a man who has not managed to get as much happiness as he might have, or the hostility of the spirit toward the "humiliating impulses of the flesh"? In any case, it's hostility—and cold, as in *Anna Karenina*. About the "humiliating impulses of the flesh" he spoke very well on Sunday, discussing Rousseau's

---

* Tolstoy worked on this story of monasticism, spiritual ambition, and sexual temptation between 1890 and 1898. It was published only posthumously, in 1911.

Confessions with Chekhov and Elpatievsky.* Suler took down his words and
then, in brewing coffee, managed to burn the note over the spirit-lamp. The
time before he burnt L. N.'s judgment about Ibsen and lost a note about the
symbolism of wedding rituals (where L. N. had expressed some very pagan
views, coinciding to some extent with those of V. V. Rozanov†).

XXIII

In the morning some Shtundists‡ from Theodosia came to see him, and today all day long he has been speaking about the peasants with enthusiasm.

At breakfast:

"They came, both of them such solid, strong fellows. One said, 'We've
come unbidden,' and the other added: 'And, God willing, we'll leave un-
beaten.'" And he broke into childlike laughter, shaking all over.

At lunch, on the terrace:

"Soon we'll cease understanding the language of the people altogether.
We say the 'theory of progress,' the 'role of the individual in history,' the 'evolution of science,' 'dysentery,' while a peasant will say, 'You can't hide an awl
in a sack,' and all our theories and histories and evolutions become pitiful and
ridiculous because the common people don't understand them and don't
need them. But the peasant is stronger than we are, he has more vitality in him,
and it could be that what will happen with us is what happened with the tribe
of the Attsurs, about whom some scholar was told: 'All the Attsurs have died
out, but there is one parrot here who knows a few words of their language.'"

* Sergei Yakovlevich Elpatievsky (1854–1933), a district doctor and writer, published
memoirs of Tolstoy, Chekhov, and Gorky, among others.

† Vasily Vasilievich Rozanov (1856–1919), iconoclastic literary critic and paradoxalist-
provocateur, wrote extensively on religious questions. His views on most matters were diametrically opposed to Gorky's; nonetheless, the two corresponded, and Gorky admired
him deeply.

‡ "Shtundists" was the term adopted in Russian Orthodox circles to designate members
of a variety of Christian sects which had grown up in the later nineteenth century among the
peasantry of Ukraine and Russia under the influence of Western Protestantism. Shtundists did
not recognize the Orthodox church, regarding the Bible as their sole authority.

XXIV

"With her body woman is more sincere than man is, but her thoughts are false. When she lies, though, she doesn't believe herself, whereas Rousseau lied—and believed what he said."

XXV

"Dostoyevsky wrote about one of his crazy characters that he lived revenging himself and others for having served what he did not believe in. He wrote that about himself; that is, he could well have said the same thing about himself."

XXVI

"Certain church expressions are amazingly obscure. For instance, what sense is there in the words, 'The earth is the Lord's and the fullness thereof'? That's not from the Bible, it's from some popular-science materialism."

"You've interpreted those words somewhere," Suler said.

"I've interpreted all kinds of things. 'Some of it's smart, but only part.'"

And he grinned slyly.

XXVII

He likes to ask difficult and malicious questions:

"What do you think of yourself?"

"Do you love your wife?"

"What do you think, is my son Lev talented?"

"Do you like my wife?"

It is impossible to lie to him.

Once he asked, "Do you like me, A. M.?"

This is the mischief-making of a folk hero; Vaska Buslayev, the Novgorod prankster, played such games in his youth. He's "testing," constantly probing, as if getting ready for a fight. It's interesting, but I can't say I like it much. He is the devil, and I am still a babe, and he should leave me alone.

XXVIII

Perhaps the peasant is simply a bad smell to him—something he is aware of constantly and has to talk about willy-nilly.

Last evening I told him about my battle with the wife of General Cornet. He laughed till the tears came, till his chest ached, groaning and crying out in a thin little voice:

"With a spade! On her [. . .] With a spade, right? Smack on her [. . .] Was it a broad spade?"

Then, after a pause to catch his breath, he said seriously:

"You were actually generous hitting her there, another would have banged her on the head for that. Very generous. You understood of course that she wanted you?"

"I can't remember. I don't think I did . . ."

"Come on, it's obvious! Of course she did."

"That didn't interest me at the time . . ."

"Even so! It's clear you're not much of a ladies' man. Another man would have turned that to account, become a homeowner, and spent the rest of his days drinking himself into a stupor with her.

After a pause:

"You're a funny one. Don't be offended, but you're really very funny! And the strange thing is that you turned out good-natured, when you had every right to be resentful. Yes, you could well have turned out resentful. You're strong, and that's good . . ."

Then, after another pause, he added musingly:

"I don't understand your mind, it's a very confused mind, but you've got a wise heart . . . It really is a wise heart!"

N.B.: When I lived in Kazan I got a job as janitor and gardener to the widow of General Cornet. She was a Frenchwoman—young, fat, with the skinny legs of an adolescent girl; she had amazingly beautiful eyes, restless, always wide open and avid. I think she had been a shopgirl or a cook before she married, maybe even a tart. She started drinking in the morning and would come out into the yard or the garden in just her nightgown with an orange robe over it, wearing red morocco Tartar slippers. Her thick hair was like a mane; pinned up carelessly, it kept falling down over her red cheeks and her shoulders. A young witch. She used to walk around the garden humming French songs and watching me work; from time to time she'd go up to the kitchen window and say:

"Pauline, let me have something."

The "something" was always the same, a glass of vodka with ice . . .

Three young ladies, the orphan Princesses D.-G., lived on the ground floor of her house. Their father, a general in the Quartermaster Corps, had gone off somewhere and their mother was dead. Madame Cornet had taken a dislike to the young ladies and was trying to get them to move out by playing various dirty tricks on them. Her Russian was bad but she could curse magnificently, like a drayman. I really disliked her attitude toward those poor young ladies—they were so sad, constantly frightened of one thing or another, and defenseless. Once around midday two of them were walking in the garden when the general's widow suddenly came out, drunk as usual, and began shouting and chasing them out of the garden. Saying nothing, they started to leave, but the general's widow stood in the gateway, stopping it up like a cork with her body, and began addressing them using the kind of serious Russian words that would make even horses shudder. When I asked her to stop cursing and let the young ladies pass, she screamed:

"I know yu! Yu crawl their window at night . . ."

I lost my temper, took her by the shoulders and pushed her out of the gateway. But she broke free, whirled around to face me, pulled open her robe, lifted her nightgown, and yelled:

"I am better zan zose rats!"

That did it. I turned her around and hit her on the backside with the spade, so that she bounded through the gate and ran around the yard, saying three times, in great astonishment:

"Oh! Oh!! Oh!!!"

After that I collected my passport from her companion Pauline, also a lush but a very sly one, tucked my belongings under my arm, and walked out of the yard, while the general's widow, standing in the window clutching a red handkerchief, called to me:

"I doan call police—is nuthing—lissen! Come back! Doan be 'fraid . . ."

XXIX

I asked him:

"Do you agree with Poznyshev* when he says that doctors have killed and continue to kill hundreds of thousands of people?"

"Are you very curious to know?"

"Very."

"Then I won't tell you!"

And he grinned, twiddling his thumbs.

I recall that in one of his stories[†] there is a comparison between a quack, a village horse-doctor, and a doctor of medicine: "The words 'the staggers,' 'piles,' 'let blood'—aren't they simply another way of talking about nerves, rheumatism, constitution, and so on?"

And that after Jenner, Behring, Pasteur. Talk about mischief!

XXX

How strange that he likes to play cards. He plays seriously, emotionally. And his hands become so nervous when he takes up his cards—as if he were holding live birds in his hand and not dead pieces of cardboard.

---

* From Tolstoy's story "The Kreutzer Sonata" (1890).
† "Polikushka" (1863).

XXXI

"Dickens said very wisely: 'Life is given us strictly on condition that we defend it valiantly right up to the end.'* In general he was a sentimental, prolix, and not very intelligent writer. All the same, he could construct a novel like no one else—much better, of course, than Balzac. Somebody has said, 'Many are possessed by the passion for writing books, but few are ashamed of them afterwards.' Balzac was not ashamed, nor was Dickens, and both of them produced a good deal of bad writing. And yet Balzac was a genius, the real thing—there's no other word for it . . ."

Somebody brought him Tikhomirov's book *Why I Stopped Being a Revolutionary.* Lev Nikolayevich picked it up from the table and said, waving the book in the air:

"Everything he says here about political assassination and how that form of resistance has no clear idea behind it is good. Such an idea, according to this reformed assassin, could only be the anarchic, absolute power of the individual, together with a contempt for society and humanity in general. He's right, but anarchic, absolute power was a slip of the pen; he should have written, monarchic. The idea is a good one, a correct one, and it will trip up all the terrorists. I mean all the honest ones. Whoever by his nature likes to kill won't be tripped up; there's nothing for him to trip over. Somebody like that is simply a murderer who accidentally wound up being a terrorist."

XXXII

At times he is smug and intolerant, like a dogmatic sectarian from beyond the Volga, and that is a terrible thing for a man who is heard clear across this world like a sonorous church bell. Yesterday he told me:

* Daniel Doyce's words in *Little Dorrit.*

"I am more of a peasant than you, and can feel things the way peasants do better than you can."

My God! He shouldn't boast of that! He mustn't!

XXXIII

I read him a scene from *The Lower Depths;* he listened attentively and then asked:

"What made you write that?"

I explained as best I could.

"You're constantly pouncing on everything like a rooster. And another thing: you always want to paint over all the nicks and cracks with your own paint. Remember Andersen's line: 'The gilt wears off, the pigskin remains.' Our peasants say, 'Everything passes, only truth remains.' Better not lay it on so thick or you'll be sorry later. And then there's your language: It's too showy. Too many tricks. Let it go. You need to write more simply. That's how ordinary people speak—simply. It can sound disjointed, but it's good. A peasant won't ask as one educated young lady did, 'Why is a third more than a fourth, if four is always more than three?' Stay away from tricks."

He spoke irritably; it was clear how strongly he disliked what I'd read. He paused, and then said, looking past me and frowning:

"That old man in your play is not likable; his goodness isn't believable. The Actor is all right, he's fine. Do you know [my play] *The Fruits of Enlightenment*? I have a cook there who resembles your Actor. It's not easy to write plays. Your prostitute comes off well too, that's the way they really must be. Have you seen some like that?"

"I have."

"Yes, that's clear. Truth always shows. But a lot of what we hear is really the author speaking—you don't have characters, and when it comes right down to it, all the people are actually one person. It must be that you don't understand women. Yours don't come off well, not a single one. One doesn't remember them . . ."

His son Andrei's wife came in to call us to tea; he rose and hurried off as if glad of a reason to end the conversation.

XXXIV

"What is the most terrible dream you ever had?"

I seldom dream and don't remember them well, but there are two dreams that remain in my memory—and will, most likely, till I die.

In one I saw a scrofulous, rotting, greenish-yellow sky; the stars in it were round and flat, with no rays, no lustre, like the sores on the skin of an emaciated man. Slithering sluggishly among them in the putrid sky, reddish lightning, snakelike, would touch a star and that star would expand into a sphere and pop noiselessly, leaving behind a dark stain like a puff of smoke, which quickly vanished in that purulent, liquid sky. So, one after another, all the stars burst and died; the sky turned darker and more frightful and then began to bubble and boil and, disintegrating into gelatinous shreds, started falling on my head, while in the spaces between the shreds could be seen the glossy blackness of roofing iron. L. N. said:

"Well, that came from some science book; you must have been reading something about astronomy and it gave you a nightmare. What was the other dream?"

The other dream: A snowy plain, smooth as a sheet of paper, with not a hill or a tree or a bush—only, barely visible, occasional birch switches sticking up out of the snow. Through the blank wilderness of snow, from horizon to horizon, a faintly perceptible road stretches like a yellow stripe, and down that road gray felt boots are slowly striding—empty ones.

He lifted those shaggy, wood-sprite's eyebrows of his, and looked at me fixedly. After a moment he said:

"That's terrible! You actually dreamt it? You didn't make it up? Because there's something bookish in it, too."

And suddenly he seemed to lose his temper. In a voice cranky and stern, tapping his knee with one finger, he said:

"You say you're not a drinker. And it's not likely that you ever drank much. All the same there's something drunken in these dreams. There was a German writer, Hoffmann, who has a story where card tables run down the streets, and other things like that—but he was a drunkard, a 'calaholic' as the literate coachmen say. Empty boots walking—that's genuinely terrifying! Even if you made it up, it's very good. Terrifying!"

He suddenly smiled through his beard so broadly that even his cheekbones glowed.

"Just imagine a card table suddenly running down Tverskaia Street on little curved legs, with its planks rattling and sending out little clouds of chalk where the score can still be made out on the green baize. Excise clerks have been playing whist on it for three straight days and nights, till it couldn't take it anymore and ran off."

He laughed, and then must have noticed that I was a bit hurt by his doubting me:

"Are you offended that your dreams struck me as bookish? Don't be. I know that at times a person can inadvertently make something up, something so strange as not to be believable, and so he thinks that he didn't invent it but dreamed it. One old landowner told how he dreamed he was walking in a wood, came out onto the steppe and saw two hills there, and suddenly they turned into women's tits, and between them arose a black face with two moons instead of eyes, like white discs, and he's standing between the woman's legs, and in front of him there's a deep black ravine and it's sucking him in. After that he began to turn gray, his hands started shaking, and he went abroad to take the water cure with Dr. Kneip. The man was bound to see something of the sort; he was a lecher."

He patted me on the shoulder.

"But you're not a drunk or a lecher. Why should you have such dreams?"

"I don't know."

"We know nothing about ourselves!"

He sighed, screwed up his eyes, thought a moment, and added in a quieter voice:

"Nothing!"

This evening when we were out talking he took my arm and said:

"Those boots marching—it gives you the shivers, doesn't it? Absolutely empty—crunch, crunch—and the snow squeaks! No question, it's good! But you're very bookish all the same. Really. Don't be angry, it's just that it's a bad thing and will hamper you."

I'm hardly a more bookish person than he is, and in this case he struck me as a heartless rationalist, whatever he might say to the contrary.

XXXV

At times you have the impression that he has just arrived from somewhere far away, where people think differently, feel and relate to each other differently, even move differently from us, and speak in another language. He sits in a corner, tired, gray, as if covered with the dust of some other earth, observing everybody attentively with the eyes of an alien and a mute.

Yesterday, just before dinner, he came into the parlor looking precisely that way, like someone who'd been far away, and sat down on the couch. After a minute of silence, he said suddenly, rocking slightly, rubbing his knees with his palms and wrinkling up his face:

"That's not the whole of it. No, there's more."

Some person, as stupid and stolid as a flatiron, asked:

"What are you talking about?"

He gave him a long look, leaned lower, gazed at the terrace where Doctor Nikitin,* Elpatievsky, and I were sitting, and asked us: "What are you talking about?"

"About Plehve."†

"About Plehve . . . Plehve . . ." he repeated pensively, with a pause, as if he were hearing that name for the first time. Then he shook himself like a bird and said, with a faint smile:

---

* D. V. Nikitin (1874–1960), the Tolstoy family's physician from 1902 to 1904.

† Vyacheslav Konstantinovich Plehve (1846–1904), minister of the interior, 1902–1904. Harsh in treatment of arrested revolutionaries, he was assassinated by terrorists in 1904.

"All day something silly has been running through my head. Somebody told me he'd seen this epitaph in a graveyard:

> Under this stone Ivan Yegoriev lies.
> A tanner by trade, he used to soak his hides.
> He labored righteously, had a kind heart, but died
> And left the tannery to his wife.
> He was not yet old, and might have been able
>   to do a lot,
> But God took him to His bosom in the night
> Between Good Friday and Holy Saturday.

And other things in the same vein . . ."

He paused and then, shaking his head, added with a faint smile:

"There's something in human stupidity—if it's not mean—that's really very touching, even lovable . . . There always is . . ."

Dinner was announced.

XXXVI

"I don't like drunks, but I know people who when they've had a little become interesting, show a wit they don't have when sober, along with elegance of thought, adroitness, and richness of expression. Then I am ready to bless alcohol."

Suler told how he had been walking on Tverskaia Street with Lev Nikolayevich when Tolstoy noticed two cuirassiers in the distance. With the copper of their breastplates ablaze in the sunlight, spurs jingling, they walked in step as if conjoined, and their faces, too, gleamed with the self-satisfaction of strength and youth.

Tolstoy began to rail against them:

"What majestic stupidity! Absolute animals, trained with a whip . . ."

But when the cuirassiers passed close to him, he stopped and, following them with an affectionate glance, said admiringly:

"Aren't they beautiful, though! Ancient Romans, eh, Lyovushka? The vitality, the beauty, my God! How good it is when a man is handsome, how very good!"

XXXVII

One very hot day he caught up with me on the low road. He was on a docile little Tartar horse, riding in the direction of Livadia. Gray, shaggy, in a hat of thin white felt shaped like a mushroom, he was like a gnome.

He reined in his horse and started talking; I walked alongside the stirrup. When I mentioned in passing that I had received a letter from V. G. Korolenko, Tolstoy shook his beard angrily:

"Does he believe in God?"

"I don't know."

"Then you don't know the most important thing. He believes, only he's ashamed to admit it in front of atheists."

He spoke querulously, capriciously, his eyes narrowed in anger. It was clear that my presence was unwelcome, but when I tried to walk away he stopped me:

"Where are you going? I've slowed down."

And he started grumbling again:

"That Andreyev* of yours is also afraid of the atheists, but he believes in God too, and God terrifies him."

At the boundary of Grand Duke A. M. Romanov's estate, standing close to each other in the road, three Romanovs were talking: the master of the Ai-Todor estate, Georgy, and one other—Pyotr Nikolayevich from Diulber, I think—all of them solid and manly fellows. A one-horse drozhky and a saddle horse blocked the road; Lev Nikolayevich could not pass. He stared at the Romanovs sternly and demandingly. But they had their backs

* The writer Leonid Nikolayevich Andreyev. See below, pp. 115–163.

to him when we arrived. The saddle horse shifted in place, then moved to the side a little, letting Tolstoy's horse through.

After we'd gone on a minute or two in silence, he said:

"They recognized me, the fools."

And a minute after that:

"The horse understood that it had to make way for Tolstoy."

XXXVIII

"Take care of yourself in the first place, for your own sake; then much will be left for other people, too."

XXXIX

"What does it mean to know something? I know, for instance, that I am Tolstoy, a writer, that I have a wife, children, gray hairs, an ugly face, and a beard—they put all that in passports. But they don't put anything in passports about the soul. About the soul I know one thing: the soul desires closeness to God. And what is God? That, of which my soul is a particle. That's the whole of it. Anyone who has learned to think finds it hard to believe, yet to live in God is only possible through faith. Tertullian said, 'Thought is evil.'"

XL

Despite the monotony of his preaching, this fabulous man is infinitely various.

Today, in the park, chatting with the mullah of Gaspra, he acted like a trusting country bumpkin for whom the hour had come to think about the end of his days. Small as he was, he seemed to have deliberately shrunk even more; next to that strong and solid Tartar he looked like a little old man whose soul had just begun to ponder the meaning of existence and feared the questions he found it confronting. He raised his shaggy eyebrows in astonishment and, timidly blinking his sharp little eyes, extinguished their unbearably penetrating brilliance. His searching glance rested motionless on the mullah's broad face; his pupils lost that keenness that usually makes people so uneasy. He asked the mullah "childish" questions about the meaning of life, the soul, and God, deftly replacing verses of the Koran with verses from the Gospels and the prophets. Basically he was playing, and doing it with the astonishing art that only a great actor and wise man can command.

A few days ago, speaking with Taneyev* and Suler about music, he was as delighted as a child with its beauty, and it was clear that he took pleasure in his own delight—or rather, in his ability to be delighted. He said that the best and deepest writing about music was Schopenhauer's, told in passing an amusing story about [the poet] Fet, and called music "the mute prayer of the soul."

"What do you mean mute?" Suler asked.

"Because it is wordless. There is more soul in sounds than in thoughts. A thought is a purse with coins in it, but a sound is internally pure, unsullied by anything."

He spoke with obvious enjoyment, using affectionate, childish words as the best and tenderest of them surfaced in his memory. Then, suddenly, grinning into his beard, he said softly and almost caressingly:

"Musicians are all stupid people, and the more talented the musician, the narrower he is. It's strange that they're almost all religious."

XLI

To Chekhov, on the telephone:

"Today is such a good day for me, there is such gladness in my heart, that I want you to feel gladness, too. You in particular! You are a very, very good person!"

* Sergei Ivanovich Taneyev (1856–1915), composer, pianist, teacher, and author.

XLII

He doesn't listen—and doesn't believe it—when people say the wrong thing. Basically, he doesn't ask, he interrogates, like a collector of rarities taking only what will not spoil the harmony of his collection.

XLIII

Going through the mail:

"They make a fuss, they write me letters, but I'll die, and a year later they'll be asking: 'Tolstoy? Oh, that's the count who tried to stitch boots and something happened to him—that one, right?' "

XLIV

Several times I've seen on his face, in his look, the sly and contented grin of a man who has unexpectedly come upon some thing he himself had hidden, hidden it and forgotten where. For long days he's lived in secret alarm, thinking all the time: "I need that thing. Where did I put it?"—and in fear that people would notice his alarm, his loss, that they would notice and do something unpleasant, something bad to him. Then suddenly he has remembered and found it. Filled with joy and no longer at pains to conceal it, he looks at everyone slyly, as if to say:

"You can't get at me now!"

But about what he's found, and where, he is silent.

One never tires of marveling at him; all the same, it's difficult to see him too often, and I could never live in the same house—let alone the same room—with him. That would be like trying to live in a desert where everything has been burnt by the sun, while that sun itself is also burning down, threatening a dark night without end.

A LETTER

I had just sent off a letter to you when the telegrams about "Tolstoy's flight" arrived. And here I am, still not disconnected from you in thought, writing again.

Everything I want to say about this news will probably get said confusedly, maybe even harshly and angrily. If so, forgive me. I feel as if I'd been taken by the throat and were being throttled.

He talked with me many times and at length. When I lived at Gaspra in the Crimea I was often at his place; he also liked to come to mine. I read his books with care and love—and so I think I have the right to say what I think about him, even if it seems presumptuous, and even if it goes counter to the prevailing attitude toward him. I am no less aware than others that there is not a man more worthy of being called a genius, not a man more complex, contradictory, and great in everything—yes, yes, in everything. Great in a special, broad sense that defies formulation in words—there is something in him that has always made me want to shout to all and sundry: "Look what an amazing man is living on the earth!" For he is, so to speak, all-encompassingly and above all a man—a man among men.

But I have always been repelled by that stubborn and despotic urge of his to turn the life of Count Lev Nikolayevich Tolstoy into "the vita of our holy father, the blessed boyar Saint Leo." You know how long he began wanting "to suffer"; he has told Evgenii Solovyov and Suler of his regret at not succeeding. But he has wanted to suffer not simply, not out of a natural desire to test the resilience of his will, but rather with the plain and, I repeat, despotic intention of intensifying the weight of his teaching, making his preaching irresistible, sanctifying it in people's eyes through his suffering, and forcing them to accept it—you understand, forcing! For he knows that this doctrine is not convincing enough; in his diary you will read—in time—good examples of his skepticism about his own teaching and personality. He knows that "martyrs and sufferers rarely escape being despots and oppressors"—he knows everything! And yet he says: "If I suffered for my

ideas they would produce a different impression." This has always repelled me, for I can't help feeling in it an attempt to coerce me, a desire to
take over my conscience and dazzle it with the radiance of a martyr's blood,
to fasten the yoke of dogma around my neck.

He has always been lavish in his paeans to immortality in the next
world, but he likes it better in this one. A national writer in the truest sense,
he has embodied in that enormous soul of his all the nation's faults, all the
mutilations inflicted on us by the torments of our history; his cloudy
preaching of "nonactivity" and "nonresistance to evil"—a doctrine of
passivism—is all an unhealthy ferment of the old Russian blood, tainted
with Mongolian fanaticism and chemically, if one can put it that way, hostile to the West with its ceaseless creative labor. What people call "Tolstoy's anarchism" is essentially an expression of our Slavic antistatism,
another truly national trait . . . [When at length] people appeared who
sensed that we should seek light not from the East but from the West, he—
the culminating figure of our old history—wished (both consciously and
unconsciously) to lie like a mountain across the road that leads to Europe,
to that active life which demands of men the utmost concentration of all
their spiritual powers. His attitude toward science is also, of course, deeply
national, a remarkable reflection of the old-Russian, traditional village
skepticism, born of ignorance. In him everything is national, and his whole
teaching is reaction, an atavism which we were on the point of shaking off
and overcoming.

Think of his letter "The Intelligentsia, the State and the People," written in 1905—what an offensive and gloating piece, with its implicit insistence: "I told you so, but you wouldn't listen!" I wrote him an answer at the
time based on his own admission to me that he had "long since forfeited the
right to speak about the Russian people and in its name," for I had witnessed his unwillingness to listen to or understand the people when they
would come to him for a heart-to-heart talk. My letter was a harsh one, and
I never sent it.

And now he is making what is probably his last leap, in order to lend
his ideas the greatest possible significance. Like Vasily Buslayev, he has al-

ways been fond of leaps—but always toward the confirmation of his saintliness and his quest for a halo. This smacks of the Inquisition, although his teachings find justification in Russia's long history, and in the personal sufferings of genius. Sanctity is achieved by the rapt contemplation of one's sins, and the enslavement of the will-to-life . . .

There is much in Lev Nikolayevich that at times has evoked something close to hatred in me, much that has been like an oppressive burden on my soul. His hypertrophied personality is a monstrous thing, a thing almost deformed; he has something in him of Sviatogor, the legendary hero whom the earth cannot hold. Yes, he is great! I am utterly convinced that beyond everything he talks about there is a great deal about which he remains silent, even in his diary—remains silent, and will probably never speak of to anyone. This "something" would only occasionally get hinted at in his conversation, as it is hinted at in the two diaries he gave me and L. A. Sulerzhitsky to read; I see it as something like the "denial of all affirmations"—a profound and evil nihilism that has sprung up on the soil of an endless and intractable despair and loneliness, of a sort that probably no one before him ever experienced with such appalling clarity. He has often struck me as a man who is fundamentally, in the depth of his soul, indifferent to people, being so much higher and more powerful than they that they all seem like midges to him, and their frantic concerns ludicrous and pitiable. He has gone too far off from them into some wilderness where, concentrating all the powers of his spirit to the utmost, he gazes in solitude at "the main thing"—death.

He has hated and feared it all his life; all his life the "Arzamas horror"* has flickered at the edges of his consciousness: can it really be that

* Passing through the town of Arzamas in early September 1869, Tolstoy had stopped in a hotel there and been overwhelmed by feelings of "melancholy, fear, and horror" for reasons he could not explain; he described the experience in his story "Notes of a Madman." In an unpublished article of 1931 Gorky refers to this "Arzamas horror" as "the horror of man's aloneness in the cosmos," "the horror of man's awareness that he must inescapably perish as an individual." ("O samoubijstve," in M. Gor'kij, *Xudožestvennye proizvedenija. Stat'i. Zametki* [Arxiv A. M. Gor'kogo, 12], [Moscow: "Nauka," 1969], 141.)

he, Tolstoy, should have to die? The eyes of the entire world—the whole earth—are on him; from China, India, America—from everywhere—living, quivering threads stretch out to him; his soul is for all men and all times! Why shouldn't nature make an exception to its laws and grant one person physical immortality—why? He of course is too rational and intelligent to believe in miracles, but, on the other hand, he is a trickster, a tester, and like a young recruit wild with fear and desperation as he approaches the door of an unfamiliar barracks. I remember how, in Gaspra, after his recovery, when he'd read Lev Shestov's book *Good and Evil in the Teaching of Nietzsche and Count Tolstoy,* he said in reply to Chekhov's remarking that he hadn't liked the book:

"I found it amusing. Pretentiously written, but not bad. Interesting. I actually like cynics if they're sincere. He says, for instance, 'Truth is not required,' and he's right. What does he need truth for? He'll die all the same."

Then, evidently noticing that his words had not been understood, he added with an ironic smile:

"Once a person has learned to think, whatever else he may be thinking about, he is always thinking about his own death. You can see it in all the philosophers. And what kind of truths can there be if death is on the way?"

He went on to begin explaining that there is one truth for everyone, love for God—but he spoke coldly and wearily on that subject. Then after lunch, on the terrace, he picked up the book again, and when he found the place where the author writes, "Tolstoy, Dostoyevsky, and Nietzsche couldn't live without an answer to their questions, and for them any answer was better than nothing," he burst out laughing and said:

"There's a daring barber for you. He says straight out that I deceived myself; that means I deceived others, too. It follows clearly enough . . ."

Suler asked: "Why barber?"

"It just came into my head," he answered pensively. "He's chic and modish—and I recalled a barber from Moscow at the village wedding of his peasant uncle. The best manners, and dances the latest dances, and so looks down on everyone."

I am reproducing this conversation almost verbatim; I remember it very well and even wrote it down, like much else that struck me. Suler and I both wrote down a lot, but Suler lost his notes on the way to see me in Arzamas—he was careless in general, and although he loved Lev Nikolayevich almost like a woman, he treated him strangely, a touch condescendingly. I too put my notes away where I can't lay my hands on them; someone in Russia has them. I studied Tolstoy very attentively because I was looking, as I am looking still, and will be until I die, for a man of genuine, living faith. I studied him also because Chekhov once complained, a propos of our lack of culture:

"Every word of Goethe's got written down, but Tolstoy's thoughts are lost in the air. That, my friend, is intolerably Russian. Afterwards people will come to their senses and start writing memoirs, and they'll be full of lies."

But to come back to Shestov:

"He says one can't live always gazing at frightening apparitions. How does he know whether one can or can't? If he really knew, if he saw apparitions himself, he wouldn't write such rubbish but would occupy himself seriously with what occupied Buddha all his life."

Someone observed that Shestov was a Jew.

"Not likely," L. N. said mistrustfully. "No, he's not like a Jew; there are no nonbelieving Jews—you can't name a single one!"

It sometimes seemed that this old sorcerer was toying with death, flirting with it and trying to get the better of it somehow: *I'm not afraid of you, I love you, I'm waiting for you.* All the while peering out with those sharp little eyes: *So what exactly are you? And what is there beyond you, farther along? Will you destroy me utterly or will something of me go on living?*

"I am happy, terribly happy, too happy": those words of his produced a strange impression. And, immediately after: "Oh, to suffer." To suffer: that too was truth in him; I don't doubt for a moment that he, even while he was convalescing, would have been genuinely happy to land in prison or exile—to receive a martyr's crown one way or another. It may well be that martyrdom can justify death somewhat, make it more understandable and acceptable from an external, formal point of view. But I am convinced that he has never been satisfied; that never and nowhere—neither poring over tomes of wisdom nor racing on horseback nor lying in the arms of a woman has he ever known earthly bliss in all its fullness. He is too rational for that; he knows life and people too well. Here are more of his words:

"Caliph Abdurahman had fourteen happy days in his life. I have probably not had as many—and all because I never lived, never knew how to live, for myself, for my soul, but only for show, for other people."

A. P. Chekhov said to me as we were leaving him: "I don't believe that he hasn't been happy." But I do. He hasn't. What is not true is that he has lived "for show." Yes, he has given to people, as to beggars, what he didn't need himself; it has pleased him to make them do things—"make them" read, take walks, eat only vegetables, love the muzhik, and believe in the infallibility of the rationalistic-religious conjectures of Lev Tolstoy. You have to give people something that will either satisfy them or keep them busy if you want to get rid of them in order to sink back into your habitual, tormenting but sometimes cozy solitude and confront again the fathomless enigma of "the main thing."

All Russian preachers—with the exception of Avvakum and, perhaps, Tikhon Zadonskii*—have been cold individuals, for they did not possess a living and efficacious faith. When I wrote the part of Luka in *The Lower Depths* it was precisely that kind of old man I wanted to represent: "all kinds of answers" interest him, but people don't. When, inevitably, he comes into contact with people he tries to offer comfort, but only to keep them from interfering with his life. And the whole philosophy and all the preaching of such individuals is a kind of alms which they bestow on the beggars around them while hiding their aversion; and between the lines of the sermons a querulous and beggarly message of their own remains unspoken:

"Go away! Love God or your neighbor—just go away! Or curse God and love someone who's not a neighbor—but go away! Leave me alone, for I am a man and doomed to die!"

---

* Tikhon Zadonskii (1724–1783), saint, bishop of Voronezh, prototype for Father Zosima in Dostoyevsky's *Brothers Karamazov*.

Alas, that is how things are, and how they will continue to be! Nor can it be otherwise, for people are exhausted, tormented, terribly isolated, and they are all shackled by a loneliness that sucks the soul out of them. It would not at all surprise me if L. N. were to reconcile with the church. That would have a certain logic to it: all people are equally insignificant, even if they are bishops. Actually, it would not be a reconciliation at all; for him personally this act would be merely a logical step: "I forgive those who hate me"—a Christian act, but performed with a secret grin, betokening a clever man's requital of fools.

But none of this is what I wanted to say; I keep going on about the wrong things, in the wrong way. A dog is howling in my soul and I am full of foreboding. And now the newspapers have come, and it's clear: back in Russia they're already beginning to "create a legend": *Once upon a time there were idlers and drones—and lo! they brought forth a saint.* Just think how pernicious that will be for the country at a time when people are disappointed and downcast, the souls of the majority empty and the souls of the best full of sorrow. Hungry and tattered, they are all desperate for a myth. They want so much to slake their pain and quiet their torments! And they will be creating just what he wanted but what we do not need—the story of a holy man and a saint. In fact he is great and holy because he is a man, an insanely and maddeningly beautiful man, a man of all mankind. I know I'm contradicting myself here, but it's not important. He is a man seeking God not for himself but for others, so that God might leave him, a man, in peace, alone in the wilderness he has chosen. He gave us his Gospels,* and to make us forget about Christ's contradictions he simplified his image, played down the militancy in him and accentuated his submissiveness to "the will of Him who sent me." There is no question but what Tolstoy's gospel is more easily acceptable, for it accords more with the "ailment" of the Russian people. And those people had to be given something, for they were complaining, shaking the earth with their groans, and

* Gorky is referring to three works of Tolstoy's, printed in England and banned in Russia: *A Short Account of the Gospels, How to Read the Gospels and What Is Their Essence,* and *A Harmony, Translation and Study of the Four Gospels.*

distracting him from "the main thing." Nor could *War and Peace* and the other things of that sort appease the sorrow and despair of our great drab Russia.

About *War and Peace* he himself said: "Putting aside false modesty, it is like *The Iliad.*" M. I. Chaikovsky heard from his own lips the same appraisal of *Childhood* and *Boyhood.*

Reporters from Naples have just been here—one of them had hurried down from Rome. They asked me to tell them what I thought about Tolstoy's "flight"—that's what they call it: "flight." I refused to talk with them. You understand of course that my soul is in a state of wild alarm. I don't want to see Tolstoy made a saint; let him remain a sinner, close to the heart of this thoroughly sinful world, and close forever to the heart of each of us. Pushkin and he—we have nothing more majestic or precious . . .

Lev Tolstoy is dead.

The telegram has come, and it says in the most ordinary of words that he has died.

It is a blow to the heart; I have howled out my grief and injury, and now, in a half-crazed state, I picture him as I have seen and known him, and feel an agonizing need to speak of him. I picture him lying in his coffin like a smooth stone at the bottom of a brook, with that deceptive half-smile of detachment hidden in his gray beard. His hands, at last, are serenely folded, their arduous labor done.

I remember his keen eyes—they saw through everything—and the movements of his fingers, which always seemed to be sculpting something from the air; and his conversation, his jokes, his favorite peasant words and the indeterminate timbre of his voice. And I see how much life the man embraced, how inhumanly intelligent he was, and how awful.

Once I saw him as perhaps no one else ever has: I was on the way to visit him in Gaspra, walking along the seashore, when suddenly, just below the Yusupov estate, among the rocks at the very edge of the water, I caught sight of his small angular figure, clothes gray and rumpled, a crushed hat on his head. He was sitting with his chin in his hands, the silvery hairs of his beard straggling out from between his fingers, and gazing far out to sea, while the greenish wavelets rolled in to lap obediently at his feet as if confiding something about themselves to the old wizard. It was a day of changeable weather; the shadows of clouds crept over the rocks, and the old man would be alternately lit up and covered in shade together with the rocks. The rocks were huge, deeply fissured, and littered with pungent seaweed; the surf had been high the night before. And he himself looked like an ancient rock that had come to life, one that knew the beginnings and ends of all things and was considering when and how the end would come for the rocks and grasses of the earth, for the water of the seas, for humankind, for everything from a pebble to the sun. The sea was like a part of his soul, and everything around seemed to have come from him and be one with him. In the sight of that old man, motionless and lost in thought, one felt something magical and prophetic, plunging down into the darkness beneath him and towering above him into the blue void over the earth, as if it were he, his concentrated will, that was summoning the waves and sending them out again, directing the movements of the clouds and shadows which appeared to be pushing against the rocks, trying to awaken them. And suddenly, for one mad moment, I felt that he might be about to stand up and wave his arm, and that the sea would grow calm and glassy, and the rocks would move and begin to shout, and everything around would stir and come to life and start talking in different voices about itself, and about him, and against him. I cannot put into words what I felt then; I was filled both with rapture and horror, and then everything came together in one happy thought:

"I am not an orphan on the earth so long as this man is alive."

Then, taking care that the pebbles under my feet should make no sound, I turned back, not wanting to disturb his reverie. And now, today, I feel myself an orphan. I write and weep—never before have I wept so inconsolably, so despairingly and so bitterly. I can't say whether I loved him, but love or hate, what difference does it make? He always aroused enormous, fantastic sensations and emotions in me; even the disagreeable and hostile feelings that he provoked in me assumed forms that didn't oppress my heart but, so to speak, blasted it open, expanding it and making it more capacious and sensitive. How fine he was when, shuffling along as if smoothing out the roughness of the road with the soles of his boots, he would suddenly appear from behind a door or around a corner and walk toward you with the short, light, rapid steps of a man long accustomed to walking the earth. Sticking his thumbs in his belt, he would pause for a second, looking around with that prehensile glance of his that took in everything new and extracted its meaning on the spot, before saying:

"Hello!"

I always translated that word as meaning: "Hello—there's not much pleasure for me or use for you in this, but hello all the same!"

He would come out, a little man, and immediately everyone around would become smaller than he. His peasant beard, his rough but extraordinary hands, his simple clothing—that whole comfortably democratic exterior of his—deceived many people, and I often had occasion to see how Russians, who are used to dealing with a person according to the way he is dressed (an ancient, slavish habit!), would fall into that odious "straightforwardness" which might better be called vulgarity and presumption.

"Oh, you dear man! Look at you! At long last I have the honor of beholding with my own eyes the greatest son of my native land! Accept my respects, and may you flourish forever!"

That is the Moscow variant, simple and heartfelt. But there is also a "freethinking-Russian" variant:

"Lev Nikolayevich! Disagreeing though I do with your religious-philosophical views, but deeply respecting the great artist in you . . ."

And suddenly from under the peasant beard, from under the democratically rumpled blouse would emerge the old Russian nobleman, the splendid aristocrat, and in a flash the noses of these people—plainspoken or educated or whatever—would turn blue from the intolerable cold. It was wonderful to see this pure-blooded creature, wonderful to witness the nobility and grace of his gestures, the proud reserve of his speech, and the elegant precision of his icy words. There was just as much of the nobleman in him as was needed to deal with these lackeys. And when they called forth the nobleman in Tolstoy, the nobleman surfaced freely and easily and crushed them so effectively that they could only curl up and whimper.

I once found myself returning from Yasnaya Polyana to Moscow with one of those "plain-spoken" Russians, a Muscovite, who for a long time could not recover his breath but kept smiling plaintively and repeating in dismay:

"He really let me have it! What a hard man!"

"And I thought he was actually an anarchist," he added ruefully. "Everybody keeps repeating 'anarchist, anarchist,' and I believed it . . ."

This was a rich man, a major industrialist. He had a big belly and a shiny face the color of raw meat; why did he need Tolstoy to be an anarchist? It is one of the "profound mysteries" of the Russian soul.

If, on the other hand, L. N. wished to please, he could do it more easily than a clever and beautiful woman. I remember one such scene. Various callers are sitting with him: the Grand Duke Nikolai Mikhailovich, the house-painter Ilya, a Social Democrat from Yalta, the Shtundist Patsuk, some musician, a German, Kleinmichel the Countess' steward, the poet Bulgakov, and they are all looking at him with identically enamored eyes. He is expounding to them the teaching of Lao Tse, and he seems to me to be some sort of extraordinary one-man orchestra, able to play several instruments simultaneously—the trumpet, the drum, the accordion, and the flute. I looked at him the way they were all looking at him. And now I long for another look, and I shall never see him again.

Reporters have been here, claiming that a telegram was received in Rome "denying the rumor about the death of Lev Tolstoy." They fussed and chattered, fulsome in their expressions of sympathy for Russia. The Russian papers leave no room for doubt.

It was impossible to lie to him, even out of pity—though he never elicited that, even when he was dangerously ill. To pity people like him is fatuous. They need to be cared for and cherished, not sprinkled with the verbal dust of worn-out, mechanical phrases.

He would ask:

"You don't like me?"

The answer had to be: "No, I don't."

"You don't love me?"

"Not today I don't."

He was unsparing in his questions and reserved in his replies, as befits a wise man.

He talked most wonderfully about the past, and best of all about Turgenev. About Fet he would talk with a good-humored grin, and always tell something amusing. About Nekrasov he spoke coldly and skeptically; in general he spoke about writers as if they were his children and he their father, who knew all their shortcomings and—*come and get it!*—preferred to stress the bad in them over the good. And whenever he spoke ill of someone I had the impression that he was giving alms to his hearers out of regard for their poverty. It was uncomfortable listening to him then; when he turned that sharp little smile on you, you involuntarily lowered your eyes—and nothing stayed in your memory.

Once he had argued heatedly that G. I. Uspensky wrote in the language of the Tula province and was utterly without talent. And yet in my presence he said to A. P. Chekhov:

"There's a writer for you! In the strength of his sincerity he reminds you of Dostoyevsky, only Dostoyevsky was an intriguer and a showoff, while Uspensky is simpler and more sincere. If he had believed in God he'd have wound up as some kind of sectarian."

"Then how could you have said that he was a Tula writer and had no talent?"

His eyes disappeared under his shaggy brows and he said:

"He wrote badly. Think of his style: more punctuation marks than words. Talent is love. Whoever loves is talented. Look at lovers—they're all talented!"

About Dostoyevsky he spoke reluctantly and evasively, trying to overcome something: you felt the strain.

"He should have acquainted himself with the teachings of Confucius or the Buddhists, that would have calmed him. That is the main thing anyone and everyone needs to know. He was a violently physical man; when he got angry he'd get bumps on his bald spot and his ears would twitch. He felt a lot but thought poorly; he learned to think from those people, the Fourierists, Butashevich* and others. And then he hated them for the rest of his life. There was something Jewish in his blood. He was suspicious, proud, difficult, and unhappy. It's strange that he's read so much, I can't understand why! It's painful and it's futile, because all those Idiots, Adolescents, Raskolnikovs, and the rest—they're not how it was; things were simpler and more understandable. Whereas Leskov is neglected in vain; he's a real writer. Have you read him?"

"Yes. I like him a lot. Especially his language."

"He knew the language marvelously, with all its tricks. It's strange that you should like him; there's something un-Russian about you, your thoughts are not Russian—you don't mind my saying that? You're not offended? I'm an old man and it may be that I just don't understand what people are writing these days—still, I can't help thinking that it's not Russian. And the peculiar poems they're publishing—I don't know why they're poetry, or who they're for. They should learn to write poems from Pushkin, Tiutchev, Shenshin [Fet]. But you"—he turned to Chekhov—"you're Russian! Very, very Russian."

And with an affectionate smile he put his arm around A. P., who got flustered and began saying something in a low voice about his dacha and about Tartars.

He loved Chekhov, and whenever he looked at him his glance, turning almost tender for the moment, seemed to caress A. P.'s face. Once A. P.

---

* Mikhail Vasilievich Butashevich-Petrashevsky (1821–1866), better known in English simply as Petrashevsky, was the organizer of a circle for the study and propagation of utopian socialist ideas in Petersburg; for his membership in the Petrashevsky circle the young Dostoyevsky was condemned in 1849 to four years in a Siberian prison, followed by four more as a soldier.

was walking on the garden path with Alexandra Lvovna. Tolstoy, still ill at
the time and seated in a chair on the terrace, leaned in their direction and
said under his breath:

"What a fine man, and what a dear one, modest and demure like a
young lady! And he walks like one. He's just wonderful!"

One evening, at dusk, squinting, his eyebrows twitching, he read us a
version of the scene in "Father Sergius" where the woman goes to seduce
the hermit. He read it clear through, raised his head, closed his eyes, and
said with great clarity:

"The old man really could write!"

He said it with such amazing simplicity—his delight at the beauty of
what he'd written was so sincere—that I will always remember the thrill I
felt then, a joy I could find no words for, and one that cost me an enormous
effort to control. My heart even seemed to stand still, and then everything
around me became bracingly fresh and new.

You had to witness the way he spoke to have any sense of the special
and indefinable beauty of his speech, with all its apparent incorrectness, its
incessant repetition of particular words, its saturation with peasant-like simplicity. His words took their force from his intonation and the expressiveness of his features—particularly from the play of his shining eyes, the most
eloquent eyes I have ever seen. L. N. had a thousand eyes in that single pair
of his.

Suler, Chekhov, Tolstoy's son Sergei, and someone else were sitting
in the park and talking of women. He listened in silence for a long time and
then said suddenly:

"I'll tell the truth about women when I have one foot in the grave.
Then I'll jump into my coffin and pull the lid down over me—just try and
catch me then!" And his eyes shone with such unnerving provocation that
for a minute no one spoke.

As I see it, he combined the daring and inquisitive mischievousness of
a Vaska Buslayev with something of the Archpriest Avvakum's stubbornness of soul, while above (or beside) all this lay hidden the skepticism of a

Chaadayev.* The Avvakum element preached, lacerating the soul of the artist in him; it was the Novgorod mischief-maker in him that denied the greatness of Shakespeare and Dante; while the Chaadayev in him grinned at these soulful vagaries—and, incidentally, at the agonies they entailed.

At the same time it was the ancient Russian in him, moved by the failure of his myriad efforts to build a more humane life, that turned to passive anarchism and took to thundering against science and government.

It is amazing, but Olaf Gulbranson, the caricaturist for *Simplicissimus*, grasped the Buslayev trait in Tolstoy by some mysterious intuition. Look closely at his drawing and marvel at its likeness to the real Lev Tolstoy. How much daring intelligence there is in that face with its deep-set, shrouded eyes! Here is a mind that holds nothing inviolably sacred, believing "neither in sneezes, nor dreams, nor the croaking of birds." [†]

The old wizard stands before me, alien to everyone, a solitary traveler searching vainly through all the deserts of thought for an all-embracing truth. I gaze at him and, for all my grief that he is gone, still the pride at having seen this man lightens my pain and sorrow.

It was strange to see L. N. among the "Tolstoyans." A majestic belfry, whose bell peals incessantly across the whole world—and around it timid little dogs scurry, adding their yelps to the tolling of the bell and looking

---

* Vaska (Vasily) Buslayev is the hero of two old-Russian folk narratives—a devil-may-care, hard-drinking antihero at war with all respectable society who later came to be admired for his valor, daring, and freethinking. The Archpriest Avvakum was a seventeenth-century cleric, an Old Believer who vigorously and unbendingly opposed even the slightest modifications to Russian Orthodox ritual, for which he courted and ultimately achieved martyrdom; he was burned at the stake in 1681. Pyotr Chaadayev (1793–1856), an early convert to mystical Catholicism, wrote his *Philosophical Letters* on the meaning of history around 1830; in the first of them he is unsparing in branding Russian history as a paltry thing, unable to sustain comparison with the history of Western Europe. For this he was officially declared a madman; for the same reasons he was revered by the Europe-oriented youth of the time.

[†] A common formula in Old Russian literature signifying disdain for pagan belief in signs and omens.

sidelong at each other to see who is howling the best. It always seemed to me that these people brought to both his house at Yasnaya Polyana and the palace of Countess Panina [where he stayed in the Crimea] a taint compounded of hypocrisy, cowardice, petty haggling, and vying for the inheritance. There is something in common between the "Tolstoyans" and those wanderers who traverse Russia from one end to the other, carrying dogs' bones which they pass off as fragments of holy relics and selling "Egyptian darkness" and "the tears" of the Virgin Mary. I remember one such apostle refusing to eat eggs at Yasnaya Polyana out of sympathy for the hens—and then, at the station in Tula, eating meat with gusto, saying:

"The old man overdoes it!"

Almost all of them are given to sighing and bestowing kisses; they all have limp sweaty hands and shifty eyes. At the same time these are practical people, quite shrewd when it comes to arranging their earthly affairs.

L. N. of course understood very well what these "Tolstoyans" were, as did Sulerzhitsky, whom he loved so tenderly and about whom he always spoke with youthful enthusiasm and delight. Once someone at Yasnaya Polyana was describing eloquently how good his life had become, and how pure his soul, since he had adopted the teachings of Tolstoy. L. N. leaned over to me and said softly:

"He's lying, the scoundrel, but he's doing it to please me . . ."

Many people tried to please him in this way, but few that I observed did it well or effectively. He almost never talked to me about his usual subjects—universal forgiveness, love for one's neighbor, the Gospels and Buddhism—evidently because he'd seen from the beginning that it wouldn't go down well. I deeply appreciated that.

When he wanted he could be wonderfully tactful, sensitive and gentle, his speech charmingly simple and elegant, but there were times when it was hard and unpleasant to listen to him. I never liked what he had to say about women; in that area he was excessively crude. There was something artificial about it, something at the same time insincere and very personal. It was as if he'd been hurt once in a way that he could neither forget nor forgive. The evening I first met him he took me into his study—it was in Moscow— sat me opposite him and began to talk about my stories "Varenka Olesova" and "Twenty-Six Men and a Girl." I was upset by his tone and even lost my head, so plainly and harshly did he speak, arguing that modesty was not natural in a healthy girl.

"If the girl is over fifteen and healthy, she wants to be hugged and squeezed. Her mind fears what it doesn't yet know or understand—that is what people mean when they talk about chastity and modesty. But her flesh already knows that what is incomprehensible is nevertheless inevitable and legitimate, and that it demands fulfillment, her mind's fears notwithstanding. You describe your Varenka Olesova as being healthy, but her feelings are anemic and that is false!"

He then started talking about the girl from [my story] "Twenty-Six Men and a Girl," uttering a stream of "indecent" words with a casualness that struck me as unseemly and even somewhat offensive. Later I came to understand that he used such obscenities simply because he found them more pointed and precise, but at the time they were unpleasant for me to hear. I let the matter pass, however, and suddenly he became kind and considerate, asking me about my life, my education, and my reading.

"They say you're very well read. Is it true? What about Korolenko? Is he a musician?"

"I don't think so. I don't know."

"You don't? Do you like his stories?"

"Very much."

"That's because of the contrast. He's a lyrical writer and you're not. Have you read Veltman?"*

"I have."

---

* Alexander Fomich Veltman (1800–1870), Russian novelist best known for his cycle of whimsical, Sternean novels published between 1846 and 1863.

"He's good, isn't he? Lively, exact, no exaggeration. At times he's better than Gogol. He knew Balzac. Whereas Gogol imitated Marlinsky."*

When I said that Gogol in all likelihood had been influenced by Hoffmann, Sterne, and maybe Dickens, he glanced at me and then asked:

"You must have read that somewhere, yes? Well, it's not true. Gogol hardly knew Dickens. But you really have read a lot—be careful, it can be dangerous! Koltsov ruined himself that way."

Seeing me out he put his arms around me, kissed me, and said:

"You're a real muzhik! You'll have a hard time rubbing elbows with our writers, but don't let anything intimidate you. Always say what you feel; if it comes out crudely, don't worry. Intelligent people will understand."

I came away from this first meeting with mixed feelings. I was both happy and proud to have met Tolstoy, but his conversation with me was a bit like an examination. It was as if I had met not the author of *The Cossacks,* "Strider," and *War and Peace,* but rather a condescending nobleman who felt constrained to speak to me like "an ordinary fellow," in "the language of the street," and this tended to upset my idea of him, an idea I had gotten used to, and one that was dear to me.

I saw him for the second time at Yasnaya Polyana, on a dank autumn day. It was drizzling, and he, in a heavy outercoat and waterproof boots, took me walking in the birch grove. He leapt across the ditches and puddles like a young man, shaking raindrops from the branches onto his head while he gave a marvelous account of how Shenshin had explained Schopenhauer to him in this very grove. Tenderly and lovingly, he stroked the moist and satiny trunks of the birches and said:

"I recently read these verses somewhere:

> The mushrooms are gone but the hollows are filled
> With the reek of mushroom damp . . .

* Marlinsky, pseudonym of Alexander Alexandrovich Bestuzhev (1797–1837), probably the most popular Russian story-writer and novelist of the 1830s, a romantic celebrated for his sparkling dialogue and Byronic themes, soon to be eclipsed by the emerging realists in the decade following his death.

How good! How true!"

Suddenly a hare started under our feet. L. N. jumped up in excitement, his face flushed, and whooped like some ancient animal-hunter. Then he looked at me with an indescribable smile and laughed a wise, very human little laugh. He was wonderfully sympathetic at that moment.

On another occasion in the same place he was watching a hawk hover over the cattle yard. The hawk would circle, then float motionless in the air, barely rocking on outstretched wings, undecided whether to strike or wait a bit. L. N. straightened up, shaded his eyes with his hand and whispered anxiously:

"The rascal is after our chickens. Look at him! He's about to—he's about to—there he goes—no! He's afraid! Is the coachman there? We should call to the coachman . . ."

And he did. When he shouted, the hawk took fright, shot upward, streaked off, and vanished. L. N. sighed, plainly blaming himself, and said:

"I shouldn't have shouted. If I hadn't, he'd have gone ahead and pounced . . ."[20]

Once in telling him about Tiflis I mentioned the name of V. V. Flerovsky-Bervi.*

"You knew him?" L. N. asked eagerly. "What's he like?"

I began describing Flerovsky—tall, thin, with a long beard and enormous eyes, wearing a long canvas tunic with a bundle of rice cooked in red wine hanging from the belt, and carrying an enormous canvas umbrella. I told him how the two of us had been hiking the mountain trails of the Caucasus once, when on a narrow path we met a buffalo, from whom we prudently retreated, threatening the menacing beast with the open umbrella as we backed off—and risked falling into the abyss as we did.

---

* Some scholars have conjectured that Gorky's travels through the Caucasus with Flerovsky (1829–1918), author of "The ABC of the Social Sciences: Modern Western Civilization" (*Azbuka social'nyx nauk: Sovremennaja zapadno-evropejskaja civilizacija*), an original attempt at a history of universal human culture (whom Gorky called "almost a genius") may have played a significant role in Gorky's later interest in "Godseeking." Flerovskij-Bervi—or Bervi-Flerovskij—was a major ideologist of the "religion of humanity" in Russia.

Suddenly I noticed that there were tears in L. N.'s eyes and I stopped in confusion.*

"Never mind! It's nothing. Go on. It's only from pleasure at hearing about a good man. What an interesting fellow! That's the way I'd pictured him, as someone special. Of all the radical writers he's the most mature and intelligent; in his *Primer* he proves very well that our whole civilization is barbaric and that culture is the work of peaceable tribes, the work of the weak and not the strong, and that the struggle for existence is a false invention for justifying evil. You, of course, don't agree? But Daudet agrees. You remember his Paul Astier?"[†]

---

* Bervi-Flerovsky had been a fellow student of Tolstoy's at Kazan University. Boris Eikhenbaum, in the course of his work on Tolstoy, wrote Gorky in 1933 to ask whether there was anything he could add concerning Tolstoy's attitude toward Flerovsky. Gorky's reply, written on March 14, 1933, from Sorrento, is doubly interesting:

> I think I can say the following: in the attitudes of people there exists something that might be termed national aristocratism. You feel that aristocratism particularly in Englishmen; despite all his good breeding, an Englishman almost always seems to be saying to a foreigner, "Yes, you're good, you are Tolstoy, or Goethe, or Balzac, but—you are not English!" It's a little stupid, sometimes it may be funny, but it exists in Germans and Frenchmen, and it is characteristic of us Russians too. Thus when Lev Nikolayevich would speak of N. F. Fedorov or V. V. Rozanov or Vladimir Solv'ev or Nikolayev, or anyone else of their standing, it seemed to me that in each case he was thinking, "He's good, but he's no Tolstoy!" One can of course think that condescendingly or regretfully or disdainfully, but it is always done from on high and by a mind that is not a broad one.
> I have come to believe that the real drama of Tolstoy lay in the constant struggle of his enormous and wonderful talent with his mind, which was, comparatively speaking, not a large one, and which was at the same time officious and volatile. The great artist did not like the mind of the Other, because his own was hostile to it. There is hardly to be found, among the great of the world, another such, in whom the disparity between talent and mind would approach the disparity between a lion and a rat.
> (*Literaturnyj sovremennik,* 1937, no. 6: 28–29.)

[†] An ambitious young architect in Alphonse Daudet's novel *The Immortal* (L'immortel, 1888), and his play *The Struggle for Life* (La Lutte pour la vie, 1889), who justifies his cynical careerism by reference to Darwin's theories.

"How would you square the role of the Normans in the history of Europe with Flerovsky's theory?"

"The Normans—that's a different matter!"

If he didn't want to answer, he would always say: "That's a different matter."

I always felt (and I do not think I was mistaken) that L. N. didn't much like talking about literature but was intensely interested in the personality of the writer. "Do you know him? What's he like? Where was he born?" are questions I heard from him very often. And almost always his comments opened up a new angle on the person.

About V. G. Korolenko he said thoughtfully:

"He's Ukrainian, not Russian, so he must see our life better and more clearly than we see it ourselves."

About Chekhov, for whom he had great tenderness and affection:

"Medicine hinders him. If he weren't a doctor he would write even better."

About one of the young writers:

"He pretends to be an Englishman, and Moscow people are no good at that."

To me he said more than once:

"You make things up. All those Kuvaldas of yours are made up."

I told him that Kuvalda was an actual person.

"Tell me where you saw him."

He was vastly amused at the scene in the courtroom of Kolontayev, the Kazan justice of the peace, where I first saw the man I was later to describe under the name of Kuvalda.

"Blue blood!" he said, laughing and wiping away the tears. "That's it—blue blood! But what a nice fellow, and what an amusing one! You know, you talk better than you write. No, you're a romantic, an inventor—admit it!"

I said that probably all writers are to some extent inventors, depicting people as they would like to see them in life. I said too that I like active people, who are ready to resist the evil in life by all means, even violence.

"But violence is the chief evil!" he exclaimed, taking me by the arm.

"How do you get out of that contradiction, inventor? Take your story 'My Traveling Companion': that's not made up, and it's good precisely because it's not made up. It's when you start inventing that your people come out knights, Amadises* and Siegfrieds . . ."

I observed that so long as we live cheek by jowl with those half-human and unavoidable "traveling companions" of ours, everything we build will be on shaky ground, and in hostile territory.

He grinned and nudged me with his elbow.

"That can lead to very, very dangerous conclusions! You're no true socialist. You're a romantic, and romantics should be monarchists. That's what they've always been."

"What about Hugo?"

"Hugo is a different matter. I don't like him. He's too strident."

He would frequently ask me what I was reading, and invariably accuse me of what he considered a poor choice of books.

"Gibbon is worse than Kostomarov, you should be reading Mommsen—very boring but very solid."

When he learned that the first book I'd read was *The Brothers Zem-ganno*† he actually showed exasperation.

"See what I mean? It's a silly novel. That's what spoiled you. The French have three writers: Stendhal, Balzac, Flaubert—well, maybe Maupassant too, but Chekhov's better than he is. As for the Goncourts, they're clowns; they only pretended to be serious. They studied life from books written by inventors like themselves and thought they were up to something serious, but it's nothing anyone needs."

I didn't agree, and that rather irritated L. N. He did not easily brook contradiction, and his judgments could be capricious and bizarre at times.

"There is no such thing as degeneracy," he said. "That's something invented by the Italian Lombroso, and the Jew Nordau picks it up, screeching

* Amadis of Gaul is the hero of a fourteenth-century Spanish chivalric romance published in 1508 and remembered today as the favorite reading of Cervantes' Don Quixote.
† A novel of circus life by Edmond de Goncourt, published in 1879.

like a parrot. Italy is a country of charlatans and adventurers—only Aretinos, Casanovas, Cagliostros, and the like are born there."

"And Garibaldi?"

"That's politics, that's a different matter!"

In response to a whole range of facts from the history of Russia's merchant families he said:

"That's not true. That's only what they write in clever books . . ."

I told him the story of three generations of a merchant family I knew, a story in which the law of degeneracy could be seen working with particular ruthlessness. When I'd finished he began tugging excitedly at my sleeve, urging me:

"Now that's the truth! I've seen it myself, there are two such families in Tula. You should write it. A big novel, sparely written, you understand? You must do it!"

His eyes flashed eagerly.

"But there would be knights, L. N.!"

"Stop it! I'm speaking seriously. The one who joins the monks to pray for the whole family—that's marvelous! That's something real: You sin, and I'll go atone for your sins by prayer. And the other one, the bored and money-grubbing builder, that's the truth, too! And for him to drink, and be a dissolute beast, and love everybody, and then suddenly commit murder—that's really good! You've got to write that instead of searching for heroes among thieves and beggars! Heroes are a lie and an invention; there are only people, just people."

He often pointed out exaggerations in my stories, but once, speaking of the second part of [Gogol's] *Dead Souls,* he said, smiling good-naturedly:

"It's terrible what inventors we all are, myself included. Sometimes you'll be writing and suddenly you begin to pity someone, so you add some slightly better trait, and then you take a little away from another character, so that those around him don't look too black by comparison."

And immediately, in the severe tones of an implacable judge, he added:

"That's why I say that art is a lie and a deception, an arbitrary thing, and harmful to people. You find yourself writing not about real life, what and how it is, but about what you think about life, you personally. Who needs to know how I see that tower, or the sea, or a Tartar? Why is that interesting or needful?"

Sometimes his thoughts and feelings struck me as capriciously, even deliberately, perverse, but it was common for him to astonish and unsettle people precisely by the severe directness of his thought, like Job, the fearless questioner of a cruel God.

Once he told this story:

"It was the end of May and I was walking down the Kiev highway. The day was heavenly, everything seemed to be rejoicing. The sky was cloudless, the birds singing, the bees buzzing, the sun so pleasing, everything around me festive, human, magnificent. I was moved to tears and felt that I, too, was a bee that had been given all the best flowers of the earth, and I felt the presence of God close at hand. And then in the bushes by the side of the road I saw two vagabonds, a man and a woman, lying there squirming against each other, both of them gray, filthy, old—sliding around like worms, panting and mumbling, while the pitless sun lit up their naked blue legs and flabby bodies. What a blow that was to my soul! Lord God, creator of beauty—You should be ashamed of Yourself! I felt miserable . . .

"So you see. Nature—which the Bogomils* considered the devil's creation—torments man only too cruelly and mockingly: it takes away his strength but leaves desire. That's how it is for everyone whose soul is still alive. Only to man is it given to experience all the shame and horror of this torment, which is visited on him through the flesh. We bear it like an ineluctable punishment—but for what sin?"

While he was saying this his eyes changed strangely, childishly plaintive at one point, at another blank and harsh. His lips were trembling, and his mustache bristled. When he'd finished, he took a handkerchief out of

---

* The Bogomils were a Christian sect that arose in Bulgaria in the tenth century. They rejected the teachings, sacraments, and ceremonies of the Orthodox church, believing the earth and the whole material world to be the creation of the evil god Satanail, whose name became Satan after Jesus vanquished him. The true church as they construed it was an interior spiritual thing, the equal possession of all believers.

the pocket of his blouse and wiped his face vigorously, though it was dry. Then he ran the hooklike fingers of his strong peasant's hand through his beard and asked again softly:

"For what sin?"

Once I was walking with him on the low road from Diulber to Ai-Todor. Striding along like a young man, he spoke rather more nervously than usual.

"The flesh should be the obedient dog of the spirit, going wherever the spirit bids it go, but look how we live. The flesh rampages while the spirit follows after, helpless and pitiable."

He rubbed his chest hard just above his heart, raised his eyebrows, and went on to recall:

"In Moscow one autumn day, in a back alley near the Sukharev Tower, I saw a woman lying drunk in the gutter. A stream of filthy water from a courtyard flowed right under her neck and back. She lay in that cold liquid muttering, squirming, floundering in the wet, unable to get to her feet."

He shuddered, half-closed his eyes, and said softly, shaking his head:

"Let's sit down here . . . There is nothing more horrible, more repulsive, than a drunken female. I wanted to help her get up, and I couldn't, it made me queasy. She was all slimy and slippery, if you touched her it would take a month to wash it off, it was terrible! And on the curb sat a fair-haired, gray-eyed little boy, tears running down his cheeks, who kept snuffling and repeating helplessly:

" 'Ma-ma. Come on mama, stand up . . .'

"She would move her arms, grunt, lift her head—and drop it back into the filth."

He paused and then, looking around, repeated uneasily, almost whispering:

"Terrible, terrible! Have you seen a lot of drunken women? You have? Oh, God! You mustn't write about that, you mustn't."

"Why not?"

He looked me in the eye, smiled, and repeated my words: "Why not?" Then he said, thoughtfully and slowly:

"I don't know. It just came out . . . It's shameful to write about horrors. But actually, why not write about them? One should write all about everything . . ."

There were tears in his eyes. He wiped them away and, smiling all the time, stared at his handkerchief while fresh tears ran down his wrinkles.

"I'm crying," he said. "I'm an old man. When I recall something horrible it cuts me to the heart."

And, nudging me gently:

"As for you, when you've lived out your life and nothing has changed, then you, too, will weep, and harder than I do—'more streamingly,' as the peasant women say . . . And we should write about everything, otherwise that fair-haired little boy will be offended and reproach us, saying it's not true, not the whole truth. He's strict for the truth!"

Suddenly he gave himself a shake and said in a kindly voice:

"Now, tell me some story; you tell them well. Something about a child, about yourself when you were a child. It's hard to believe that you too were once little. You're such a strange one—as if you'd been born a grownup. Your ideas have a lot of childishness and immaturity in them, but you know a good deal about life, and that's all you need. Come on, tell me something . . ."

He lay down on the exposed roots of a pine tree, made himself comfortable, and watched the ants scurrying among the gray pine needles.

Here in this southern landscape, so foreign to the eye of a northerner in its spectacular variety and unstinting lushness, he, Lev Tolstoy, the very name suggesting his inner strength,* a gnarled little man with tenacious and profoundly earthy roots of his own, was at the same time out of place and in his element. He seemed some very ancient creature, the master of all he surveyed—master and creator both—back after an absence of centuries to the demesne he had created. There are many things he has forgotten, and many others that are new to him; it is all as it should be, but not entirely as it should be, and he needs to find out at once what is amiss and why it is amiss.

* "Lev" is the word for lion; "Tolstoy" suggests stoutness.

He walks along the roads and pathways with the rapid, intent gait of the expert he is, and with his keen eyes, from which not a single stone or a single thought can be hidden, looks, measures, probes, and compares. And he scatters around him the living seeds of his untamable thought.

He said to Suler:

"Lyovushka, you read nothing and that is bad because it's arrogant, whereas Gorky here reads a lot and that is also bad, because he does it out of self-mistrust. I write a lot, and that is bad because it comes from an old man's egotism and a desire that everyone should think my way. Of course, thinking my way is right for me, but Gorky thinks it would be wrong for him, while you don't think anything, you just blink and keep an eye out for something to catch hold of. And you're liable to catch hold of something that isn't right for you—it's already happened. You'll catch hold, hang on for a while, but when that something begins to slip away you won't even try to hold it back. Chekhov has a wonderful story, 'The Darling'—you're almost like her."

"In what way?" Suler asked, laughing.

"You know how to love all right, but you don't know how to choose and you'll fritter away your energy on trifles."

"Isn't everybody like that?"

"Everybody?" L. N. repeated. "No, not everybody."

And suddenly he asked me, the question coming like a blow:

"Why don't you believe in God?"

"I have no faith, L. N."

"That's not true. You are a believer by nature, and you can't get along without God. You'll feel that soon enough. As for your having no faith, that comes from stubbornness: you're offended that the world is not arranged as you would have it. There are also those who don't believe out of shyness. It happens with young men: they can worship a woman but hide the fact because they're afraid she won't understand, and because they lack courage. Faith, like love, requires courage and boldness. You need to tell yourself 'I believe'; then all will be well, everything will appear the way you want it to be, everything will explain itself to you and draw you in. You, for example, love many things; belief is simply intensified love, you only need to love a little more and then love will turn into belief. When a woman is loved she becomes the best woman on earth—every man is in love with the best woman on earth—and that already is faith. An unbeliever cannot love. He will fall in love with one today, and another a year from now. The souls of such people are vagabonds; their lives are sterile, and that is bad. You were born a believer and it's no use trying to change your character. You're always saying beauty, but what is beauty? That which is highest and most perfect—God."

Until then he had almost never broached this subject with me, and its importance, not to mention its unexpectedness, all but overwhelmed me. I said nothing. Sitting on the divan with his legs tucked under him, he smiled a triumphant smile into his beard and wagged his finger at me:

"No! You won't get out of it with silence!"

And I, who do not believe in God, for some reason looked at him very warily and a little fearfully—looked, and thought: "This man is godlike."

◄•►

Appendix

Testimony is abundant that Gorky told many stories about Tolstoy which, as Viktor Shklovsky put it, "he either failed to write down or didn't want to." As an example ("of course, not verbatim"), Shklovsky offers this:

> Tolstoy's daughters brought a rabbit with a broken leg up to the balcony. "Oh, the poor little rabbit!"
>
> Lev Nikolayevich came down the stair. Almost without stopping, he took the rabbit's head in his big hand and, with the practiced movement of a professional hunter, throttled it with two fingers.

"It's a shame," Shklovsky comments, "that this was never written down."[21]

One has to agree.

Kornei Chukovsky recalls hearing Gorky tell two other such episodes:

Walking in the woods Tolstoy once said to me: "It was in this very spot that Fet recited his verses. Fet was a ridiculous man."

"Ridiculous?"

"Yes, of course ridiculous—all people are ridiculous. You're ridiculous too. So am I—we all are."

And this:

"It was Easter. Chaliapin came up to Tolstoy with the traditional greeting:

" 'Christ is risen, Lev Nikolayevich!'

Tolstoy remained silent, gave Chaliapin his cheek to kiss, and then said in grave and measured tones:

" 'Christ did not rise, Fyodor Ivanovich . . . He did not rise . . .' "[22]

Even in cases where the unpublished material rings variations on passages in Gorky's published memoir, it can contribute to the larger effects of that memoir, precisely because the form Gorky chose is an open one, easily accommodating— indeed, drawing much of its force from—contradictions large and small. The following specimen passages, fascinating in themselves, show how.

The first comes from N. V. Vol'skij, who offers a striking variant of the view of Tolstoy as pagan that runs through Gorky's memoir. Vol'skij (1879-1964), who wrote under the pseudonym N. Valentinov, was an economist, journalist, and author of philosophical and sociological works. He met Gorky in 1905 and renewed the acquaintance when Gorky left his seven-year exile on Capri to return to Russia at the end of 1913. For the next four and a half years they met and corresponded frequently. In the course of a trenchant and revealing account of these contacts, Vol'skij recalls a long walk during which Gorky expatiated on the reasons for Tolstoy's "ruination" [*gibel'*]. These lay, he quotes Gorky as saying, in his late religious writings, and in his "constantly talking about death and trying to subdue himself with vegetarianism."

> "But you know who Tolstoy actually was? The pagan god Pan. He should have girded his loins with the skin of some wild animal, picked up some hundred-pound cudgel, and gone off to live in the woods where he could fight with bears and smash in the heads of wolves. Nobody was better at describing how the grass and the trees, the dew and the wild berries smell. Why? Because he was the god Pan, and who better to know all the forest smells? Remember that nose of his, with the huge flaring nostrils that took in everything our olfactory sense can register. I picture Tolstoy as the god Pan so clearly: huge, naked, hair down to his shoulders, sneaking up to a riverbank where a bunch of girls are bathing and inviting them over, cackling and roaring with laughter: 'Hey girls, swim over here, never mind how many there are of you—twenty, thirty—I've got enough for everybody.' That's the real Lev Tolstoy, but he kept trying to change his character, suppressing his pagan self to denounce the sin of lust and preach abstinence. There is a portrait of the Tolstoy who wrote 'The Kreutzer Sonata' and 'God's Kingdom on Earth' that's been spread all over the world. I often get an urge to rip up that portrait and put a real one in its place. Maybe I will some day. It's only a matter of working up the nerve. Listen to this: I went to Tolstoy's house once when he was living in the Crimea. As I went in, [the poet] Balmont was hurrying out, red-faced; evidently they'd had a very unpleasant conversation. Tolstoy led me to the window and pointing to the skinny figure of Balmont striding away, said with a grin: 'In his poems that man is always cheeping like a swallow about love when the fact is he couldn't even handle one healthy peasant girl.' You have to understand that Tolstoy didn't say 'handle a peasant girl'; he used a different and maximally crude verb—and without the slightest inhibition. I blushed, dumbfounded: so that's what the preacher from Yasnaya

Polyana is like! At the time I still didn't understand that the remark about Balmont was only a minor eruption of that titanic pagan nature, which had forcibly restrained itself with the help of biblical prescriptions regarding death and the mortification of the flesh. That nature kept breaking through in his diary in the form of confessions . . ."[23]

Finally, two items which are not reminiscences but analytic passages (and ascriptions) from Gorky's fragmentary notebooks of the 1920s, written for himself and published only after his death. The first cannot be dated precisely; it may have been written at the time Gorky was adding items for new editions of his memoir. The second is dated 1928–29, well after he had stopped making additions to his work on Tolstoy:

At a certain moment in his life L. N. Tolstoy imagined himself to be capable of the greatest sins, and became terrified. That is why he wasted himself all his life on one woman, respecting but no longer loving her, and why he wore a peasant blouse so as not to have to order any particular tailcoat or kaftan, etc.

Quite capable of preaching the greatest antihumanistic heresies, he preached, utterly without imagination, the most naïve Christianity, making thin gruel of the Gospels.

A rationalist, . . . he basically hated his own rationalism and suffered from it; it was like a thorn in his side.[24]

■

In his religio-philosophical inventions Leo Tolstoy does not appear to be a wise man. The primitiveness of the thought, the straining to simplify it to the point where it could get through even to frogs and flies—all that renders the majestic image of the artist virtually invisible.

Reason for him is a braggart and a scoundrel. But reason is foppishly and seductively dressed; it is received everywhere, and it has about it something convincing; everybody respects it and many are ruled by it. Some philosophers have believed that it is precisely in reason that God is incarnated. Tolstoy sometimes doubted that, while not quite letting himself disbelieve it: What if it's true and reason *is* God? And so, regarding reason with the hostility of a pagan, he submitted with the humility of a Christian to the officiousness of its shallow and impassive impositions. He knew, he felt, that life is dark and stupid, and he tried to make it reasonable, for himself in the first place. He carried the torch of reason into the darkness, but he didn't trust in the strength of the fire and diminished the fire as far as he could through simplification. It's what I call shaving the devil—a dubious thing to do; the devil is fine precisely when he is unshaven, in his thick coat of hair.

The fact that Tolstoy can often seem stupid and clumsy does not detract from his genius. Because Tolstoy was majestic even in his stupidity. Probably "stupidity" is not the right word, but I find it clearer as a way of designating the force that exists in contrast to the deft and ingenious tricks of "despised" reason.

One wants to talk about Tolstoy constantly, but all of Tolstoy cannot be put into words.

The last true Russian.[25]

2

Anton Chekhov

In the fall of 1898, in the first flush of sudden celebrity, the thirty-year-old Gorky sent Anton Chekhov the two volumes of his *Sketches and Stories,* which he asked the older writer—Chekhov was eight years his senior and at the peak of his powers—to accept as a token "of the most sincere and ardent admiration." "How many divine moments," he wrote, "have I spent with your books! How many times have I wept over them, or raged like a trapped wolf, or laughed long and sadly."[1] Thus began a cordial correspondence based on high mutual regard and characterized by a frankness which that regard made possible. The two met for the first time in March 1899. Shortly thereafter Gorky wrote his wife that they were seeing each other daily: "He very clearly displays a great sympathy for me and says a great many things that he would not, I'm sure, say to others. I am touched by his trust in me and very glad that he—whom I consider an enormous and original talent, one of those writers who define a whole period in literary history and shape the mood of their times—that he should see in me something to be reckoned with."[2] They met frequently the following winter, at Tolstoy's temporary residence in the Crimea and elsewhere in and around Yalta; Gorky even lived in Chekhov's house in Yalta for part of November 1901. The two remained in close touch thereafter, meeting in Petersburg and Moscow, and corresponding regularly.

On July 4, 1904, two days after Chekhov's death, Gorky wrote his wife: "I think I have never before felt any death as profoundly as I do this one—with misery, outrage, and grief."

Gorky wrote most of his memoir at that time and published it the following year. The section beginning "Fifth day of fever" was written as a diary entry in 1914, and the seven fragments that follow it were apparently written in the first half of 1923; the expanded piece was published later that year. A letter he wrote in 1933, commenting on the manuscript version of his friend A. N. Tikhonov's memoir of Chekhov, adds a fresh detail and an unforgettable metaphor: "He had such limp wrists, and one often had the impression that he touched things with a combination of squeamishness and hesitancy. His gait was like that, too: he walked like a doctor making the rounds of a hospital in which there are many patients but no medicine—and the doctor himself is not quite sure about trying to treat them."[3]

Unlike Gorky's memoir of Tolstoy, which consists of notes jotted down at the time of the events it describes, the memoir of Chekhov is a product of memory, and from beginning to end a written thing, retrospective in tone, and unitary (rather than kaleidoscopic or contradictory) in emphasis. Gorky's very vocabulary, with its frequent repetition of key words such as "simple," "sad," "mournful," and "gentle," can seem restricted and restrictive.

When he first undertook this memoir, Gorky in fact complained to his friend Leonid Andreyev that he did not know "how to write about the deceased." The abrupt transition from essay to diary form (on page 98) seems to bear this out—as do, even more, the concluding lines with their open confession of defeat, their opaque gesture at what a better memoir would be like, and their final veering into that sententiousness (doubly out of place here) which was Gorky's signature temptation.

The critic Kornei Chukovsky quotes Gorky in 1919 as calling this memoir "bad" and adding: "I should have written something different: he kept consulting me all the time about whether to marry [Olga] Knipper."[4]

Moving and valuable as the memoir unquestionably is, it does stand apart from Gorky's portraits of Tolstoy and Andreyev because those two show him interacting with his subjects, judging them, and, inevitably, measuring himself against them. Chekhov, by contrast, personifies for Gorky a cherished set of values, and he does so in a way that leaves no room for any sort of conflict, in the lived relationship or in the telling. As Alfred Kazin has shrewdly suggested, "He admired in [Chekhov] all that was missing or inadequate in himself—the calmness, the humor, the gift of chiaroscuro; and so many virtues for which one hungered, and hungers still, in Russia—respect for the dignity of the individual, the freedom to declare the value of a person or a work, despite all political 'necessity,' liberalism as a way of life. It is obvious that Gorky could not bear to think of Chekhov as having a single fault."[5] So there is no drama here—only a memorable, utterly convincing and contagious declaration of love.

◄•►

A. P. Chekhov

He once invited me to visit him in the village of Kuchuk-Koi, where he had a small plot of land and a white two-story cottage.* In the course of showing me around this "estate" of his, he said with great animation:

"If I had a lot of money I would build a sanatorium here for sick village teachers. What a building it would be—full of light, with great windows and high ceilings. There'd be a splendid library, various musical instruments, an apiary, a vegetable garden, an orchard; and there would be lectures on agronomy and meteorology because, my friend, a teacher needs to know everything, absolutely everything."

* Kuchuk-Koi is about twenty miles from Yalta. Chekhov bought the land (some eight acres) in December 1898, when work on his house in Autka, on the outskirts of Yalta, was just beginning.

He stopped suddenly, coughed, gave a sidelong glance, and smiled that gentle and winning smile of his that drew you to him so irresistibly, and made you want to attend to his every word.

"Does it bore you to listen to my fantasies? This is something I love to talk about. If you knew how desperately Russian villages need good, intelligent, educated teachers! We Russians need to set up special conditions for them, and do so as quickly as possible if we know what's good for us, because without broad education for the people the state will collapse like a house made of badly baked bricks! A teacher should be a performer, an artist, someone who loves his work—whereas in Russia he is a common laborer, badly educated himself, who goes off to teach children in the village with about as much enthusiasm as he'd have for going off into exile. He's hungry, beaten down, terrified of losing his daily crust of bread. What's needed is for him to be the leading citizen in the village, for him to have answers for all the muzhiks' questions, for the muzhiks to realize that he has a power worth respecting, so that no one will dare to shout at him or put him down as everyone in our country does—the policeman, the well-to-do shopkeeper, the priest, the school supervisor, the village elder, and that official who, though his title is inspector of schools, concerns himself not with producing a better education but only with carrying out to the letter the directives that come from the district center. It's absurd to pay a man next to nothing when his job is to educate the people—you understand?—to educate the people! It's intolerable that that man should go around in rags, shiver with cold in a damp and drafty schoolhouse, breathe fumes, catch colds, suffer from laryngitis, rheumatism, and tuberculosis by the time he's thirty—it's simply disgraceful! Our teachers live like hermits eight or nine months of the year, with no one to talk to, deadened by loneliness, without books, without recreation of any kind. And if one of them invites some friends over, he is accused of being politically "unreliable"—a stupid word used by wily people to frighten fools! . . . It's all disgusting, a mockery of people who are doing enormously important work. I tell you, when I meet a teacher I am embarrassed, partly by his timidity and partly because he is shabbily dressed. I feel—seriously!—that I am somehow to blame for his miserable condition."

He paused, reflected for a moment, and, waving his arm, said softly:

"What an absurd and clumsy country our Russia is."

A profound sadness shadowed his wonderful eyes; a network of fine wrinkles like rays of light encircled them, deepening their expression. He looked around and commenced making fun of himself:

"There you have it—I've spun out a whole editorial for some liberal newspaper. Let's go in, I'll give you a glass of tea for your patience . . ."

This was a regular thing with him: he would speak so warmly, seriously and sincerely—and then suddenly laugh at himself and his own words. And in that gentle, melancholy, wry smile you felt the subtle skepticism of a man who knows both the value of words and the value of dreams—that, and his captivating modesty and instinctive tact.

We walked to the house in silence. The day was clear and hot. You could see the waves sparkling in the sun and hear them break on the shore. At the foot of the hill a dog was squealing his delight at something. Chekhov took me by the arm and said slowly, coughing as he did:

"It's sad and it's shameful, but true: there are a great many people who envy dogs . . ."

And then he added with a laugh:

"I keep using decrepit words today. I must be getting old!"

He was forever saying things like:

"Listen, a teacher has just arrived. He's unwell, has a wife—would there be any chance you could help him? I've taken care of him for the moment."

Or:

"Listen, Gorky, there's a teacher here who'd like to meet you. He's sick and doesn't go out. You should go see him, all right?"

Or:

"Here's a note from some schoolmistresses asking for books . . ."

Sometimes I would find that "teacher" in his house. Most often the teacher, awkward, red-faced, and self-conscious, would be sitting on the edge of his chair sweating; he would pick and choose his words and strain to speak more "educatedly." Or else, with the brashness of a morbidly shy individual desperate not to seem stupid in the eyes of the writer, he would

pepper Anton Pavlovich with questions, none of which, most likely, had
occurred to him before that very moment.

Anton Pavlovich would listen attentively to the man's halting speech. A
smile would flicker in his melancholy eyes. The furrows in his forehead
would twitch. And then, in a deep, gentle, velvety voice he would begin to
speak, using simple, clear, everyday words, and somehow the person they
were addressed to would relax and stop trying to be a clever fellow, with the
result that he became more intelligent and more interesting on the spot.

I remember one such teacher—tall, gaunt, with a hungry yellow face
and a long hooked nose curving mournfully toward his chin—sitting across
from Anton Pavlovich, staring him in the face with his black eyes and in-
toning in a somber bass voice:

"Out of such impressions of existence, garnered over the course of the
entire pedagogical season, there forms a psychic conglomerate which absolutely obviates any possibility of an objective attitude vis-à-vis the surrounding world. And the world is, in any case, nothing but our conception of it . . ."

He then crossed over into the area of philosophy and lurched around
in it like a drunk trying to walk on ice.

"But tell me," Chekhov asked in a quiet and friendly voice, "who is it
in your district who beats the children?"

The teacher leapt from his chair and began waving his arms in indignation:

"What do you mean?! Me beat them? Never!"

He gave an offended snort.

"Calm yourself," Anton Pavlovich continued with a reassuring smile.
"What makes you think I was talking about you? It's just that I remember
reading in the papers that somebody was beating them, precisely in your
district . . ."

The teacher sat down, wiped the sweat from his face, and with a sigh
of relief began speaking, his bass voice low now and muffled:

"It's true! There was a case. It was Makarov. I must say, it was hardly a
surprise! Bizarre, but understandable. Married man. Four children. Wife
sick, he too—consumption. Salary—20 rubles. . . . The school really a cel-

lar, and only a single room for the teacher. In conditions like that you'd thrash one of God's angels without needing a reason—and I can assure you that the pupils there are far from angels!"

Here was this man who had just been trying to impress Chekhov with his store of fancy words, suddenly, wagging his hooked nose ominously, using words that were simple but weighty as stones, that lit up the fearful and accursed truth of life in a Russian village like a searchlight . . .

Saying goodbye, the teacher took his host's small dry hand with the delicate fingers into his own two hands, and said as he shook it:

"I came here as if I were going to see my boss, cowed and shaking and puffed up like a turkey cock to make you see I was no yokel—and yet here I am saying goodbye the way one does to a good friend who understands everything. It's a great thing, understanding everything! Thank you! I'm going, but I'm taking with me a good and heartening thought: Great people are more simple and more understanding and closer to people like us than all those nonentities we live among. Goodbye! I'll never forget you . . ."

His nose quivered, his lips formed a kindly smile, and he added unexpectedly:

"When you get right down to it, even the scoundrels are also unhappy people, damn them!"

Anton Pavlovich watched him go, then grinned and said:

"A nice fellow. But he won't be a teacher long . . ."

"Why not?"

"They'll hound him and chase him away . . ."

He thought a moment, then added in a low, quiet voice:

"An honest man in Russia is something like the chimneysweep that nurses frighten little children with . . ."

I think that Anton Pavlovich's presence made everyone feel an unconscious desire to be simpler and truer, to be themselves. I had many occasions to observe how people would cast off their armature of fancy bookish phrases, modish expressions, and all kinds of other trinkets which Russians, like savages putting on their shells and fishes' teeth, adorn themselves with when they want to seem European. Anton Pavlovich didn't like fishes' teeth and cocks' feathers; everything flashy and tinkling that a person puts on to impress others made him uneasy, and I have noticed that every time he saw a person decked out in that way he was overcome with a desire to free him from all the burdensome and needless ostentation that was distorting his true face and constraining his living soul. Chekhov lived his whole life expending the capital of his soul; he was always himself, inwardly free, and he never concerned himself with what some people expected (and others, less tactful, demanded) from Anton Chekhov. He disliked conversations on "lofty" themes—conversations which Russians in their charming simplicity find so amusing, oblivious to the comedy of discoursing on the velvet suits people will wear in the future when they don't even have a decent pair of pants in the present.

Beautifully simple himself, he loved everything that is simple and genuine and sincere, and he had a way all his own to make others simple.

One time three elegantly dressed ladies came to see him. Filling his room with the rustling of their silk skirts and the fragrance of their perfume, they sat down decorously across from the host and, pretending to be interested in politics, started "posing questions."

"Anton Pavlovich, how do you think the war will end?"

"Most likely with peace . . ."

"Well yes, of course! But who will win, the Greeks or the Turks?"

"I think the ones who are stronger will win . . ."

"But who do you think are stronger?" the ladies asked, vying with each other.

"The ones who are better fed and better educated . . ."

"Oh, how witty that is!" exclaimed one of them.

"But which do you like better, the Greeks or the Turks?" asked another.

Anton Pavlovich gave her a sympathetic look and answered, with a meek and amiable smile:

"I'm fond of marmalade. Are you?"

"Oh yes!" the lady exclaimed.

"It smells so good!" one of the others concurred solemnly.

And all three began an animated conversation on the question of marmalade, revealing their impressive erudition and complex knowledge of the subject. It was quite clear how relieved they were not to have to tax their brains further by pretending to be seriously interested in the Turks and Greeks, to whom they had given no thought whatsoever up to that moment.

As they left they gaily promised Anton Pavlovich:

"We'll send you some marmalade!"

"You managed that marvelously," I remarked when they were gone.

Anton Pavolvich gave a quiet laugh and said:

"Every person needs to speak in his own language . . ."

Another time I found a young and rather good-looking deputy prosecutor visiting him. He was standing in front of Chekhov, shaking his curly head and holding forth:

"With your story 'The Malefactor,'* Anton Pavlovich, you broach what is for me a very complex question. If I find in Denis Grigoriev the presence of malice aforethought, then I must, with no ifs, ands, or buts, send Denis to prison as the interests of society demand. But he is a savage, he had no awareness of the criminality of his act, and I pity him! And yet if I give in to a feeling of compassion and regard him as a person who did not realize that what he was doing was wrong, how can I guarantee society that Denis will not unscrew the bolts on the rails again and perhaps cause an accident? There's the question! What's the answer?"

He stopped, threw back his head, and fixed Anton Pavlovich with a searching glance. The uniform he wore was brand-new and the buttons on the front of it glittered as confidently and stupidly as did the eyes in the freshly scrubbed face of this young apostle of justice.

"If I were the judge," Anton Pavlovich said seriously, "I would acquit Denis . . ."

"On what grounds?"

"I would tell him: 'Denis, you haven't yet matured into a conscious criminal. Go and mature!'"

* An early story (1885), also translated as "The Culprit," about a peasant who is hauled before a magistrate for stealing from the railroad. He has taken one of the nuts used to bolt the rails to the ties in order to use it as a sinker in his fishing.

The jurist began to laugh but quickly got hold of himself and went on solemnly:

"No, my dear Anton Pavlovich, the question you have posed can be decided only in favor of the interests of society, the life and property of which I am sworn to safeguard. It's true Denis is a savage, but he is still a criminal, and that's the truth!"

"Do you like the gramophone?" Anton Pavlovich asked suddenly, in a kindly tone.

"Oh yes, very much! An astonishing invention!" the young man replied.

"And I can't stand gramophones!" Anton Pavlovich confessed mournfully.

"Why not?"

"They talk and sing all right, but without feeling anything. And everything comes out caricatured, dead . . . Do you go in for photography?"

It turned out that the lawyer was a passionate fan of photography. On the spot he began talking about it enthusiastically, quite uninterested in further discussion of the gramophone despite his resemblance to that "astonishing invention," which Chekhov had so shrewdly noted. Once again I saw behind the uniform a lively and amusing enough individual, in this case one whose responses to the world still seemed to be those of a puppy in a hunting party.

After seeing the young man out, Anton Pavlovich said glumly:

"And it's pimples like that on the backside of justice that dispose of other people's fates."

After a pause he added:

"Prosecutors love to fish. Especially for perch!"

He possessed the art of detecting and exposing vulgarity* wherever it occurred. It is an art available only to one who makes the highest demands on

---

* The word he uses is *poshlost'*, a word that combines the notions of banality, self-righteous conventionality, extreme moral and spiritual poverty—as well as, in Nabokov's gloss, "the obviously trashy," "the falsely important, the falsely beautiful, the falsely clever, the falsely attractive." Here and throughout the word I translate as "vulgarity" should be understood as standing for this complex of meanings.

life, and it arises only from a burning desire to see simplicity, beauty, and harmony in people. He was always a merciless and implacable judge when it came to vulgarity.

Someone said in his presence that the publisher of a popular magazine, a man who was forever urging the necessity of love and compassion toward others, had quite gratuitously insulted a train conductor and was in general extremely rude in his dealings with subordinates.

"But of course," said Anton Pavlovich with a somber chuckle. "After all, he's an aristocrat, an educated man, he's even studied in a seminary! His father went around in bast sandals, but he wears patent-leather shoes . . ."

And something in his tone immediately made the "aristocrat" trivial and ludicrous.

"Quite a talented fellow!" he said of one journalist. "His writing is so noble, so humane, so saccharine. He calls his wife a fool in front of others. The servants' room in his house is damp and the maids are constantly coming down with rheumatism . . ."

"And do you like N—, Anton Pavlovich?"

"Yes . . . Very much. A pleasant man," he said with a little cough. "Knows everything. Reads a lot. He borrowed three books from me. Never returned them—but he is a little forgetful. One day he'll tell you you're a marvelous person, and the next he'll report to somebody that you stole the silk socks of your mistress' husband—the black ones, with the blue stripes . . ."

Somebody was complaining in his presence about how dull and ponderous the "serious" sections of the leading journals were.

"But you shouldn't be reading those articles," Anton Pavlovich advised him. "That is the literature of friendship—in fact, the literature of friends. It's written by Mr. Brown, Mr. Black, and Mr. White. One writes an article, another publishes a rejoinder, and the third sorts out their disagreements. It's as if they're playing a game of whist with a dummy. And it never occurs to any of them to wonder why a reader needs all this."

Once a plump lady came to see him—healthy, attractive, attractively dressed—and started speaking like a character out of Chekhov:

"Life is tedious, Anton Pavlovich! Everything is so dismal: people, the sky, the sea, even flowers—they're all so dismal. And there is nothing worth desiring—my soul is awash in melancholy, it's like a disease—."

"It *is* a disease!" Anton Pavlovich assured her. "No question. In Latin it is called *morbus pretenditus.*"

Fortunately for her, the lady seemed not to know Latin, or perhaps she concealed the fact that she knew it.

"Critics are like the horseflies that bother plow horses," he said, smiling that wise smile of his. "The horse is pulling the plow, his muscles are tense as the strings on a bass viol, and along comes a horsefly to settle on his hindquarters, buzzing and tickling, obliging the horse to shake its coat and flick its tail. What is the fly buzzing about? The fly has no idea. He simply has a restless character and wants to make his presence known, as if to say, 'I live in this world too! Just look: I even know how to buzz—I can buzz about anything I want!' I've been reading criticisms of my stories for twenty-five years, and I can't recall a single stricture or a single bit of advice that was of any use. Once, it's true, the critic Skabichevsky did make an impression on me. That was when he wrote that I would die drunk in a ditch . . ."

In his mournful gray eyes there was almost always a gentle and ironic little smile lurking, but there were times when those eyes became cold, sharp, and hard; at such moments a firmness came into his supple and candid voice that told me this modest and kindly man could, if necessary, stand up to a hostile force, stand up to it and never yield.

I sometimes sensed a tinge of hopelessness in his attitude to others, something akin to despair, cold and vast.

"The Russian is a strange creature!" he said once. "He's like a sieve, he can't hold anything for long. In youth he stuffs his soul with whatever comes to hand, and after thirty nothing is left of it but some kind of gray rubbish. To live well, like a human being, one has to work—work with love and with faith! But we don't know how to do that. An architect will build two or three not-bad buildings and then sit down to play cards for the rest of his life, or else start hanging around the backstage of theaters. A doctor, once he has a practice, stops keeping up with the progress of science, reads nothing except the *Therapeutic News,* and at the age of forty believes seriously that all illnesses come from the common cold. I've never met an official who had the slightest understanding of the significance of his job; they usually sit in their office in the capital or the county seat concocting documents which they then send to Zmiev or Smorgon to be acted on. And the question of who is going to lose his freedom of movement in Zmiev or Smorgon as a result of these documents—that is something that concerns the official as little as the torments of hell trouble an atheist. The lawyer who's made his name through one successful defense ceases to care about defending the truth and defends only the rights of property, bets on the races, eats oysters, and passes himself off as a connoisseur of all the arts. The actor who's played two or three roles, more or less adequately, stops studying his lines, puts on a top hat instead, and regards himself as a genius. Russia is a country of greedy and lazy people who eat and drink on a terrifying scale, like to nap in the afternoon, and snore in their sleep. They marry for the sake of order in their houses, and take mistresses for prestige in society. Their psychology is that of dogs: beat them and they slink back to their kennels whimpering, pet them and they roll over and wag their tails . . ."

A cold and sorrowful contempt suffused these words. But, feeling contempt, he was capable of feeling pity at the same time, and if you happened to speak ill of anyone in his presence, Anton Pavlovich would immediately speak up for him:

"Why talk that way? Remember: he's old, he must be seventy . . ."

Or: "Remember, he's still young, he doesn't know any better . . ."

At such moments I could find not a hint of irony in his face.

When we are young, vulgarity can seem no more than an amusing and trivial thing, but by degrees it envelops a person in its gray fog, penetrates his brain and blood like poison or noxious fumes, and the person comes to resemble an old sign eaten away by rust. Something was evidently written on it, but what? Impossible to make it out.

In his very first stories Anton Chekhov already knew how to sound the dull sea of vulgarity and discover its tragically sad jokes. One need only read his "humoristic" stories with care to realize how much that was cruel and repellent the author saw behind his comic words and situations—saw and deplored, saw and concealed, ashamed.

His modesty had a kind of chaste quality about it. He would never let himself say to people straight out, "Try to be more decent!"—hoping vainly instead that they would come on their own to recognize the urgent necessity of being more decent. Hating everything that was vulgar and mean, he described life's abominations in the noble language of a poet and with the gentle smile of a humorist, leaving barely perceptible beneath the beautiful surface of his stories their inner sense, their bitter reproach.

The esteemed public, reading "A Daughter of Albion," laughs and most likely fails to see how in this story a well-fed aristocrat makes contemptible sport of a lonely individual without ties to anyone or anything. Similarly, in every one of Chekhov's humorous stories I hear the deep and quiet sigh of a pure and genuinely human heart, a hopeless sigh of compassion for people who do not know how to respect their own human dignity, and who live like slaves, bowing without resistance to brute force, believing in nothing except the daily need to ingest as much thick cabbage soup as possible, and feeling nothing but the fear of being beaten by the strong and insolent.

No one understood as clearly and astutely as Anton Chekhov the tragic nature of life's trifles; no one before him ever depicted with such unrelenting accuracy the shameful and tedious nature of their everyday dismal, chaotic, and philistine lives.

Vulgarity—*poshlost'*—was his enemy; all his life he fought it, ridiculing it, painting it precisely and impassively, managing to find the mold of vulgarity even in places where at first glance it would seem that everything had been ordered very well, very comfortably, very attractively . . . And vulgarity took its revenge by playing him the nasty trick of transporting his corpse—the corpse of a poet—back to Russia in a freight car marked "Oysters."

I see that dirty green freight car as vulgarity's broad smile of triumph over its exhausted foe, and I see the endless "reminiscences" in the gutter press as expressing a hypocritical sadness, behind which I sense the cold and stinking breath of that same *poshlost'*, secretly rejoicing at the death of its enemy.

You read Chekhov's stories and you feel transported to one of those sad days in late autumn when the air is so transparent and the bare trees, and the houses huddled together, and the drab people all stand out so sharply against it. Everything is strange, lonely, motionless and feeble. The remote blue distance is empty; merging with the pale sky, it breathes a dreary chill across the frozen earth. The mind of the author, like that autumn sun, shines a cruelly clear light on the rutted roads, the cramped and dirty houses in which pitiful little people are suffocating from boredom and laziness as they bustle about mindlessly, like automatons. "The Darling" scurries past, anxious as a gray mouse—a sweet and meek woman with a knack for loving, and loving slavishly. You can slap her face and the long-suffering little slave won't even dare to moan aloud. Standing glumly next to her is Olga from *Three Sisters;* she too is full of love, yet submits to the caprices of her lazy brother's vulgar slut of a wife. The lives of her sisters are coming apart around her, while she weeps, unable to help in any way, or to find in her heart a single strong or vital word of protest against vulgarity.

And here are the lachrymose Ranevskaya and the other former owners of *The Cherry Orchard,* egotistical as children and flabby as old people. They've passed up the chance to die when they should have, and now they whine, unable to see or understand anything around them—parasites, without the strength to reconnect with real life. The shabby little student Trofimov speaks eloquently about the need to work—and fritters away his time, venting his boredom in stupid mockery of Varya, who works untiringly for the well-being of these idlers.

Vershinin [in *Three Sisters*] dreams about how beautiful life will be in three hundred years and lives without noticing how everything around him is falling apart, how before his very eyes Solyony is ready, out of boredom and stupidity, to kill the pitiable Baron Tusenbach.

Before us passes an endless parade of slaves—slaves to love, to their own foolishness and sloth, their own greed for earthly blessings. Marching among them are the slaves to an obscure fear of life; dully anxious, they fill

their lives with incoherent speeches about the future, sensing that there is
no place for them in the present.

From time to time a shot rings out in the midst of their colorless mass:
it is Ivanov or Treplev realizing what he needs to do—and ending it all.

Many of them harbor beautiful dreams of how wonderful life will be in
two hundred years, yet the simple question of who will make it good if all
we do is dream never occurs to them.

Before this whole dismal and tedious crowd of ineffectual people there
passed a great and intelligent man, noting everything. He looked at his dull
countrymen and, with a sad smile, in a tone of gentle but profound reproach, with the ache of despair in his face and in his heart, said in that
beautiful and sincere voice of his:

"You live wretchedly, my friends!"

Fifth day of fever, but no desire to stay in bed. The gray Finnish rain falls
lightly, turning the dust to mud.* The cannons of Fort Inno thunder as
they try to find the range. At night the long tongue of a searchlight licks the
clouds—a revolting spectacle, for it is a constant reminder of this nightmar-
ish war.

Have been reading Chekhov. If he hadn't died ten years ago, the war
would surely have begun by poisoning him with hatred for people—and
ended by killing him. Recalled his funeral.

The coffin of Moscow's "dearly beloved" writer arrived in a green freight
car, on the doors of which was written in large letters: "FOR OYSTERS."† A part

---

* In 1914 Gorky was living in Finland, at Mustomäki. Fort Inno was a few kilometers
away on the northern shore of the Gulf of Finland, opposite Kronstadt.

† The report of the newspaper *Novosti Dnja* for 9 July 1904 noted that these words on
the side of the boxcar had in fact been painted over in Petersburg, but including that detail
could only have diluted the expression of Gorky's rage at the public and its philistine behavior.
A letter to his wife of 11 July 1904 makes clear his determination to see everything connected
with Chekhov's funeral as grounds for his indictment. "That boxcar," he writes, "represents
precisely that Russian vulgarity and lack of culture which always outraged the deceased." (M.
Gor'kij, *Polnoe sobranie sočinenij. Pis'ma v dvadcati četyrex tomax,* 4 [1998]: 103–4.)

of the smallish crowd that had gathered at the station to receive the writer's body went off behind the coffin of General Keller, which had arrived from Manchuria, and was astonished that they should be burying Chekhov to the accompaniment of a military band. When the mistake was discovered, some of the more jovial in the crowd began to snicker and giggle. A hundred people, not more, followed Chekhov's coffin.* I particularly recall two lawyers, both of them in new shoes and bright neckties, looking like bridegrooms. Walking behind them, I heard one of them, V. A. Maklakov, talking about the intelligence of dogs, while the other, whom I did not recognize, went on praising the conveniences of his summer house and the beauty of the landscape around it. And a lady in a lilac-colored dress, walking under a lace parasol, kept assuring an old man in horn-rimmed glasses, "Oh, he was wonderfully sweet—and so witty . . ."

The old man coughed incredulously. The day was hot and dusty. Heading the procession was a stout district police captain on a stout white horse. All this and much more was painfully vulgar, and glaringly incompatible with the memory of a great and subtle artist.

In one of his letters to [his publisher], old A. S. Suvorin, Chekhov wrote:

"There is nothing drearier and, so to speak, more unpoetical than the prosaic struggle for existence, which saps the joy of life and drives people into apathy."

* Gorky's memory confuses the reception of Chekhov's coffin in Petersburg and in Moscow. There were in fact few people meeting the coffin at the Warsaw and Nikolayevsky stations in St. Petersburg, as the newspapers noted at the time. In Moscow, by contrast, thousands of people followed Chekhov's coffin, as Gorky himself noted in a letter to his wife of 11–12 July 1904. He writes: "At the funeral of a writer like Anton Chekhov I would have preferred to see a handful of people who really loved him, but what I saw was a crowd of 'the public,' perhaps three and a half thousand people, who for me merged into a single thick and oily cloud of triumphant vulgarity" (Ibid., 104). To Leonid Andreyev he wrote on the same day: "I am all splattered by the gray mud of the speeches, the inscriptions on the wreaths, the conversations one overheard. And thinking involuntarily of my own death, this is how I imagine the ideal funeral: a dray horse pulls the carriage containing my coffin, while a single indifferent policeman walks behind it. A writer in Russia cannot be buried better, more nobly, or more decently than that." (Ibid., 106.)

These words express a very Russian sentiment, but one that was not, in my view, generally characteristic of Chekhov. In Russia, where you find a lot of everything except love for work, that is the way the majority thinks. The Russian admires energy but doesn't much believe in it. A writer with an active temperament—Jack London, for example—would be impossible in Russia. Though his books are eagerly read in Russia, I don't see them doing much to incline Russians toward any activity; they merely stir the imagination of their Russian readers. But Chekhov is not very Russian in that respect. As a young man he experienced the "struggle for existence" in the not very attractive or colorful form of constant petty concern over securing a crust of bread—and a big one, not just for himself but for others as well. To this concern, devoid of joys, he devoted all the energy of his youth, and one has to wonder how, under the circumstances, he contrived to preserve his sense of humor. He saw the life around him as no more than a tedious quest for enough to eat and a little peace; a thick layer of ordinariness covered over the great dramas and tragedies of life. And only once he had freed himself from worrying whether those around him had enough to eat did he allow himself to look deeply into the heart of these dramas.

I never knew a man who grasped the significance of work as the basis for culture so profoundly and so variously. This found expression in all the details of his domestic economy, in the choice of objects and in that noble love for objects which, utterly excluding any desire to accumulate them, never tires of admiring them as the product of man's creative spirit. He loved to build, plant gardens, beautify the land; he had a keen feeling for the poetry of labor. With what touching care he watched the growth of the fruit trees he had planted, and the decorative shrubs! Amid all the concerns of building his house in Autka he said:

"If every person did all that he could on his little piece of land, how wonderful our earth would be!"

When I'd begun writing my play *Vaska Buslayev* I read him Vaska's boastful monologue:

Ah, if I but had more strength!
I'd blow and melt the snow with my breath,
I'd walk the whole round earth and plow it,
Walk all my life—found cities,
Build churches and plant gardens!
I would adorn the earth as if it were a girl,
Embrace her as my bride,
I'd lift the earth to my chest,
Lift it and carry it to the Lord, saying:
"Look you, Lord, at what the earth is now,
See how Vaska has beautified it!
You launched it into the sky as a rock.
But I have turned it into a precious emerald!
Look you, Lord, and rejoice.
How it shines green in the sunlight!
I would have made a gift of it to you,
But cannot, finding it too dear!

Chekhov liked that monologue. Coughing excitedly, he said to me and Dr. A. N. Alexin:

"It's good—very real and human! There you have 'the meaning of all philosophy.' Man has made the world habitable, and he will make it cozy for himself." Nodding his head vigorously, he repeated: "He will!"

He proposed that I read Vaska's eulogy again and listened, looking out the window.

"You should cut the two last lines. They're impertinent—and unnecessary."

About his own writings he spoke little, and always reluctantly—I'm tempted to say bashfully, with something like the reserve he showed in talking about Lev Tolstoy. Only on rare occasions, when he was feeling expansive, would he smile and tell us about some new idea for a story (always a humorous one).

"I'm thinking of writing about a schoolteacher, an atheist who adores Darwin and is committed to battling the prejudices and superstitions of the people—while going herself, at midnight, to the bathhouse, where she boils a black cat in a cauldron so as to get a wishbone for attracting a man and making him love her. There actually is such a bone."

He always spoke of his plays as "amusing" [*veselye*] and seemed genuinely to believe that they were simply that. It is probably from hearing him say that that Savva Morozov used to insist: "Chekhov's plays should be staged as lyrical comedies."

But he paid very serious attention to literature in general, and it was particularly touching to see him extend this to "beginning writers." He showed astonishing patience in reading the copious manuscripts of B. Lazarevsky, N. Oliger, and many others.

"We need more writers," he used to say. "Literature is still a novelty in our daily life and is regarded as being "for the select." Norway has one writer for every two hundred and twenty six inhabitants, while we have one for every million . . ."

His illness at times turned him into a hypochondriac, and even into a misanthrope. On such occasions he would be capricious in his judgments and difficult in his dealings with people.

Once, lying on the couch, coughing a dry cough and playing with the thermometer, he said:

"To live merely to die is hardly amusing. But to live knowing that you will die before your time—that really is idiotic."

Another time, as he sat at an open window gazing at the sea in the distance, he said in an unexpectedly angry voice:

"We are used to living with hopes for good weather, a good harvest, a happy romance, dreams of getting rich or being made chief-of-police, but the hope of getting a little wiser is one thing I never see in people. We think things will be better under the new Tsar, and better still in two hundred years; yet no one shows any interest in making things better tomorrow. Life in general gets more complicated with every passing day and is moving somewhere on its own, while people grow markedly more stupid, and more and more of them stand apart from life."

He thought a moment and, wrinkling his brow, added:

"Like crippled beggars in a church procession."

He was a physician, and a physician's illness is always harder than those of his patients. The patients feel only what is happening to them; the doctor understands, in addition, how his organism is being destroyed. This is one of those situations where knowledge can be said to hasten the person's death.

He had fine eyes. When he smiled they became warm and caressing, like a woman's. And his laughter, almost soundless, was somehow particularly fine. Laughing, he was enjoying the laughter, rejoicing. I don't know anyone else who could laugh so—if one can put it that way—"spiritually."

He never found coarse jokes amusing.

Laughing so winningly and soulfully, he said to me:

"Do you know why Tolstoy treats you so inconsistently? He's jealous. He thinks Sulerzhitsky likes you better than he likes him. It's true, that's what he thinks. Yesterday he told me: 'I can't be sincere with Gorky. I don't know why, but I can't. I actually dislike the fact that Suler is living with Gorky.* It's not good for Suler. Gorky is an angry man. He's like a seminarist who's been forcibly tonsured as a monk and is furious with the whole world. He has the soul of a spy; he's come from somewhere into the alien land of Canaan, where he inspects everything closely, observes everything, and reports about it all to some god of his own. But that god is a monster, like the wood demons or the water sprites that peasant women believe in.' "

As he told me this he laughed until the tears came. Wiping them away, he went on:

* Sulerzhitsky lived at Gorky's country place in Oleiz, in the Crimea, from the end of 1901 to the beginning of April 1902. He was instrumental in Gorky's almost daily contact with Tolstoy, who was then staying nearby in Gaspra. See Gorky's memoirs of Tolstoy and of Sulerzhitsky in this volume.

"I said to him: 'Gorky is a good man.' But he says: 'No, no. I know what I'm talking about. He has a duck's bill for a nose; the only people who have noses like that are the unhappy and the angry. Besides, women don't like him, and women can smell out a good man the way dogs can. Take Suler, he has a really exquisite capacity for disinterested love. He's a genius at it. If you can love, you can do anything . . . '"

Catching his breath, Chekhov repeated:

"Yes, the old man is jealous. What an amazing fellow . . ."

When he spoke of Tolstoy it was always with a certain scarcely perceptible, gentle and embarrassed smile in his eyes. He spoke, lowering his voice, as if he were speaking about something spectral and mysterious that required words at once careful and soft.

He complained constantly that there was no Eckermann around Tolstoy, no person to keep a careful record of the old sage's sharp, surprising, and (often) contradictory observations.

"You're the one who ought to do it," he would tell Sulerzhitsky. "Tolstoy likes you so much, he's so open with you, and he says such wonderful things."

About Suler, Chekhov said to me:

"He is a wise child."

Most true.

Once Tolstoy was expressing his enthusiasm for a story of Chekhov's—it may have been "The Darling." He said:

"It's like lacework woven by a virgin; in the old days there were girls— 'old maids'—who put their whole lives, all their joys and dreams, into their designs. Their dreams of happiness came out as patterns; all their love, vague and pure, they plaited into their lace."

Tolstoy said this with real emotion. There were tears in his eyes.

But that day Chekhov was running a temperature. He sat there with red splotches on his cheeks, his head bent forward, carefully cleaning his

pince-nez. For a long time he said nothing. Finally, with a sigh, he mur-
mured in embarrassment:

"It's got misprints in it . . ."

There is a lot to be written about Chekhov, but it needs to be done very finely
and precisely, in a way that is beyond my ability. The writing should be like
his own in *The Steppe*—the atmosphere light and fragrant, the story so Russian in its pensive sadness. A story written for oneself.

It is good to reminisce about a man like him; instantly it brings energy
and clarity of meaning back into one's life.

Man is the axle of the world.

But, it may be objected, what about his vices, his failings?

Love of our fellow-man is something we all hunger for, and when you
are hungry even badly baked bread can taste sweet and give sustenance.

3

L. A. Sulerzhitsky

The third and least-known of the figures around Tolstoy in Gorky's memoir, Sulerzhitsky, was memorialized by Gorky soon after his death in December 1916 at the age of forty-two. This sketch explains a good deal about Tolstoy's attitude toward the man—and, as always in these reminiscences, it reveals the memoirist himself in a new light.[1]

◄•►

L. A. Sulerzhitsky

Leopold Sulerzhitsky, or Suler, as L. N. Tolstoy nicknamed him, was the son of a Kiev bookbinder, born in a cellar and educated on the street.

"The street is the best of all academies," he used to say cheerfully . . . "The street can give you a lot if you know how to take it. It's the sparrows who taught me how to face life without fear . . ."

Stocky and powerful, he had wonderfully expressive eyes, an oval face framed by a broad dark beard, and an infectious laugh.

"It's one thing for an eagle to soar in the emptiness of the sky—there's no one up there except eagles. But you try hopping around on a paved street the way sparrows do, with monsters looming all around you—a horse that's ten thousand times bigger than you, a man who can crush half a dozen creatures like you with one foot . . . And the thunder, and the noise, the dogs and cats—life is tremendous, overwhelming. I've always been amazed how cheerfully these brave little creatures live surrounded by the terrible chaos of life! And I'm sure that it's precisely from them that

I learned stubbornness in fighting for what's mine, and for what I love . . ."

A sparrow was the last thing that Suler himself resembled; rather, he suggested some other, longer-distance, freedom-loving bird—strong, independent, fueled by a fierce appetite for life.

"Of course they beat me, I was a rotten bookbinder. But everybody gets beaten. It does you no harm, though it doesn't teach you anything either. The good thing is that without crippling me they did make me abhor violence."

At the age of twelve Suler began to draw; he was particularly good at rendering birds, and later drew them like a Japanese master. After finishing school in Kiev he enrolled in the Moscow School of Painting and Sculpture or else Count Stroganov's school, I don't remember which.* He went around half-starved, of course, painting shop signs and submitting little news stories to Pastukhov's *Moscow Paper;* at Easter, at Yuletide, and during Lent he sang in fairground choruses at Maidens' Field. But six years later we find him working with V. Vasnetsov and Vrubel on the murals in the cathedral in Kiev.† He seems at this time to have met the well-known "Tolstoyan" Evgenii Popov, one of the most sincere martyrs to the idea of "non-resistance to evil". . . .

Tolstoy's anarchism fascinated Suler from the start. . . . [Being] above all a man of action, he immediately quit his work as a painter and traveled to a Ukrainian village in the Kanev district where, while practicing truck farming, he openly preached Tolstoy's doctrine to the peasants, distributing copies of his banned works by the hundreds. When the local police chief tried to catch him, Suler hid in a neighboring district, and when the Kanev authorities forgot about him, relieved to find this subversive gone,

---

* It was the former. One of his fellow students there was Tolstoy's daughter Tatiana.

† Viktor Mikhailovich Vasnetsov (1848–1926) and Mikhail Alexandrovich Vrubel (1856–1910) were two of the leading Russian painters of the late nineteenth century. Both drawn to folkloric and literary themes, they worked together in Kiev between 1884 and 1889 painting controversial frescoes for St. Vladimir's Cathedral.

he came back to his vegetables and clandestine printing. He had a boat in which he carried his vegetables down the Dnepr to Kiev, where he used his profits to stock up on paper for the production of hectographed brochures, which he printed beautifully.

Called to military service, Suler refused to take up a rifle, for which he was slapped into a series of jails and declared to be mentally ill; confined for half a year to the Krutitsky barracks, he taught his guards to read and write—"out of boredom and nothing to do," as he put it. At length he was exiled to Kushka, on the Afghan border.

"I haven't got anything for you to do, and it would be a shame to shoot you," the Kushka commandant told Suler, and sent him to Seraks, a desolate military post in the Koshan valley amid the sparse settlements of the local tribes. On the way there Suler encountered "an unpleasant situation."

"My escort and I were following a barely visible trail through the sand dunes, he with a single-shot rifle slung across his back. We ride into a little village and there we find a crowd of Turkmen, most of them young men, who have caught some handsome tiger-like animal and tied him to a tree by his paws so that he seemed to be crucified, and they're shooting arrows and throwing clumps of dry clay at him, shouting and laughing. Several arrows are already sticking out of his stomach and chest; blood is foaming out of his mouth; he is shaking spasmodically, howling and snarling. His eyes, I remember, were glittering amazingly, and his golden eyebrows were quivering so mournfully. I whipped my horse and galloped into the crowd, but the Turkmen pulled me off my horse, and if my escort hadn't come to my aid I'd have been a goner. In the end they only roughed us up a little before we managed to gallop off. Later my escort said to me: 'Such a desperado, and yet you refuse to be a soldier—I don't get it.' I explained how it was with me, and we became friends."

The commander at Seraks turned out to be a good-natured man, though he also declared to Suler that irrepressible people like him should be hanged.

"But you're lucky; around here we need every Russian we can get. Besides, my children need a teacher."

Suler was put down as a noncombatant. He taught the commander's children to read and write, worked in the bakery and the tailor shop, carved toys for the children and pipes for the soldiers out of the roots of the *saksaul* tree, and soon became the favorite of the whole population of Seraks. He became everyone's favorite everywhere he went; that was his natural role.

Unflaggingly cheerful and witty, physically sturdy and adroit, there was no work he shunned, and he brought with him an ardent and contagious sense of the joy of existence. As a fish is filled with roe, so he was filled with the seeds of competence in the most diverse activities; that was the gift of the environment that produced him. He had a highly developed talent for observation; he improvised little genre sketches beautifully; skillfully combining humor and fantasy, he drew deft and subtle and genuinely amusing caricatures; he was a wonderful singer of Ukrainian songs; and he was forever thinking up clever jokes and games.

Stranded out in the torrid sands of Asia with a handful of Russian peasants dressed up as soldiers, ten thousand kilometers from home, Suler naturally became a source of joy and animation for those people. Many years later he showed me a letter from the soldiers of Seraks. I particularly remember a passage in it that sums up Suler's role in Seraks—and, I think, in life generally:

"When you were with us, it was like being home, but without you it's foreign parts again, brother."

But such a restless fellow was not proof against boredom, and once Suler made an attempt to flee Seraks, taking with him, most ill-advisedly, a woman, the wife of one of the post officials. The deserted husband caught up with the fleeing pair in the steppe and at first tried to stab them both.

"But," Suler said, "I talked him out of doing anything foolish. He was a fine fellow; I was as fond of him as he was of me, and his wife had gotten mixed up in this escapade only because she didn't have enough to do—she was bored, there were no children, so she says to me, 'Carry me off!'—and I say, 'Sure, why not?' So I carried her off. But when her husband caught up with us I realized that I'd done a rotten thing—to leave a man by himself in the deserts of Asia! I began trying to persuade the lady to go back where she belonged. She was tired, worn out, both of us were hungry, and it ended by the three of us going back to Seraks together. Soon after that I was transferred to Kushka."

I don't remember what led to Suler's receiving permission to return to Russia, but he did return and lived for a time in the Crimea at the house of a well-known follower of Tolstoy's, Maria Schultz, working as a janitor, gardener, and water carrier, and distributing among the evangelists of the Crimea the banned brochures of the anarchist of Yasnaya Polyana.

After that I think he worked as a sailor on a freighter.

At the end of the 1890s Suler was living near Moscow, on Moose Island, in somebody's empty summer house; there once again he took up the clandestine reproduction of Tolstoyan literature. At this time he was already personally acquainted with Tolstoy.

The local policeman, curious about the hermit who called himself a painter, would drop in on him from time to time, and Suler would give him tea, play checkers with him, sing him romances while accompanying himself on the guitar, and all the while in the next room freshly printed sheets of subversive literature were drying on all the chairs and tables.

I believe that if the policeman had actually discovered what this jovial fellow was up to, he would not have turned him in—such was the power of Suler's personal charm.

It was not long before Lev Nikolayevich proposed to Suler that he organize the resettlement of the Dukhobors from the Caucasus to Canada. That epic operation is interestingly described by Suler in his book *With the Dukhobors to Canada,* published by Tolstoy's firm "The Mediator" [Posrednik]. The book is written somewhat chaotically, and it omits a great many interesting moments that depict Suler's personal adventures. Reading the manuscript, I urged him to add some of that material, but he refused. "I'm not relevant," he said. "The story is about the Dukhobors and I'm only an incidental figure in that unnatural combination of religion and politics . . ."

We decided that after publishing that book he should start work on another, which would be called "Notes of a Restless Man." Suler, who was living with me in the town of Arzamas at the time, was enthusiastic about starting it, but his restlessness nipped the project in the bud. He, like so many people with an abundance of talents, had no liking for persistent and regular work. Still, there is no question but what he had a flair for literature; his sketches, printed in one of the Znanie volumes, are evidence of that.

In 1904 [during the Russo-Japanese war] Suler served as a medical orderly in Manchuria. He was, of course, an ardent participant in the tragedy of our society in 1905 and 1906*; bold and ubiquitous, he worked with all groups and parties without belonging to any of them. He was even a highly dubious Tolstoyan. Lev Nikolayevich once said of him: "Really, what kind of Tolstoyan is he? He's simply "The Three Musketeers"—not one of them, but all three!"

The observation is true and could not be bettered as a description of the vivid individuality of this man, with his love for getting things done, his inclination to quixotic adventures, and his romantic passion for everything beautiful.

It must have been in 1906 that Sulerzhitsky started working at the Moscow Art Theater; a year or two later he was already putting on *The Bluebird* in the Théâtre Réjane in Paris. His work in the Moscow Art Theater Studio is well known thanks to Dickens' *Cricket on the Hearth* and other productions, and has been hailed as the work of an outstanding artist.

When I met Sulzerzhitsky I experienced an unforgettable feeling of joy, realizing it was precisely such a person that that I had been needing to meet in order to appreciate more fully the beauty of a free personality and the generative power of the soil that had created that personality.

We made friends quickly, the way children do. He always showed up unexpectedly, like the sun in winter, and always from someplace remote—from the Caucasus, from Vologda, from the Butyrki prison—filled with new impressions, amusing stories, and fresh joy. Dressed in the same

* Reference is to the failed revolution of 1905.

heavy wool jacket winter and summer, wearing an English sailor's blue jersey and an American cap, noisy and effervescent, he was not someone you could miss in any company; he drew all eyes to himself.

A truthful man who could express his opinions sharply, he was astonishingly cultivated, tolerant of the opinions of others, and able to respect others' ideas even when they were distasteful to him. But that tolerance never kept him from standing up for what he believed.

"There is a reason for everything," he used to say. "Not a single thought is accidental; each one has roots in the past. It's very sad and it does a lot of harm, but we live with the deceased and in many ways as they willed it. We should and must struggle against dead ideas; but it's the living man who needs to be respected. That doesn't mean you shouldn't argue with him; on the contrary, you should!"

" 'I came into the world to dissent'?"*

"Absolutely! Each of us is a creation of the past, and anyone who understands that should try to overcome the past for the sake of the present and the future."

Once he got into an argument with Tolstoy about the Dukhobors, trying to convince him that the Dukhobor anarchism couldn't hold out against the temptations of American life. Lev Nikolayevich answered with some heat, pointing to examples of religious ferment in America itself, among them the Mormons and the sect of Mary Baker Eddy.

"All the same, you're not really sure of what you're claiming," Suler said abruptly, with a smile.

Lev Nikolayevich gave him a sharp look, burst out laughing, wagged his finger at him, but said not a word.

He loved Leopold like a son, and admired him, as one would a woman.

"Just think," he said, observing Suler with those all-seeing little eyes of his, "in someone else that would have been rude, or comical, but coming

---

* The only surviving line of Gorky's first attempt at an epic poem, "The Song of the Ancient Oak," the young author having burned the manuscript in response to the criticism of V. G. Korolenko.

from him it's all right! He does everything his own way, and it's full of truth because he's obeying his heart. What a rare and astonishing fellow . . ."

Watching Suler play skittles with his daughter Alexandra and some others at the entrance to the park in Gaspra, Tolstoy said, smiling his wonderful and subtly expressive smile:

"I always understood the injunction to 'be as little children' intellectually, but I never felt it. How can a grown-up man with a lot of experience be a child? But I look at Suler and I feel it. He can! How much joy he brings to everything, how much there is of the child in him! Despite all he has suffered. How rare it is to see a man who can forget his sufferings, who doesn't boast of them or shove them down the throat of his neighbor . . ."

In the town of Arzamas a man of quite other views and temperament, cultivated and ascetic, Father Fyodor Vladimirsky (who was subsequently one of the deputies in the Second Duma) spoke of Suler in the same terms: "In truth, that man is a pure child of God!"

Chekhov regarded Suler every bit as lovingly and tenderly as Tolstoy.

"There's a talent for you, my friend," he said, frowning softly. "Make him a bishop, a plumber, a publisher—he'll bring something special, all his own, to whatever he does. And in the most tangled situation he'll remain honest."

They were hilarious conversationalists, Suler and Chekhov. They would think up the most improbable things, telling each other (for example) about the impressions of a cockroach from the poverty-stricken hut of a peasant who landed by accident in the apartment of a high-ranking nobleman, where he promptly died of hunger. They both possessed to perfection the art of mixing the real with the fantastic, and those mixings, always unexpected, were memorable for their humor and their knowledge of life. Suler felt himself the equal of any man fate brought him together with; what a Negro feels among white people and what not seldom puts very gifted people at a loss in surroundings that are alien to them—these things were utterly unknown to him.

With Lev Nikolayevich, Suler became a philosopher and boldly took issue with the great "teacher of life," despite the fact that Tolstoy did not like to be contradicted. With Chekhov Suler was a literary man. With Chaliapin he sang the moving Ukrainian song *Beyond the Danube,* and sang it magnificently. He had a lot in common with Chaliapin—understandably enough, since they grew up in the same milieu. And strange as it seems, Suler, for all his activism, was an essentially apolitical man.

Boasting a very high and flexible tenor voice, Suler loved to sing and often performed at concerts for workers; an extreme individualist, he was enraptured by the crowd, felt in its presence like a fish in water, and never passed up a chance for contact with it.

Like all sensitive people who have been through the school of hard knocks, he contained a great many contradictions, which were resolved in his touching faith that goodness would triumph—a kind of social idealism that is so characteristic for many—almost all, in fact—of our Russian "diamonds in the rough."

I recall how, in 1901, when Tolstoy was ill and living at Gaspra, the estate of Countess S. V. Panina, there came a terrible day: his illness had taken a dangerous turn, his friends and family were terribly upset, and to cap it all a rumor was circulating that a prosecutor had arrived in Yalta from Simferopol to inspect and confiscate the papers of the great writer. The rumor seemed to be confirmed when certain inquisitive people showed up in the park at Gaspra, making strenuous efforts to act like carefree tourists. They took a lively interest in everything except the state of Tolstoy's health. Tolstoy's daughter Alexandra galloped over to Oleiz, where I was living with Suler, and proposed that the two of us hide certain documents. I rushed up to Gaspra while Suler went to some workers on a neighboring estate who were good friends of ours. As a result of his meeting with those workers all of the carefree strollers suddenly ran off from Gaspra like hares from a wolfhound. Then Suler stuffed a mass of documents into his shirt and his broad Ukrainian trousers, and galloped back with them on his doughty steed. All this he accomplished in the blink of an eye, as in a fairy tale.

He was in many ways like someone out of a fairy tale. The memory of him kindles joy in one's soul and makes the colors of life more radiant. . . .

4

Leonid Andreyev

Leonid Nikolayevich Andreyev (1871–1919) was, with Chekhov and Gorky, one of the most popular prose writers of the early twentieth century in Russia. His fiction, expressionist in manner, centers on the objectification of inner states; it orchestrates emotional and philosophical abstractions, and has at its best (as in "The Red Laugh" and *The Seven That Were Hanged*) a genuine and unsettling hypnotic power. In its time it spoke to a widespread mood of enervation and foreboding in Russia and led Western readers to regard him as the latest incarnation of the Slavic soul, passionate and extreme, grappling portentously with profundities that could seem at once exotic and universal. (There would appear to be a good deal of Andreyev in Max Beerbohm's satirical sketch "Kolniyatch."[1] Russian critics, too, found the parodic tone hard to resist; one of them observed that "he pronounced the word 'death' as some voluptuaries pronounce the word 'woman.'") Time has not been kind to Andreyev. Both in Russia and outside it he remains in a kind of limbo, not quite dead as a writer but not quite alive, either.

As a personality, however, he comes to vibrant life in Gorky's memoir. They had been friends, closer even than Gorky's account may suggest. They wrote to each other and about each other, and when the news of Andreyev's death reached Gorky (then forty-one), he wept and declared: "Strange as it may seem, he was my only friend. The only one."[2]

Gorky's memoir was an immediate response to that news, and it came just after he had completed his memoir of Tolstoy. Both deal, strikingly, with writers who were obsessed with death—a subject that Gorky (like Dostoyevsky before him)

115

could muster no interest in.[3] And both, for all their many differences, offer remarkable insights into the temperament of the notoriously reticent memoirist himself.

What we have, then, is the account of a complex friendship—though one that the reader is at no point tempted to call unlikely. Given the many ways in which the two men differed radically, that fact alone suggests the richness of Gorky's achievement in the writing. We learn a good deal here about Andreyev, and it is humanly affecting. But we learn even more, much of it fresh and unexpected, about Gorky himself—about his attitudes not just to Andreyev and friendship in general but to people, important and unimportant, and, of course, to literary and philosophical questions.[4] There are astonishing examples of the nature and breadth of his reading; of his matter-of-fact dealings with the tawdry minutiae of "dissolute" life in the spectral Russian capital; and of the first-hand experience he transmuted in his own writing. We see all these in action, and they emerge naturally as aspects of the doomed efforts he describes to shore up both Andreyev's talent and psyche.

Being Gorky's only extended account of a friendship between equals, this memoir is a double portrait, as fascinating in its detail as it is suggestive in its broader implications.[5]

◄•►

Leonid Andreyev

In the spring of 1898 I read in the Moscow *Courier* a story called "Bergamot and Garaska"—an Easter story of the usual type. Aimed at the heart of the holiday reader, it reminded him once again that at times, under certain special circumstances, a person's heart may be open to a feeling of generosity, and that sometimes enemies can become friends, even if not for long— say, for a day.

Since Gogol published "The Overcoat," Russian writers must have written hundreds or even thousands of such designedly moving stories; they are dandelions planted around the authentic flowers of Russian literature, allegedly to beautify the paltry life of the sick and dessicated Russian soul.*

But this story exuded talent in a way that reminded me of Pomyalovsky, and you could sense besides, in the tone of the narration, a shrewd little smile suggesting a mistrust of the facts; that little smile by itself made the inevitable sentimentalism of Eastertide and Christmas writing palatable.

I wrote the author a letter about his story and received from L. Andreyev an amusing answer. In a singular hand, half printing and half writing, he sent a high-spirited and very funny message, which included an underlined aphorism, unpretentious enough, but skeptical: "For one who has eaten his fill, magnanimity is as pleasant as drinking coffee after dinner."

Thus began my acquaintance with Leonid Nikolayevich Andreyev. That summer I read a few more little stories of his, and the feuilletons he signed as James Lynch, noting as I did how quickly and boldly and originally the talent of this new writer was developing.

Passing through Moscow that autumn on my way to the Crimea, I was introduced to L. Andreyev in the Kursk railway station. Wearing a worn overcoat and shaggy sheepskin hat tilted at an angle, he looked like a young actor in some Ukrainian theatrical troupe. His handsome face struck me as not very mobile, but in the fixed gaze of his dark eyes there shone the same smile that sparkled to such effect in his stories and feuilletons. I don't remember his words, but they were unusual, as was his excited manner of speaking. He spoke quickly in a flat but booming voice, coughing as if he had a cold, choking slightly on his words, and waving his arm mechanically as if conducting an orchestra. To me he seemed a healthy, inveterately cheerful man who knew how to live and laugh at the vicissitudes of existence. I found his excitement pleasing.

---

* Gorky's note: It is quite possible that at the time I did not see things that way, but I have no interest in recalling my own ideas.

"Let's be friends!" he said, shaking my hand.

I too was happy and excited.

That winter, returning from the Crimea to Nizhnii, I stopped in Moscow, and there our relations quickly took on the character of a cordial friendship.

I saw that this man had a poor grasp of reality and was not much interested in it—so that I was all the more astonished by the strength of his intuition, the fertility of his fantasy, and the tenacity of his imagination. A single phrase—and sometimes merely a pointed word—would suffice for him to take an insignificant datum and develop it on the spot into a picture, an anecdote, a character, or a story.

"What do you make of S?" he asked, referring to a then-popular writer.

"A tiger from a fur salon."

He laughed and, lowering his voice as if communicating some secret, said in a rush:

"You know, there's a story to write about a man who convinces himself that he is a hero, a real destroyer of the status quo, so terrifying he even scares himself, that sort of thing! And everyone believes him because he's so thoroughly deluded himself. But in his own house, in real life, he is simply a pitiful nonentity, afraid of his wife and even of the cat."

Gaily, adroitly stringing word after word on the thread of his nimble thought, he was forever creating something unexpected and original.

The palm of one hand had been pierced by a bullet, leaving the fingers crooked. I asked him about it.

"The fruits of youthful romanticism," he answered. "You know yourself that a man who hasn't tried to kill himself isn't worth much."

He sat down on the sofa close to me and gave a wonderful account of how, as an adolescent, he had once thrown himself in front of a freight train and how, luckily, he had landed between the rails, so that the train thundered over him, bruising only his ears with its deafening roar.

There was something unclear and unreal about his story, but he embellished it with an amazingly vivid description of what a person feels when ten tons of iron are rumbling over him. I'd had that experience myself. As a boy of ten I would lie between the rails when a freight train was coming, matching my bravery against that of my chums, one of whom, the son of a switchman, could do it with particular nonchalance. The trick is almost without danger if the locomotive tender is raised high enough and if the train is going uphill and not downhill, because in that case the wagon couplings are stretched taut and can't hit you or catch and drag you along the ties. For some seconds you experience a giddy feeling of terror. You try to press yourself into the ground while fighting back an intense urge to move and lift your head. You feel that the torrent of iron and wood hurtling above you wants to tear you from the earth and bear you away somewhere, while the rumbling and scraping of the iron seems to be pulsing in your very bones. And when the train has passed you lie there on the ground for a minute or more, unable to get to your feet, and feel as if you're floating along behind the train and your body is stretching out to infinity and growing and getting light and airy, so that any second now you'll be flying. It's a very pleasant sensation.

"What made us play such a crazy game?" L. N. asked.

I said that perhaps we were testing our will, countering the mechanical movement of a tremendous mass by the conscious immobility of our insignificant bodies.

"No," he objected, "that's too intellectual. It's not how children think."

I reminded him how children "rock the ice," jumping on the springy surface of a pond or river inlet just after it's frozen. I suggested that children in general like dangerous games.

He said nothing, lit a cigarette, threw it away immediately, and gazed into the dark corner of the room with narrowed eyes.

"No, that's probably not right. Almost all children fear the dark. Someone* said:

> There's ecstasy in battle
> And on the grim abyss' brink—

* Pushkin, in *A Feast in the Time of Plague.*

but that's only fine words. I have a different idea, but I can't quite express it."

And he suddenly started, as if singed by an inner flame.

"There's a story to write about a man who spends his whole life suffering unspeakably in pursuit of the truth, only to have it suddenly appear before him. But he shuts his eyes, covers his ears, and says, 'I don't want you, even if you're beautiful, because my life and my sufferings have filled my heart with hatred for you.' What do you think?" and, then said:

"Yes, first we need to decide where the truth is, in man or outside him. You think it's in him?"

He burst out laughing.

"If so, it's really bad, really trivial."

There was hardly a fact or an issue that we saw eye to eye on, but for years our myriad differences didn't keep us from relating to each other with an intensity of interest and concern rare even between very old friends. We talked endlessly. Once I remember we sat more than twenty hours without a break, emptying two samovars of tea, which Leonid put away in incredible quantities.

He was amazingly interesting to talk with—witty and indefatigable. Although his mind showed a stubborn tendency to dwell on the very darkest sides of the human heart, it remained spirited, capricious, and idiosyncratic, easily sliding into grotesquerie and humor. He knew how to use humor very deftly in private conversation, but when he wrote his stories, alas, that talent, rare enough for a Russian, deserted him.

The possessor of a lively and sensitive imagination, he was lazy; he took much more pleasure in talking about literature than in producing it. He was all but unacquainted with the monklike pleasure of working at night, alone and in silence, over a clean sheet of white paper; and he was innocent of the joy that comes from filling that page with traceries of words.

"Writing is hard for me," he confessed. "The pens feel uncomfortable, the whole process is too slow, and even a little humiliating. My thoughts flit like jackdaws around a fire and I easily tire of trying to catch them and lay them out in the right order. Or something like this will happen: I write the word 'cobweb,' and I suddenly think of geometry, algebra, and the teacher in my Orel high school (a dull man, it goes without saying). He often cited the words of some philosopher: 'True wisdom is calm.' But I know that the best people in the world tend to be restless. To hell with calm wisdom! But what else is there? Beauty? Here's to it! There's just one hitch: though I've never seen Venus in person, in pictures she looks to me like a pretty stupid female. Generally speaking, whatever is beautiful tends to be a little stupid—the peacock, the borzoi hound, woman . . ."

You'd have thought that, with his indifference to facts and his skepticism regarding man's reason and will, he would hardly be drawn to the sort of didacticism inevitable in those who know reality only too well. But it was clear from our earliest conversations that this man, possessing all the qualities of a superb artist, craved recognition as a thinker and philosopher. That struck me as not only dangerous but almost hopeless, chiefly because his store of knowledge was so oddly limited. You always sensed that he felt an invisible enemy lurking nearby, that he was in an intense argument with someone he was trying to get the better of.

He didn't like to read, and while he himself was a maker of books, a creator of miracles, he treated old books mistrustfully and carelessly.

"For you a book is a fetish, the way it is for a savage," he used to tell me. "That's because you didn't wear out the seat of your pants in a high school or have any contact with higher education, whereas for me *The Iliad* and Pushkin and the rest are all beslobbered with teachers' spit and prostituted by hemorrhoidal officials. [Griboedov's classic comedy] *Woe from Wit* is as boring as Evtushevsky's book of math problems. [Pushkin's novel] *The Captain's Daughter* is as tedious as one of the girls who work Tverskoy Boulevard."

I've heard these platitudes about how schooling spoils literature for a person all too often, and always found them unconvincing, because I always sensed they were just an excuse for Russian laziness. L. Andreyev was much more original in laying out the ways that reviews and critical articles crushed and ruined books: he did it by using the language found in newspaper accounts of urban street life.

"They're mills that grind Shakespeare, the Bible, and all the rest into the dust of banality. Once I was reading a newspaper article about Don Quixote and realized suddenly, to my horror, that this Don Quixote was a little old man I knew; he ran a government office, had a chronic head cold, and his mistress was a girl who worked in a pastry shop. He called her Milly, but out on the street they called her Bubbles . . ."

For all his casual and sometimes hostile attitude toward books and learning, however, he always evinced a keen interest in what I was reading. One time he caught sight of Alexei Ostroumov's book on Synesius, the bishop of Ptolemais, in my room in the Moscow Hotel and asked in astonishment:

"What do you need that for?"

I told him about the strange half-pagan bishop and quoted from his composition, "In Praise of Baldness": "What can be balder than a heavenly sphere?"

That fervent exclamation from the descendant of Hercules sent Leonid into gales of laughter, but then, wiping the tears from his eyes and still smiling, he said:

"You know, there's a terrific idea there for a story about an unbeliever who wants to test the stupidity of those who believe. He puts on a mask of holiness, lives like an anchorite, and preaches a new doctrine about God— a really silly one—and wins the worshipful love of thousands, after which he tells his disciples and followers: 'It's all nonsense.' But they have a need to believe, and so they kill him."

I was struck by his words; in fact, there is just such an idea in Synesius:

"If they were to tell me that a bishop should share the outlook of the people, then I would reveal who I really am to everybody. For what can philosophy and the rabble have in common? Divine truth must be hidden, for the people have need of something else."

But I didn't mention that to Andreyev, and didn't tell him about the unusual position of this unbaptized pagan philosopher in the role of bishop of the Christian church. When I finally did later on, he exclaimed with a triumphant laugh:

"You see, a person doesn't always have to read in order to know and understand."

Leonid Nikolayevich was talented by nature; it was inborn. His intuition was amazingly acute. In everything connected with the dark sides of life, contradictions in the human heart, turmoil in the domain of the instincts, his perspicacity was uncanny. The example involving Bishop Synesius is far from unique; I could cite a dozen like it.

So, speaking with him about various questers after unshakeable faith, I summarized the contents of the priest Apollov's manuscript "A Confession," one of those works by an obscure martyr of thought—works called into being by the example of Leo Tolstoy's *Confession*. I also told him about my own observations of people of dogma, how they are often the voluntary prisoners of blind, inflexible faith—and how, the more tormenting their doubts about it, the more fanatical they become in defending its truth.

Andreyev became thoughtful, stirred his tea slowly, and then said with a grin:

"I'm surprised you understand that. You talk like an atheist but think like a believer. If you die before me, I'll write on your tombstone: 'While summoning people to revere reason, he secretly mocked its feebleness.'"

Two or three minutes later, nudging me with his shoulder, the dilated pupils of his dark eyes staring into mine, he said in a half-whisper:

"I'll write about a priest, you'll see! And I'll do it well, my friend!"

And wagging his finger at somebody and rubbing his brow hard, he smiled.

"I'll be going home tomorrow and I'll start it! I even have the first sentence: 'He was alone in the midst of people, for he had come into contact with a great mystery.'"

The next day he left for Moscow, and within a week—not longer—he wrote me that he was at work on the priest and that it was going well, "like downhill skiing." That was how he always snagged in passing whatever met the needs of his spirit concerning the most acute and tormenting mysteries of life.

He responded to the enormous success of his first book as only a young man can. When he showed up in Nizhnii he was in high spirits, sporting a new tobacco-colored suit, a devilishly flashy tie set off against a crisply starched shirt, and yellow shoes.

"I looked for straw-colored gloves, but some lady in a shop on the Blacksmiths' Bridge in Moscow said they were no longer fashionable and scared me off. I suspect she was lying. Probably she simply prized her heart's freedom and was afraid to see how irresistible I would be in straw-colored gloves. But I'll tell you a secret: all this finery is uncomfortable. An ordinary shirt is much better."

And suddenly, putting his arm around my shoulder, he said:

"You know, I'd like to write an anthem. I don't know to whom or what, but it has to be an anthem! Something Schilleresque, you know? Something rich and resounding—bommmmm!"

I made fun of him.

"Never mind!" he cried out happily. "It's all there in Ecclesiastes: 'Even a poor life is better than a good death.' No, that's not right, it's about the lion and the dog: 'A bad dog is more useful in the house than a good lion.' Or—what do you think, could Job have read Ecclesiastes?"

In his excitement he fantasized about taking a trip down the Volga on a fancy steamer and hiking through the Crimea.

"And I'll drag you along—otherwise you'll wall yourself in completely with these bricks," he said, pointing to my books.

His joy resembled the active satisfaction of a child who, after going too long without eating, now thinks that his stomach will be full forever.

We were sitting on a large sofa in a small room and drinking red wine. Andreyev reached down from the shelf a notebook filled with poems.

"May I?"

And he began to read aloud:

>Columns of copper pines,
>The monotonous tollings of the sea . . .

"Could that be the Crimea? The fact is, I don't know how to write verse. Or have much desire to. In general I like ballads best:

>I love everything that's new,
>Romantic, incoherent
>Like a poet
>Of the past.

"This is from an operetta—*The Green Island,* I think:

>And the trees sigh,
>Like a poem without rhymes.

"I like that. But tell me: why do you write poems? It's not up your alley. Still, a poem is a thing of artifice, whatever you may say."

We went on to invent parodies on the writer Skitalets:

>I'll take up a big log
>In my mighty hand
>And beat you all
>To the seventh generation.
>I'll slaughter you!
>I'll flabbergast you besides!
>Yippee! Go on, tremble! Be my guests!
>I'll chuck Mt. Kazbek at you
>And drop Ararat on your heads!

He shook with laughter, tirelessly turning out amiable idiocies, and then, abruptly, leaned toward me with a glass of wine in his hand and said, softly and seriously:

"A while ago I read an amusing story: There's a monument to the poet Robert Burns in some English town. But there's no sign about who it is dedicated to. At the foot of the monument a boy is selling newspapers. A writer comes up and says, 'I'll buy a paper if you can tell me whose statue that is.' 'Robert Burns,' says the boy. 'Good. Now I'll buy all your papers if you can tell me why they put up a monument to Robert Burns.' The boy says, 'Because he died.' How do you like that?"

I didn't particularly like it. The labile nature of Leonid's moods always worried and alarmed me.

For him fame was not only what Pushkin called it—"a bright patch on the singer's tatters." He was greedy for all he could get of it, and made no secret of the fact. He said:

"When I was only fourteen I told myself that I would be famous, otherwise life wouldn't be worth living. I'm not afraid to say that whatever may have been accomplished before my time does not strike me as better than what I feel myself capable of producing. If you think that's arrogance, you're wrong. It's what anyone has to assume if he doesn't want to take his place as one of the faceless multitudes. It is precisely a belief that one is exceptional that should—and can—be a source of creative energy. If at first we tell ourselves that we are not like all the others, then it will be easy later on to prove it to all the others."

"In short, you're a baby who doesn't want to feed at its nurse's breast."

"Exactly. The only milk I want is the milk of my own soul. A man needs love and attention—or else to be feared. Even a peasant understands that when he puts on the mask of a sorcerer. The luckiest of all are those who are loved and feared simultaneously, like Napoleon."

"Have you read his *Memoirs*?"

"No. I don't need to."

He winked and grinned:

"I keep a diary myself, so I know how it's done. Memoirs, confessions, all that sort of thing—it's just the excrement of a soul that has been poisoned by bad food."

He liked to come out with epigrams of that sort, and when they were successful he was visibly happy. Despite his tendency to pessimism, there was something ineradicably childlike in him—for instance, the naïve and childish way he flaunted his own verbal adroitness, which in fact worked much better in talk than on paper.

Once I was telling him about a woman so proud of her "honest" life, so concerned to convince one and all of her purity, that all the people around her, bored to death, either contrived to get away from this paragon of virtue, or else trembled with hatred for her.

"It was like saying, 'I'm an honest woman so I don't need to clean my nails'—am I right?"

With these words he caught the character and even the habits of the person I had been describing just about perfectly: she was in fact careless of her appearance. When I told him, he was very pleased and began to boast in a guileless and childlike way:

"You know, I'm sometimes amazed myself at how succinctly and precisely I can get at the very essence of a thing or a person."

And he began a long speech in his own praise. But, being an intelligent fellow, he saw that this was slightly ridiculous, and his tirade ended in humorous hyperbole:

"In time I will so refine my genius as to be able, with a single word, to pinpoint the meaning of the entire life of a man, a nation, a historical epoch . . ."

But a critical attitude toward himself was not for all that very highly developed in him—a fact which at times cost him dearly both in his work and his life.

Leonid Nikolayevich was strangely and deeply self-divided, and it caused him pain. In one and the same week he could sing "Hosanna" to the world and call down imprecations on it.

He would say:

"I hate individuals who avoid the sunny side of the street out of fear that their faces will get sunburned or their jackets fade—I hate all those who let dogmas constrain the free and capricious play of their inner selves."

He once wrote quite a caustic column about people who keep to the shady side, and immediately after that, in connection with the death of Emile Zola from monoxide poisoning, a piece in which he polemicized with the barbaric asceticism fairly common among intellectuals at the time. But, talking with me about that polemic, he unexpectedly declared:

"All the same, you know, my opponent is more consistent than I am. A writer should live like a homeless wanderer. Maupassant's yacht is an absurdity!"

This was not said in jest. We began to argue, and I asserted that the more various the needs of a man are, the more greedy he is for the joys of life—even if they are trivial ones—the more quickly his physical and spiritual culture develops. Leonid's answer was that, no, Tolstoy was right, culture is rubbish and only warps the free growth of the soul.

"An attachment to things," he said, "is the fetishism of a savage; it's idol worship. Don't make yourself an idol or you're a goner—that's the truth! Make a book today, a machine tomorrow—yesterday you made a boot, but you've already forgotten about it. We need to learn how to forget."

But, I said, we need to remember that each thing is an embodiment of the human spirit, and often the inner value of the thing is more significant than the man who made it.

"To say that is to worship inert matter," he shouted.

"Immortal thought is embodied in it."

"What is thought? It is two-faced and repulsive in its impotence . . ."

We found ourselves arguing more and more often, and more and more heatedly. Our most intense disagreements centered on our attitudes toward thought.

I feel myself to be living in an atmosphere of thought, and seeing how much that is great and majestic is the product of thought, I believe that its impotence is only temporary. It may be that I romanticize and exaggerate the creative power of thought, but that is so natural in Russia, where no spiritual synthesis exists—a paganly sensual country.

Leonid regarded thought as "an evil trick played on humanity by the devil"; it seemed to him a thing false and repugnant. Carrying man right up to the edge of abysses of irresolvable mystery, it deceives him by leaving him there in painful and impotent isolation, while itself simply dying away.

Just as irreconcilable were the differences in our respective views of man, the source and crucible of thought. For me man is always victorious, even when mortally wounded or dying. His quest for self-knowledge and knowledge of nature is a wonderful thing, and though his life is a torment he keeps pushing back its limits, creating with his thought the wisdom of science and the marvels of art. I felt that I sincerely and truly loved man— man as he lives and acts around me today, and the wise, good, strong man who will appear at some point in the future. Andreyev saw man as beggarly in spirit, jumbled together out of the irreconcilable contradictions between instinct and intellect, and perpetually barred from any possibility of achieving inner harmony. All his doings are "vanity of vanities," decay and self-deception. And the main thing is that he is the slave of death and goes around his whole life dragging its chain.

It's very hard to speak of a person to whom you are particularly well attuned.

That may sound like a paradox but it is the truth. When the mysterious throbbing of another person's self is something you can sense, something that moves you, you fear confronting the invisible rays of the soul that is dear to you with an ill-chosen or heavy-handed word—you fear saying the wrong thing, or saying a thing the wrong way: you don't want to distort the barely graspable thing you feel by giving it a name, you can't bring yourself to force what is humanly valuable (albeit of general significance) in another person into the straitjacket of your speech.

It is much easier and simpler to talk about something that you do not feel clearly enough; you can add a lot—anything you want, in fact—as your own commentary.

I do believe that I was very well attuned to L. Andreyev. To put it more concretely: I saw how he walked a path bordering the precipice above the quagmire of madness, above the abyss into which the eye of reason cannot look without being extinguished.

Great was the strength of his imagination, but, for all his constant and intense attention to the humiliating mystery of death, he could never picture anything beyond it, nothing majestic or consoling, and he remained too much of a realist to try to invent a consolation for himself, though he would have liked to do that.

It was his walking the path on the edge of the void that increasingly divided us. I myself had experienced Leonid's mood much earlier, but my natural human pride made dwelling on death organically repellent and offensive to me.

Once I told Leonid about having gone through a difficult period when the "prisoner dreams of existence beyond the walls of his prison," of "the stony darkness" and "being frozen in position for all eternity." He jumped up from the sofa and, running about the room, waving his crippled hand up and down like a conductor, speaking rapidly and indignantly, gasped out:

"It's cowardice, my friend, to close a book without reading it to the end! That book contains your indictment—in it you are being denied—don't you see? You and everything you care about are denied there—humanism, socialism, esthetics, love—it's all nonsense according to the book. It's ridiculous and pitiful: they've condemned you to death. For what? And you pretend you don't know this and that it doesn't offend you, and you go around admiring the flowers, deceiving yourself and others . . . The stupid little flowers! . . ."

I pointed out that there was a certain futility in protesting against earthquakes and tried to make him see that protests cannot affect the spasms of the earth's crust, but that only made him angrier.

The talk took place in Petersburg, in autumn, in an empty and depressing fifth-story room. A dense fog shrouded the city, and inside that gray mass the spectral, rainbow spheres of the streetlights hung motionless like huge soap bubbles. Through the thick cotton wool of the fog absurd sounds rose up from the street below; among them the clattering of horses' hooves on the pavement was especially irksome.

Down below a fire brigade was rushing noisily past. Leonid came over, slumped down on the sofa, and suggested:

"How about going to see the fire?"

"Fires in Petersburg aren't interesting," I said.

He agreed:

"It's true. Whereas out in the provinces—in Orel, say—when the wooden streets burn and the townsfolk are fluttering around like moths—then it's good! And the pigeons circling over the cloud of smoke—you've seen them?"

Putting his arm around me, he said with a grin:

"You've seen everything, damn you! That 'stony darkness'—that was really good—stony darkness and the void!"

And butting me with his head:

"Sometimes I hate you for that."

I told him I felt that.

"Yes," he agreed, putting his head on my lap. "You know why? I'd like you to suffer with the same pain I do, then we'd be closer. You know how lonely I am!"

I did. He was very lonely—although at times it seemed to me that he jealously guarded that loneliness as the source of his fantastic inspirations and the fertile ground of his originality.

"You're lying when you say that scientific thought satisfies you," he said, fixing the dark and melancholy glance of his frightened eyes on the ceiling. "Science, my friend, is a kind of mysticism too, the mysticism of fact. The truth is, nobody knows anything. And the question of how I think and why I think—the main source of people's torment—that is the most terrible truth of all. Please, let's go somewhere . . ."

Talking about the mechanism of thinking agitated him more than anything. And frightened him.

We put on our coats, went down into the fog, and for an hour or two navigated the Nevsky Prospect like sheatfish on a slimy river bottom. Then, as we were sitting in a coffee shop, three girls glommed onto us and would not go away; one of them, a shapely Estonian, said her name was El-frieda. She had an expressionless face and kept her big dull gray eyes on

Andreyev—her seriousness was hair-raising—while she sipped some poisonous green liquor out of a coffee cup. It gave off a stench of burnt leather.

Leonid was drinking cognac and quickly grew tipsy. He turned bois-
terous, made the girls laugh with surprisingly funny and elaborate jokes,
and wound up deciding to go home with them as they kept importuning
him to do. It was impossible to let Leonid go by himself; once he started
drinking it woke something terrifying in him, a vengeful appetite for
destruction, the blind hatred of the "captive beast."

I went with him. We bought wine, fruit, sweets, and somewhere on
Razezhaya Street, in the corner of a filthy courtyard piled high with barrels
and firewood, on the second floor of a wooden outbuilding, in two small
rooms whose walls were squalidly and pitiably adorned with postcards,
we began to drink.

Before he got to the point of passing out, Leonid became alarmingly
excited. His brain bubbled, his imagination took fire, his speech became
almost unbearably vivid.

One of the girls, plump, soft, and agile as a mouse, told us with something like delight about how an assistant prosecutor had bitten her leg
above the knee. She plainly considered the jurist's act the most interesting
event of her life, for she showed the scar from the bite and, spluttering with
excitement, her beady little eyes shining with joy, said:

"He loved me so much—it's scary just recalling it. I mean, he bit me,
and he had a false tooth, and it got stuck in my flesh!"

This girl got drunk very quickly, collapsed on a couch in the corner,
and fell asleep snoring. An ample brunette with thick hair, sheep's eyes,
and monstrously long arms was playing the guitar, while Elfrieda set the
bottles and plates on the floor, jumped up on the table, and danced word-
lessly, twisting her body like a snake, without taking her eyes off Leonid.
Then she began to sing in an unpleasantly thick voice, her eyes wide and
angry, leaning over Andreyev at times as if broken in two, and he would
shout out the words he caught from that alien song in a foreign language,
nudging me with his elbow and saying:

"She understands something. Look at her. You see? She understands!"

At certain moments Leonid's eyes would seem to go blind; turning even darker, it was as if they were receding into his skull in an effort to see into his brain.

Exhausted, the Estonian girl jumped down from the table onto the bed, stretched out, and with her mouth open began stroking her little breasts, which were pointed like a she-goat's.

Leonid said:

"The highest and most profound sensation we can have in life is the spasm of the sexual act, yes indeed! And maybe the earth like that bitch over there is whirling in the void of the universe expecting me to impregnate her with an understanding of the goal of existence, and I, with everything wonderful in me, am only a spermatozoon."

I suggested that we go home.

"You go, I'll stay here . . ."

By now he was seriously drunk, and he had a lot of money on him. He sat down on the bed and, stroking the girl's shapely legs, started telling her playfully that he loved her, while she, with her hands folded behind her head, stared unblinking into his face.

"When the ram has tasted radish he grows wings," Leonid said.

"No, he doesn't," the girl said seriously. "That's not true."

"I tell you, she understands a thing or two!" Leonid cried out in drunken happiness. A few minutes later he left the room. I gave the girl money and asked her to persuade Leonid to go for a ride. She agreed at once:

"He scares me. Men like him use guns," she muttered.

The girl with the guitar had fallen asleep sitting on the floor near the couch where her friend slept snoring.

When Leonid came back the Estonian girl was already dressed. He started shouting:

"I don't want to! Let there be a banquet of the flesh!"

And he began trying to undress the girl, but she fought him off, all the while looking him in the eye so obstinately that her glance tamed him and he agreed:

"Let's go."

But when he tried to put her hat on his own head à la Rembrandt he broke off all the feathers.

"You going to pay for that hat?" she asked in a businesslike way.

Leonid raised his eyebrows and burst into laughter, shouting:

"Tha-hat does it! Whoopee!"

Out on the street we found a cab and drove through the fog. It wasn't very late, somewhere around midnight. Between the huge beads of its streetlights the Nevsky Prospect seemed a path descending to distant depths; wet specks gleamed around the streetlamps; black fishes struggled upward in the gray dampness, while the hemispheres of umbrellas seemed to be lifting the people who held them off the ground—the whole scene was spectral in the extreme, strange and melancholy.

Out in the air Andreyev became completely drunk and dozed off, swaying. The girl whispered to me:

"I'll jump out, all right?"

And springing from my lap into the thick mud of the street, she disappeared.

At the end of Kamennoostrovsky Prospect Leonid opened his frightened eyes and asked:

"We still driving? I want to go to a tavern. You got rid of the girl?"

"She left."

"That's a lie. You're a sly one—and so am I. I left the room to see what you'd do. I stood there behind the door and heard what you said to her. You acted innocently and nobly. In general you're a bad sort, you drink a lot but don't get drunk, and that means that your children will be alcoholics. My father drank a lot without getting drunk and I'm an alcoholic."

Then we sat smoking on the embankment under the idiotic bubble of the fog, and when the end of a cigarette would flare up you could see how gray our overcoats looked covered with the beady condensation of the damp.

Leonid spoke with unconstrained frankness, and it was not the frankness of a drunk; his mind hardly became intoxicated until the moment when the poison of the alcohol brought the functioning of his brain to a complete halt.

"If I had stayed with the girls it would have ended badly for someone. That's true. But that's just it, that's why I don't like you! You stop me from being myself. Leave me alone and I'll expand. You may be the hoop on the barrel: take you away and the barrel falls to pieces. But let it fall to pieces! You understand what I'm saying? No reason to hold back anything, let it all be destroyed. It may be that the true meaning of life lies precisely in the destruction of something that we don't know—or of everything we've thought up and done."

His dark eyes stared mournfully into the gray mass around and over him; sometimes he lowered them to the wet and leaf-strewn ground and stamped his feet as if gauging the firmness of the soil.

"I don't know what you really think, but what you say all the time is not the expression of your faith, the words are not the words of your prayer. You say that all the forces of life come from the destruction of equilibrium, but it's precisely equilibrium—some sort of harmony—that you yourself seek, and you try to get me to do the same, even though in your view equilibrium equals death!"

I said I wasn't trying to get him to do anything, and had no interest in trying, but that I cared greatly about his life, about his health and his work.

"You only care about my work, what's external to me, but not about my self, about what can't be embodied in my work. You get in my way, you get in everybody's—go to hell!"

He leaned on my shoulder, looked into my face with a smile, and went on:

"You think I'm drunk and don't realize that I'm talking nonsense? No, I simply want to tick you off. I, my friend, am a decadent, a degenerate, a sick individual. But Dostoyevsky was sick too, like all great men. There's a book, I don't remember who wrote it, about genius and insanity, where it's proved that genius is a psychic disease! That book has been my undoing. If I hadn't read it I'd be simpler. By now I know that I'm almost a genius, but I wonder if I'm crazy enough. Do you understand? I see myself as crazy in order to convince myself that I'm talented. Get it?"

I laughed. What he said struck me as a poor invention, and therefore untrue.

When I told him that, he laughed too, and by a supple reflex of his soul skipped like a trained acrobat into a joking tone:

"So where's there a tavern where the holy rites of literature can be performed? Talented Russians absolutely have to do their talking in a tavern. That's our tradition. Our critics refuse to recognize talent outside of it."

We went to sit in an all-night tavern for cabbies, where it was stifling, smoky and damp. The sleepy "garçons" shuffled around the room angry and exhausted, the drunks cursed on cue, the wretched prostitutes screamed. One of the latter uncovered her left breast—a yellow thing, with the enormous nipple of a cow—and put it on a plate which she brought over to us, asking:

"Want to buy a pound?"

"I adore shamelessness," Leonid said. "In cynical behavior I sense the sadness—the despair almost—of a person who knows he can't help being an animal, wants not to be, but can't. You understand?"

The tea he was drinking was strong, almost black. Knowing how much he liked it and knowing how it sobered him, I made a point of ordering more. Sipping the pitchlike bitter liquid, and probing the swollen faces of the drunkards with his eyes, Leonid talked nonstop.

"I'm indecent with women. It's more honest that way, and they love it. Better to be an out-and-out sinner than a righteous person who can't quite pray himself into full sainthood."

He looked around, paused, then said:

"It's as boring here as at a gathering of clerics."

He found this funny.

"I never was at a gathering of clerics but it must be something like a fish-pond . . ."

The tea had sobered him up, and we left the tavern. The fog was thicker than ever; the opalescent globes of the streetlights were like melting ice.

"I'd like some fish," Leonid said, leaning with his elbows on the railing of a bridge over the Neva. He went on in high spirits: "You know what happens with me? It's probably how children think: they start with a word—say, carp, and come up with words that sound like it: carp, park, pork, port, fort . . . But when it comes to writing poems, I can't do it!"

He thought a moment, then added:

"It's also the way writers of ABC books think . . ."

We were sitting once again in a tavern, partaking of fish soup, and Leonid was telling how "the decadents" had been inviting him to contribute to *The Scales.**

"I won't do it, I don't like them. I don't sense any content behind their words. They 'get high' on words, as Balmont likes to say. He's another talented—and sick—fellow."

On a different occasion I remember his saying about the people around the almanac *Scorpion:*

"They abuse Schopenhauer, but I like him, and so I hate them."

But the word sounded too strong in his mouth; he didn't know how to hate; he was too soft for that. Once he had showed me "words of hate" in his diary, but they all turned out to be humorous words and he himself had a good laugh over them.

I took him to his hotel and put him to bed, but when I came round at midday I discovered that as soon as I'd gone he had gotten up, dressed, and gone off somewhere by himself. I spent the whole day looking for him, without luck.

He drank without stopping for four days and then left for Moscow.

He had an unpleasant way of testing the sincerity of people's relations with each other. It worked like this: suddenly he would ask in passing:

"You know what Z said about you?"

Or he'd report:

"But S was saying that you . . ."

And he would look you in the eye to see your reaction.

Once I told him: "Watch out or you could wind up setting all your friends against each other."

* *The Scales* (Vesy) was the influential journal of the Russian symbolists. Published between 1904 and 1909 it was, according to D. S. Mirsky, "without doubt the most civilized and European publication of its time."

"What if I did?" he answered. "If they can fall out over little things it means their relations were not sincere."

"What is it you're after?"

"Some solidity, some kind of monumentality, some real beauty in the relationship. Each of us has to know how delicate the lacework of the soul is, what gentleness and care it deserves to be treated with. A certain romanticism is needed in relationships—it was there in Pushkin's circle and I envy it. Women only respond to the erotic; *The Decameron* is their gospel."

But a half hour later he made fun of his comment on women, offering a hilarious account of the conversation between an erotomaniac and a schoolgirl.

He couldn't stand Artsybashev* and at times showed crude hostility in the way he ridiculed him precisely for his one-sided portrayal of women as representing nothing but the principle of sensuality.

He once told me the following story: When he was about eleven, in some grove or garden he saw a church deacon kissing a young lady.

"They were kissing, and they were both crying," he said, lowering his voice and hunching up. Whenever he told anything intimate he always tensed his somewhat flabby muscles.

"The young lady was very thin and fragile, with little matchstick legs, while the deacon was fat. His cassock was greasy and shiny on the belly. I already knew why people kiss, but this was the first time I saw them crying while they kissed, and I thought it was funny. The deacon's beard got snagged in a hook on her unbuttoned jacket; he kept twisting his head; and I whistled to scare them, but then got scared myself and ran away. But on the evening of that same day I decided I was in love with the daughter of a justice of the peace, a girl of about ten; I felt around—she had no breasts— which meant that there was nothing to kiss and that she was no good for love. Then I fell in love with our neighbors' maid, a short-legged girl with

---

* Mikhail Petrovich Artsybashev (1878–1927), a prose fiction writer best known for his philosophical-erotic novel *Sanin,* which enjoyed a succès de scandale when it appeared in 1907.

no eyebrows but with ample breasts—the jacket was as greasy over her chest as the deacon's cassock had been over his belly. I was very resolute in approaching her, and she was equally resolute in boxing my ears. But that didn't dampen my ardor; she was a beauty as far as I was concerned—more and more, in fact. It was almost torture, and very sweet. I have seen many really beautiful girls, and I understand with my mind that the one I loved was monstrous by comparison, and yet for me she has always remained better than them all. I felt good because I knew that nobody else was capable of loving as I did a fat tow-haired wench, and nobody else—that was the point—would be able to see her as the fairest of the fair."

His narration was wonderful, the words all suffused with that winning humor of his that I am unable to convey. What a pity that, using it so effectively in conversation, he neglected (or feared) to let it enliven his fiction, evidently worrying that flashes of humor would mar the somber tonality of his pictures.

When I remarked what a shame it was that he had forgotten how successfully he had turned that short-legged serving maid into the greatest beauty of the world, and that he no longer wished to extract golden veins of beauty from the base ore of reality, he narrowed his eyes slyly and said:

"Ah, but you like your little treats, don't you? No, I have no intention of pampering you romantics . . ."

It was impossible to make him see that he himself was the romantic.

When Leonid gave me his *Collected Works* in 1915 the inscription read: "Beginning with 'Bergamot' in *The Courier,* everything here took place and was written before your eyes, Alexei: in many ways this is the history of our relationship."

It is, alas, true—"alas" because I think it would have been better for L. Andreyev if he had not brought "the history of our relationship" into his stories. But he was only too eager to do that, and in his haste to "rebut" my views he spoiled what he was doing. It was as if he made my image the embodiment of his invisible enemy.

"I've written a story you probably won't like," he said on one occasion. "Shall we read it together?"

We did. Apart from some details, I liked the story a lot.

"The details are nothing, I can fix them," he said animatedly as he shuffled around the room, his shoes scrunching on the floor. Then he sat down next to me and, tossing back his hair, looked me in the eye.

"Look, I know—I feel it—that you're sincere in praising the story. What I don't understand is how you can possibly like it."

"There are plenty of things in the world that I don't like, but that doesn't detract from them as far as I can see."

"You can't think that way and be a revolutionary."

"You mean your idea of a revolutionary is Nechayev's 'a revolutionary is not a human being'?"*

He hugged me and laughed:

"You don't understand yourself very well. But—listen to this—when I was writing 'The Thought' I was thinking of you. Alexei Savelov is you! There's one phrase there—'Alexei was not talented'—that was probably not very nice of me, but sometimes you irritate me with that stubbornness of yours so much that I start thinking of you as untalented. That was a bad thing to write, wasn't it?"

He was agitated, even blushing.

I calmed him down by saying that I didn't consider myself an Arabian steed but only a drayhorse, and that I realized that my success was due not so much to any inborn talent as to my industry and love for work.

"You're a strange man," he said softly, interrupting me; and then suddenly, changing the level of the conversation, he began speaking thoughtfully about himself and the trouble in his soul. He had none of that very common and unpleasant Russian penchant for confession and repentence; still, he was able at times to speak about himself with a candor that was not only courageous, but even rather harsh—and do it without losing his self-respect. I liked that in him.

---

* Sergei Gennadievich Nechayev (1847–1882), revolutionary and terrorist, the prototype for Pyotr Verkhovensky in Dostoyevsky's *Demons.*

"You see," he said, "every time I write anything that particularly moves me it's as if the crust falls off my soul and I see myself more clearly—and realize that I have more talent than shows in my writing. Take 'The Idea.' I expected it would shock you, but now I see myself that it's basically a polemical work—and one that misses the mark besides."

He jumped to his feet, shook back his hair, and announced half-jokingly:

"I'm afraid of you, you villain! You're stronger than I am, but I don't want to submit to you."

Then, more seriously:

"There's something lacking in me, my friend, something important—yes? What do you think?"

I thought that he was unforgivably casual in the way he treated his talent, and that he needed more knowledge.

"You need to study, read, visit Europe . . ."

He waved away the suggestion.

"That's not it. What I need is to find God and learn to trust in his wisdom."

As always we began to argue. After one such argument he sent me the proofs of his story "The Wall." With regard to "Ghosts" he told me:

"The madman who knocks on the wall is myself; the energetic Egor is you. Confidence in your own powers really is one of your defining characteristics—and it's at the heart of your craziness and the craziness of all romantics like you, people who idealize reason and are cut off from life by their dream."

The nasty uproar over his story "The Abyss" upset him.* Those who are always ready to accommodate the public's taste for scandal started retailing

---

* Andreyev's scandalous story is about the bestiality that lurks beneath the fragile veneer of civilization. It tells of two innocent young students out for a walk who are set upon by thugs. The girl is raped, the boy beaten unconscious. When he comes to and discovers her, disheveled and still unconscious herself, he becomes inflamed with lust, and "the black abyss" swallows him. Tolstoy's wife, Sofia Andreyevna, published a letter protesting Andreyev's concentration "on the filthy moment of a human being's degradation."

all sorts of garbage about Andreyev, and some of their invented slanders
were downright comical. Thus one poet wrote in a Kharkov newspaper
that Andreyev and his fiancée had gone swimming without bathing suits.
Aggrieved, Leonid asked:

"What does he think people should do, wear a dinner jacket in the
water? Anyway, he's lying. I haven't been swimming all year, either with
my fiancée or solo. There's been no place to do it. You know, I've decided to print and stick on all the fences a short but sincere request to
readers:

Please do this:
Don't read "The Abyss"!

He was excessively, even morbidly concerned with people's reactions
to his stories, and was forever complaining, sometimes sadly, sometimes
with annoyance, about the barbaric heavy-handedness of critics and re-
viewers. Once he even complained in print about the critics' hostility to
him as an individual.

"Don't do it," he was advised.

"No, it's got to be done, otherwise in their efforts to reform me they'll
be cutting off my ears or scalding me in boiling water . . ."

He was cruelly tormented by hereditary alcoholism. Episodes were not
frequent but almost always took very severe forms when they did. He
struggled against the disease and the struggle cost him enormous effort,
but there were times when, falling into despair, he would deride these
efforts.

"I want to write a story about a man who from an early age, for twenty-
five years, is afraid to drink a glass of vodka, and because of that forfeits
many wonderful hours of life, ruins his career, and dies in the prime of life
from a splinter in his finger or a botched attempt to cut off a bunion."

And on one visit to me in Nizhnii he did in fact bring with him a manuscript on that theme.

It was there at my place that L. N. met Father Fyodor Vladimirsky, an arch-priest from the town of Arzamas who was subsequently to serve as a member of the Second Duma. He was a remarkable man whose life I will try to write someday; for now, however, I find it necessary to offer a brief sketch of the principal exploit of his life.

Practically from the time of Ivan the Terrible the town of Arzamas got its drinking water from ponds where the corpses of drowned rats, cats, hens, and dogs floated in summer, and where in winter the water under the ice grew foul and gave off a nauseating smell. So this Father Fyodor resolved to furnish the town with healthful water, and spent twelve years personally studying the groundwaters around Arzamas. Year after year, every summer, he would wander the fields and forests at sunrise like some sorcerer, observing how the earth was "rotting." And after lengthy labors he found the underground springs, traced their flow, made excavations to redirect them into a gulley in the woods about three kilometers from town, and when he had obtained upwards of one hundred twenty thousand gallons of excellent spring water for the ten thousand inhabitants of the town, proposed the construction of a water main. The town had the funds, which a merchant had left it to be used either for building a water main or for setting up a credit society. The merchants and the city authorities felt no need for a water main, since horses brought them their water in barrels from distant springs outside town, and so in their desire to use the funds to found a credit society they put all sorts of obstacles in the way of Father Fyodor. Meanwhile, the lower orders went on drinking the tainted water from the ponds, remaining—as was their ancient habit—indifferent and lethargic. As a result, once he'd found the water Father Fyodor was obliged to wage a long and tedious struggle with the obstinate self-interest of the rich and the wretched stupidity of the poor.

When I arrived in Arzamas under police surveillance he was just finishing the work of marshalling the spring water. This man, worn out with hard work and misfortune, was the first person in town to seek my acquaintance—the authorities in their wisdom had strictly forbidden municipal employees and other functionaries to visit me, and to intimidate them had set up a police post right under the windows of my apartment.

Father Fyodor came to me one evening in a heavy downpour, drenched from head to foot, spotted with clay, wearing heavy peasant boots, a gray cassock, and a faded hat so soaked through that it looked like a clump of mud. Giving me a firm handshake with the calloused and rough palm of a digger in the soil, he said in a mournful bass voice:

"Are you the unrepentant sinner who's been shipped to us in the interests of your personal correction? We'll correct you all right! Can you give us some tea?"

Hidden in his gray beard was the dried-out face of an ascetic; a quiet smile shone out of his deep-set, intelligent eyes.

"I've stopped in on my way from the woods. You wouldn't have anything for me to change into?"

I had heard a lot about him. I knew that his son was a political émigré, that one daughter was in prison "for politics" and another was preparing to follow suit. I knew, too, that he had spent all his own money on the search for water, that he'd mortgaged his house, lived like a beggar, dug ditches himself in the woods, lined them with clay, and when his own strength was not enough he asked the local muzhiks to lend a hand in Christ's name. And they helped—while the townsmen, skeptically following the labors of the "crackpot priest," refused to lift a finger to help him.

Such was the man Leonid Andreyev met at my place.

It was October, a cold, dry day; the wind was whipping debris— paper, birds' feathers, onion peels—down the street. The dust scratched against the windowpanes, while from the fields a huge rain cloud was advancing on the town. Into the room where we were sitting marched Father Fyodor, wiping the dust from his eyes, ragged and angry, cursing the thief who had stolen his rucksack and umbrella, and the governor who refused to see that running water was more useful than a credit society. Leonid opened his eyes wide and whispered to me:

"What's all this about?"

Over tea an hour later, he listened with his mouth agape as this arch-priest from the absurd town of Arzamas pounded the table with his fist and thundered against the Gnostics for fighting against the democratic character of the church by seeking to make the doctrine of the knowledge of God inaccessible to the people's understanding.

"These heretics considered themselves seekers of a higher knowledge, aristocrats of the spirit—but isn't it the people, in the persons of its wisest leaders, that embodies divine wisdom and the spirit of God?"

"Docetists," "Ophites," "pleroma," "Karpocratus" thundered Father Fyodor, while Leonid, nudging me with his elbow, whispered:

"He's the Arzamas horror personified!"*

But before long he was waving his arm in front of Father Fyodor's face, trying to convince him of the impotence of thought, while the priest, wagging his beard, offered objections:

"It's not thought that is impotent, but unbelief."

"Which is the essence of thought . . ."

"You're spouting sophisms, Mr. Writer."

The rain lashed the windowpanes, the samovar gurgled on the table, the old man and the young were clashing over ancient wisdom, while from the wall, a stick in his hand, that great pilgrim of this world Lev Tolstoy gazed down pensively at them. Long after midnight, when we had overthrown all there was time for, we went to our rooms. I was already in bed with a book in my hand when there was a knock on the door and Leonid appeared. Disheveled, flushed, the collar of his shirt unbuttoned, he sat on the edge of my bed and exclaimed in delight:

"What a priest! And what a going-over he gave me!"

Suddenly there were tears in his eyes.

"You're lucky, damn you, Alexei! You've always got amazingly interesting people around you, while I'm either alone—or else people are milling around and crowding me."

* See p. 53 above.

He made a despairing gesture.

I began telling him about Father Fyodor's life, how he searched for water; about the "History of the Old Testament" he wrote, only to have the manuscript confiscated by order of the church authorities; about his book *Love as the Law of Life,* also prohibited by the ecclesiastical censorship. In that book Father Fyodor argued, citing Pushkin, Hugo, and other poets, that one person's feeling of love for another is the very foundation of the existence and development of the world, that it is as powerful as the general law of gravity (which it resembles in all ways).

"It's true," Leonid said pensively, "I need to learn a thing or two so as not to be ashamed around the priest . . ."

Another knock at the door. This time it was Father Fyodor, who came in wrapping his cassock around him, barefoot and sad.

"You're not asleep? And I—well, here I am! I heard you talking and thought, I'll go over and apologize. I yelled at you a little too loudly, but don't you young fellows take offense. I was going to bed and thinking what fine fellows you are and, well, I decided I'd had no business getting so worked up. So I came over. Forgive me. I'm going to bed . . ."

Instead, they both sat down on the edge of my bed and another endless discussion about the meaning of life began. Leonid warmed to the company and roared with laughter:

"Seriously, what is our Russia like? 'Hold on, we haven't yet settled the question of God's existence and you're saying it's time for dinner!' That's not Belinsky talking to Turgenev, it's all of Russia talking to Europe, for Europe is basically calling us to the dinner table to eat our fill, and that's it!"

But Father Fyodor, wrapping his bony legs in his cassock and smiling, objected:

"Nonetheless, Europe remains a godmother to us, don't forget that! Without her Voltaires and without her scholars, you and I, instead of competing in philosophical knowledge, would be eating pancakes in silence—that and nothing more!"

At dawn Father Fyodor said goodbye, and an hour or two later had gone off to see to the matter of the Arzamas water main. That evening Leonid, who had slept all day, said to me:

"Just think, why should a smart, energetic, and interesting priest be living in such a rotten little town? And why should the smartest fellow in this town be the priest, eh? What nonsense! You know, Moscow is the only place to live; you've got to leave this place. It's miserable here—rain, mud . . ."

And he started packing on the spot.

At the station he said:

"All the same, that priest reflects some misunderstanding. It's a joke!"

He complained fairly often that he hardly ever encountered people who have any significance or originality.

"You clearly know how to find them, whereas I'm always snagging some thistle which I drag around on my tail—why should that be?"

I spoke of people whose acquaintance it would be worth his while to make, people of high culture or original ideas; I named V. V. Rozanov and others. It seemed to me that knowing Rozanov would be particularly useful for Andreyev. He expressed astonishment:

"I don't understand you!"

And he talked of Rozanov's conservatism, which was rather beside the point since in his heart of hearts he was deeply indifferent to politics, and only on rare occasions showed signs of a rather external curiosity about it. His basic attitude toward political events is expressed most directly in his story "Thus It Was."

I tried to make him see that you can learn just as much from the devil or a thief as from a holy anchorite—and that learning did not necessarily involve subordination.

"That's not entirely true," he answered. "Science as a whole is a matter of subordinating yourself to facts. Anyway, I don't like Rozanov."

It sometimes seemed to me that he avoided personal acquaintance with major figures because he feared their influence. He would meet once

or twice with some such person and perhaps praise the person extrava-
gantly, but soon lose interest and any desire to see him again.

That's how it was with Savva Morozov.* After the first lengthy conversation with him, Andreyev, delighted with the man's subtle mind, breadth
of knowledge, and sheer energy, nicknamed him Yermak Timofeyevich†
and said that Morozov would play an enormous role in politics:

"He may have the face of a Tartar, but he's a regular English lord!"

Nonetheless he did not continue the acquaintanceship. It was the same
story with Alexander Blok.

In these notes I am following the promptings of memory without concern
for sequence or chronology.

It was at the Moscow Art Theater, when it was still in Carriage Row,
that Leonid Andreyevich introduced me to his fiancée, a slender and delicate young lady with lovely clear eyes. Modest and taciturn, she struck me
as somewhat colorless, but I soon realized that this was a person with a
wise heart.

She clearly understood the necessity of a maternal and solicitous attitude toward Andreyev; she had been quick to sense the significance of his
talent as well as the painful volatility of his moods. She was one of those
rare women who can be passionate lovers without excluding maternal feeling; this double love made her particularly sensitive in distinguishing the
real complaints of his soul from the noisy expressions of a momentary
caprice.

According to the proverb, a Russian "will spare neither father nor
mother for the sake of a bon mot." L. N. too could get carried away with
creating verbal effects and sometimes composed maxims in quite dubious
taste.

---

* Savva Timofeyevich Morozov (1862–1905), textile manufacturer, one of the richest
men in pre-revolutionary Russia, a generous patron of the Moscow Art Theater, and of the
Bolshevik party.

† A sixteenth-century Cossack hetman who subdued western Siberia and placed it under the protection of Tsar Ivan IV.

"A year after the wedding a wife is like a well broken-in shoe—you don't feel her at all," he once said in front of Alexandra Mikhailovna. She could ignore that sort of verbal invention, and sometimes even found these sallies witty and laughed sympathetically. But because she had an unshakable self-respect she could, if she had to, be very persistent, even adamant. She was particularly alive to the forms and melodies of speech. A small and graceful woman, she was elegant and at times assumed an amusing and childlike air of importance for which I nicknamed her Lady Shura,* and the name stuck.

L. N. appreciated her, while she lived in a state of constant anxiety over him, forever tensely focused on him, utterly subordinating her own personality to the concerns of her husband.

In Moscow literary people frequently gathered at the Andreyevs', where it was crowded, cozy, and where the lovely eyes of the sweetly smiling Lady Shura had a restraining effect on those impetuous Russian natures. F. I. Chaliapin was often there, captivating everybody with his stories.

As "modernism" flowered, some there tried to understand it, but many simply condemned it, which is always much easier to do. There was no time to think seriously about literature; politics took precedence. Blok, Bely, and Briusov were seen as isolated and outlandish—at best as eccentrics and at worst as something approaching traitors to "the great traditions of Russian civic awareness." I too thought and felt that way. Was it a time for [Bely's] "Symphonies" when all of Mother Russia was grimly preparing to dance a more brutal national dance? Events were moving toward catastrophe, the signs of its imminence were more and more menacing, the Social Revolutionaries were throwing bombs and every explosion rocked the whole country, strengthening the expectation of a radical upheaval in the life of society. Meetings of the Bolshevik Central Committee were held in Andreyev's apartment, and once the entire committee, together with their, host were arrested and carted off to jail.[†]

* Shura is a diminutive of Alexandra.

[†] The arrests took place on 9 February 1905; Andreyev was freed on 25 February after posting bail of 10,000 rubles.

After about a month, L. N. emerged from jail as if from the pool of Siloam, hearty and cheerful.

"It's good when they squeeze you—you want to expand in all directions!" he said. And he teased me.

"Well, what do you say, Mr. Pessimist? Our Russia is showing signs of life, no? And you were the one who tried to rhyme 'emperor' with 'sand in gears.' "

He published his stories "The Marseillaise," "The Tocsin," and "A Story That Will Never Be Finished," but it was as early as October of 1905 that he read me "Thus It Was" in manuscript.

"Isn't it premature?" I asked.

He answered: "What's good is always premature."

Soon after that he went to Finland, and he did well to go: the senseless cruelty of the December events would have crushed him. In Finland he was active politically, speaking at a meeting and publishing acid comments on the policies of the monarchists in the Helsinki newspapers, but his mood was subdued, his view of the future one of hopelessness. In Petersburg I received a letter from him in which he wrote:

"Every horse has his inborn peculiarities, and every nation too. There are horses that will turn off from any road to get to a tavern; our fatherland has turned off in the direction of what is most congenial to it, and once again, for a long time, will live by the carafe and by the bottle."

A few months after that we met in Montreux in Switzerland. Leonid mocked the Swiss way of life.

"People like us who are used to great flat expanses don't belong in these crevices that are only fit for cockroaches," he said.

I had the impression that he had faded; he seemed somehow dimmer, his eyes glassy with fatigue, dejection, and anxiety. He talked of Switzerland flatly and superficially, saying the kinds of things that freedom-loving Russians from bustling metropolises like Chukhloma, Konotop, and Tetiush have said about that country from time immemorial. One of them summarized the Russian concept of freedom very precisely and profoundly:

"Living in our town is like being in a bathhouse—nobody there correcting you, nothing there inhibiting you."

When L. N. spoke about Russia it was reluctantly and without affect. Once, sitting by the fire, he recalled some lines from Yakubovich's melancholy poem "To the Motherland":

> What do we have to love you for,
> What kind of a mother are you to us? . . .

"I've written a play—want to hear it?"

And that evening he read me *Savva*.

While he was still in Russia Andreyev had heard accounts of young Ufimtsev and his comrades, who had tried to blow up the icon of the Kursk Madonna; deciding then and there to turn that event into a short novel, he came up with a very interesting outline, replete with three-dimensional characters. He was particularly drawn to Ufimtsev, a poet in the field of scientific technology, a young man possessing an unquestionable talent for invention. Exiled to the Semirech'e distict (I think to Karkaraly), where he lived under intense surveillance by ignorant and superstitious people, deprived of the instruments and materials he needed, he nonetheless invented an original internal combustion engine, perfected a cyclostyle, worked on a new system for dredging, and thought up a kind of "reusable shell" for hunting rifles. I showed the blueprints for the engine to some engineers in Moscow, who told me that Ufimtsev's invention was practical, ingenious, and showed a real gift. I don't know what came of all these inventions; when I went abroad I lost touch with Ufimtsev.

What I did and do know is that this young man was one of those wonderful dreamers who, under the spell of their faith and love, each in his own way, pursue a single common goal—the arousing in their people of that purposeful energy which creates goodness and beauty.

It was sad and annoying to find that Andreyev had distorted this character—a type that Russian literature had not yet seen; I had thought that in the story as originally conceived this character would be appreciated and portrayed in worthy ways. We argued, and it may be that I was a little too sharp in emphasizing the need for accuracy in the depiction of certain aspects—particularly the rarest and most positive ones—of reality.

Like all people of strongly defined personality and heightened self-awareness, L. N. did not like to be contradicted. He took offense, and we parted coldly.

It must have been in 1907 or 1908 that Andreyev came to Capri, after burying Lady Shura in Berlin, where she had died of puerperal fever. The death of this kind and intelligent companion weighed heavily on Leonid's psyche. All his thoughts and all his talk revolved around memories of the senseless extinction of Lady Shura.

"You know," he said, his pupils strangely dilated, "she was lying there still alive—but her breath was already cadaverous. It is a very ironic smell."

He was wearing some kind of black velvet lumber jacket: even outwardly he seemed crushed and crumpled. His thoughts and words revolved horrifyingly around the question of death. He happened to be staying in the Villa Caracciolo, which belonged to the widow of an artist, a descendant of the Marquis Caracciolo who had been a supporter of the French party and as such executed by Ferdinand ("the Bomb") II. The dark rooms of this villa were damp and gloomy; on the walls hung rather soiled-looking unfinished paintings looking like patches of mold. One of the rooms had a large, smoke-darkened fireplace; in front of its windows overgrown shrubbery blocked the view. Tendrils of ivy peered into the windows from the outside wall. This was the room Leonid made his dining room.

Calling on him one day toward evening I found him in an easy chair in front of the fire. Dressed in black, bathed in the crimson glow of the smoldering fire, he held his son Vadim on his lap and was telling him something, speaking softly and half-sobbing. I came in quietly. Thinking that the child was falling asleep, I took a chair near the door and listened. Leonid was telling the child how death goes around the world smothering little children.

"I'm afraid," Vadim told him.

"Don't you want to hear more?"

"I'm afraid," the boy repeated.

"Well, run along to bed then . . ."

But the child clung to his father's legs and burst out crying. It was a long time before we managed to calm him down. Leonid was in a hysterical mood himself; his words had terrified the boy, who stamped his feet and cried out:

"I don't want to sleep! I don't want to die!"

When his grandmother had taken the boy away I observed that it was hardly right to frighten the child with such fairy tales as the one about the invincible giant Death.

"And if there's nothing else I can talk about?" he asked sharply. "Now that I understand how indifferent 'beautiful nature' really is, there's only one thing I want—to rip my portrait out of that sweet little frame."

Talking with him was hard, almost impossible; he was angry, his nerves were shot; and he seemed to be deliberately rubbing salt on his own wounds.

"I'm haunted by the thought of suicide. It's as if my shadow is crawling behind me and I keep hearing it whisper, 'Leave! Die!' "

This greatly alarmed his friends, but there were times when he intimated that he encouraged this concern over him consciously and deliberately—as if needing to hear again what they could say to him in defense of living.

But the cheerful scenery of the island, the entrancing beauty of the sea, and the sympathetic attitude of the population to Russians soon enough dissipated Leonid's depression. Within two months he was avid to be working again.

I remember how one moonlit night, sitting on the rocks by the sea, he shook his head and said:

"Basta! Tomorrow morning I start writing."

"There's nothing better you could do."

"That's it!"

And with a gaiety he had not shown for a long time he began talking of his plans.

"First of all, my friend, I'm going to write a story about the despotism of friendship—it's time to get even with you, you villain!"

And on the spot, quickly and easily, he spun out a comic tale of two friends, a dreamer and a mathematician. The one spends his life concocting impossible schemes, while the other carefully calculates the cost of these imaginary voyages and by so doing torpedoes each and every dream that his friend has come up with.

But in the next breath he said:

"I want to write about Judas. Before I left Russia I read somebody's—I don't remember whose—very clever poem about him. What's your view of Judas?"

At that time I had in my study someone's translation of Julius Wecksell's tetralogy *Judas and Jesus,* the translation of Thor Hedberg's story, and a poem of Golovanov's. I suggested that he read these things.

"I don't want to. I have my own idea, and reading them would only confuse things. Better if you tell me yourself what they've written. Or no—don't."

As always in moments of creative excitement, he leapt to his feet, needing to be in motion.

"Come on!"

As we walked he told me the plan for "Judas Iscariot," and three days later he brought the manuscript. With that story he commenced one of the most productive periods of his career. On Capri he began his play *Black Masks,* wrote the caustic humoresque "Love for One's Fellow Man" and the story "The Dark," created the plan for *Sashka Zhigulev,* made sketches for his play *The Ocean,* and wrote two or three chapters of his tale *My Notes*—all this in the space of half a year. None of this serious work, however, could prevent L. N. from taking active part in the composition of the play *Alas,* a play in the classical-populist vein, in verse and prose, with singing and dancing and every sort of oppression of the unhappy Russian workers on the land. The dramatis personae gives an adequate idea of what they play was like:

Oppressius—a pitiless landowner.
Severia—his wife.

Philistinus—brother of Oppressius, a scribbler in prose.

Decadentius—the unsuccessful offspring of Oppressius.

Longsufferus—a tiller of the soil, most unhappy but not always drunk.

Mourna—Longsufferus' beloved wife, full of meekness and common sense, though constantly pregnant.

Wiktima—the beautiful daughter of Longsufferus.

Smashem—the most horrible district police chief. Bathes in his full uniform and medals.

Thunderclappis—unquestionably a genuine local policeman, but in fact the noble Count Edmond de Ptieille.

Motria La Bell—the secret wife of the Count, in reality the Spanish Marquise Donna Carmen de Unbearabia y Insupporte, who is pretending to be a Gypsy.

The ghost of the Russian critic Skabichevsky.

The ghost of Kablitz-Yuzov.

Afanasii Shchapov, completely sober.

"As We Were Saying"—a group of individuals who have no lines and do not figure in the action.

The drama is set in "Blue Mire," the estate of Oppressius, mortgaged twice in the Gentry Bank and once somewhere else.

One whole act of this play got written, full of zaniness and absurdity. Andreyev wrote the hilarious prose dialogue, helpless as a child with laughter at the things he kept coming up with.

Never, either before or after this, did I see him so primed for activity or so exceptionally hardworking. He seemed to have shed his dislike of the process of writing and was now able to sit at his desk round the clock, half-dressed, disheveled, and cheerful. His imagination had flared up, amazingly bright and productive: almost every day he spoke of the idea for some new tale or story.

"I've pulled myself together at last!" he kept saying triumphantly.

And he plied me with questions about the famous pirate Barbarossa, about Tomasso Aniello, about the local smugglers and gendarmes and the life of Calabrian shepherds.

"What a trove of stories, what variety of life!" he exclaimed. "These people have actually accumulated a thing or two for posterity. And we? Not long ago I picked up *Lives of the Russian Tsars.* What did they do? They ate! I started reading *A History of the Russian People.* What did they do? They suffered! I stopped. It was dull and disheartening."

Still, for all that he spoke so graphically and colorfully of his projects, the actual writing was careless. In the first draft of his story "Judas Iscariot" there were a number of mistakes that made it clear that he had not bothered to read even the Gospels. When you told him that "Duke Spadaro" sounded to an Italian ear as absurd as "Prince Bashmachkinov"* would to a Russian, or that the canine breed of Saint Bernards did not yet exist in the twelfth century, he replied angrily:

"Those are trivia."

"And you can't say, 'They drink wine like camels'; you have to say, 'the way camels drink water.'"

"Nonsense!"

He treated his talent the way a bad rider treats a splendid steed: he galloped on it unmercifully, but he neither loved nor tended it. His hand would not take the time to trace the intricate patterns that arose in his seething imagination; nor had he any interest in trying to develop the strength and skill of that hand. There were times when he himself understood what a serious obstacle this was to the normal growth of his talent.

"My language is petrifying. I feel that it's harder and harder to find the right words . . ."

He tried to hypnotize the reader with the monotony of his phrasing, but the phrases no longer had esthetic persuasiveness. Wrapping his thought in the cotton batting of obscure and droning verbiage, he wound

---

* The absurdity is double: the name comes from *bashmak*—shoe—and it echoes the name of Gogol's lowly copying clerk in his story "The Overcoat."

up revealing it too clearly, and the results came to look like dialogues on philosophical themes written for the popular press.

On rare occasions he would feel that and admit his distress:

"It's all a spiderweb, sticky but insubstantial! You're right, I should read Flaubert. He really is the descendant of one of those master stonemasons who built the medieval cathedrals!"

It was on Capri that Leonid heard about the incident that he used for his story "Darkness." It happened to an acquaintance of mine, a Social Revolutionary. The actual incident was very simple: one of the girls in a brothel, sensing that her client was a revolutionary, that he was being hunted by the police and had taken refuge in her establishment as a last resort, treated him with the tender concern of a mother and the tact of a woman capable of feeling respect for such a man. But he, bookish and emotionally awkward, replied to the woman's heartfelt impulse with a sermon on morality, reminding her precisely of what she wished to forget at that moment. Offended, she slapped him in the face—as I believe he deserved. Then, understanding all the coarseness of his behavior, he apologized and kissed her hand—a gesture I think he might better have forgone. And that was the whole story.

There are times—alas, too few—when reality is truer and more pleasing than even a very talented account of it.

So it was in this case, but Leonid distorted both the sense and the form of the event quite beyond recognition. In the real brothel there was no such filthy and painful mockery of the human—and none of those horrifying details with which Andreyev furnished his story so abundantly.

This distortion had a very distressing effect on me: it was as if Leonid had canceled or destroyed a feast that I had been awaiting long and eagerly. I know people too well not to prize, and prize highly, the least sign of kindly, honest feeling. Of course I couldn't help pointing out to Andreyev the seriousness of what he had done, which for me was tantamount to committing murder perversely, out of caprice. He answered by invoking the freedom of the artist, but that didn't change my view. To this day I cannot bring myself to believe that an artist is free to arbitrarily distort such rare manifestations of ideally human feeling simply to suit a dogma that he cherishes.

We talked at length about all this, and although our talk was peaceful and friendly in tone, something between me and Andreyev had been ruptured.

I remember very well the end of our talk.

"What are you after?" I asked him.

"I don't know," he said, shrugging his shoulders, his eyes closed.

"But there must be something you find yourself wanting either above all else or oftener than anything else."

"I don't know," he repeated. "I don't think there's anything like that. It's true I do sometimes feel a need for fame, lots of it, as much as the whole world could give. Then I concentrate it inside me, compress it as far as it will go, and when it becomes a critical mass—I explode, bathing the world in some new light. And after that people begin living in the light of a new reason. You see, we need a new reason, not that old phony trickster that takes all the best of my flesh, all my feelings, and, promising to give them back with interest, never does—always saying, 'Tomorrow!' Evolution, he pleads; and when my patience gives out and my thirst for life becomes suffocating, he says, Revolution. And it's all a filthy swindle. And I die having gotten nothing."

"What you need is faith, not reason."

"Maybe. But if I do, it's faith in myself in the first place."

He ran about the room in his excitement, then perched on the table and, waving his arm in front of my face, went on:

"I know that God and the Devil are only symbols, but it seems to me that the whole of human life—all its meaning—lies in endlessly, infinitely broadening those symbols, feeding them with the blood and flesh of the world. And once mankind has put absolutely all of its powers into those two extremes, mankind will vanish, and they will become fleshly realities and go on living in the void of the universe eye to eye with each other, invincible and immortal. You think there's sense in that? But there's no sense anywhere, in anything."

He had grown pale, his lips twitched, and his eyes were shining with dull horror.

Then he added in a low voice, helplessly:

"Imagine the Devil as a woman, God as a man, and they give birth to a new creature—one that is, of course, every bit as dualistic as the two of us. Every bit as much . . ."

He left Capri abruptly; a day before his departure he was still talking about how he'd soon sit down at his desk and write for three months, but on the evening of that same day he told me:

"Listen, I've decided to leave. Russia is the place to be, otherwise you risk falling into a kind of operatic silliness. You start wanting to write vaudevilles—with singing and dancing. Life here isn't real life but opera; people here spend a lot more time singing than thinking. Romeo, Othello, and the rest are Shakespeare's inventions; the Italians are not capable of tragedy. Neither Byron nor Poe could have been born here."

"What about Leopardi?"

"Leopardi . . . but who knows him? He's one of those writers people talk about but don't read."

As he was leaving he said to me:

"This, Alexei old friend, is another Arzamas—a cheery one, that's all."

"Remember how enchanted you were?"

"Everybody's enchanted before the wedding. Will you be leaving soon? You should, it's time. You're beginning to resemble a monk . . ."

Living in Italy, I felt deeply uneasy about Russia. As early as 1911 people were talking about the inevitability of a general European war and how this war would surely prove disastrous for the Russians. My worry was particularly intensified by clear indications of something morbid and perverse in the spiritual world of the great Russian people. Reading a book published by the Free Economic Society about agrarian disorders in the Russian provinces, I was appalled by the particular brutality and senselessness that attended them. Studying the reports of the Moscow district judiciary about the nature of the crimes within its jurisdiction, I was struck by the rise in crimes against the person, including the violation of women and the molestation of minors. Even before that I had been unpleasantly struck by the fact that in the Second State Duma there was a very considerable number of priests, people of the purest Russian blood, who nonetheless had not produced a single talent, a single major political figure. And there were many other things besides that contributed to my forebodings about the fate of the Great Russian tribe.

When I arrived in Finland I met with Andreyev and shared my gloomy thoughts with him. He took vehement issue with me and even seemed personally offended, but his objections, in the absence of facts to back them up, were unconvincing.

Then suddenly, lowering his voice and screwing up his eyes as if gazing intently into the future, he began speaking about the Russian people in words that were unusual for him—haltingly, incoherently, with great and unquestionably sincere conviction.

I cannot reproduce his speech—and I would not want to if I could; its power lay not in logic or in beauty, but in the feeling of tormented compassion for the people, a feeling of which—showing such power and expressed in such forms—I had not considered L. N. capable.

His whole body shook with nervous intensity and, sniffling like a woman, all but sobbing, he shouted at me:

"Would you call Russian literature a regional literature because the majority of major Russian writers come from the Moscow region? It may well be so, but all the same we are talking about a world-class literature, the most serious and powerful in Europe. The genius of Dostoyevsky alone is enough to justify even the senseless life—even the criminal life—of millions of people. And what if the Russian people are spiritually sick? Let us cure them, bearing in mind, as somebody said, that 'only the sick oyster produces the pearl.'"

"What about the beauty of the wild beast?" I asked.

"What about the beauty of human patience, meekness and love?" he retorted—and went on talking about the people and literature with increasing fervor and passion.

This was the first time that I heard him talk so passionately and lyri-
cally; up till then I had heard such strong expressions of his love only for
talents he found congenial—Edgar Allan Poe most often.

Soon after our conversation that hideous war broke out, and our dif-
fering attitudes toward it further widened the breach between us.

Only on one occasion in 1915 when a despicable wave of anti-Semitism
gushed out of the army and Leonid, together with other writers, set about
fighting the spread of that infection, did we talk. Exhausted, out of sorts, he
paced around the room, one hand stuck in his belt and the other waving in
the air. His dark eyes were gloomy. He asked:

"Can you honestly say what makes you spend your time on the fruit-
less struggle against the Jew-haters?"

I answered that I found Jews in general sympathetic, and that sympathy is a "biochemical" phenomenon not susceptible to explanation.

"Fine, and . . . ?"

"The Jew is a believer; belief is his principal quality, and I love believers, I love fanatics of all kinds—in science, art, politics—in spite of knowing
that fanaticism is a drug; drugs have no effect on me. Add to this the shame
of a Russian at the fact that in his own house—his own country—something
vile and shameful is constantly going on with reference to the Jews."

Leonid fell back heavily on the sofa and said:

"You're a man of extremes and so are they—that's the point! Somebody said, 'A good Jew is a Jesus, a bad one is a Judas.' But I don't like
Christ. Dostoyevsky is right: Christ was deeply muddleheaded . . ."

"That wasn't Dostoyevsky, it was Nietzsche . . ."

"All right, Nietzsche. Although Dostoyevsky was the one who should
have said it. Somebody was trying to tell me that Dostoyevsky secretly
hated Christ. I don't like Christ and Christianity either. Optimism is a repellent, thoroughly false invention . . ."

"You take Christianity to be optimistic?"

"Certainly. The kingdom of heaven and all that other hogwash. I think
that Judas was not a Jew but a Greek, a Hellene. He was a smart and daring
man, my friend. Have you ever thought about how many motives there are

for betrayal? They are infinitely various. Azef* had his philosophy; it's stupid to think that he betrayed only for money. You know, even if Judas had been convinced that Christ was the incarnation of Jehovah himself, he would still have betrayed him. To kill God, to humiliate him with a shameful death—that, my friend, is no small thing!"

He spoke for a long time on the subject of Herostratus,[†] and, as always when he got involved with ideas of that sort, he spoke interestingly and excitedly, whipping up his fantasy with the most extreme paradoxes. At such moments the lines of his rather coarsely handsome but cold face would turn finer and more animated, and his dark eyes, which normally flickered with undisguised terror at something, would, at such moments, shine boldly, proudly, and beautifully.

He then returned to the beginning of our conversation:

"All the same, when you talk about the Jews you're inventing something—it smacks of literature! I don't like them, they make me uncomfortable. I feel obliged to pay them compliments and treat them carefully. That makes me want to tell them funny Jewish jokes in which the wit of the Jews is always flatteringly and boastfully pointed up. But I'm no good at telling jokes, and I always have a hard time with Jews. They consider that I too am responsible for the misfortunes of their lives—so how can I feel myself an equal, when for a Jew I am a criminal, an oppressor, a fomentor of pogroms?"

"Then you did the wrong thing joining our group. Why make yourself do it?"

"Well, there's shame. You yourself use the word. And the bottom line is that the Russian writer is duty-bound to be a liberal, a socialist, a revolutionary, and God knows what all else! Least of all, in any case, himself."

---

* Evno Fishelevich Azef (1869–1918) was a famous double agent. One of the founders of the Socialist-Revolutionary party, he organized several major terrorist acts, including the assassination of the Minister of the Interior, Plehve in 1904. At the same time he was responsible for betraying a number of revolutionary agents to the Tsarist police.

† The man reputed to have burned down the great temple of Diana at Ephesus, one of the seven wonders of the ancient world, in 356 B.C., in order to secure eternal fame. The adolescent Andreyev aspired to comparable acts of pure transgressive destruction.

With a twisted smile he added:

"That is the path my good friend Gorky has taken, leaving behind a respected but empty place. Don't be offended."

"Go on."

He poured himself a glass of strong tea and, with the clear intention of getting a rise out of me, began crudely denigrating the splendid and austere talent of Ivan Bunin. He disliked him. But suddenly, in a flat voice, he announced:

"And me? I've married a Jewess!"

In 1916 when he brought me his books, we both felt again, and deeply, how much we had been through with each other and what old friends we were. But it was only the past that we could talk about without quarreling; the present was erecting a high wall of irreconcilable disagreement between us.

I can say without stretching the truth that for me that wall was transparent and permeable. On the other side of it I saw a remarkable and original man who had been very close to me over a period of ten years: my only friend among writers.

Differences in outlook need not affect our sympathies; I have never allowed theories or opinions a decisive role in my relations with others.

L. N. Andreyev felt otherwise. But I do not hold that against him, for he was what he wanted and knew how to be—a man of rare originality, rare talent, and courageous enough in his search for truth.

5

Alexander Blok

Alexander Alexandrovich Blok (1880–1921) was one of the great poets of his time and place, a symbolist, mystically inclined, attuned to questions of Russia's destiny and prophetic in his premonitions about the cultural consequences of revolution. In terms of background, temperament, life experience, and artistic method, he and Gorky were polar opposites. That fact, acknowledged by both, is crucial to an understanding of Gorky's memoir.

Still, they fascinated each other, and what Anna Akhmatova said of Blok—that he was "a monument to the beginning of a century"—might with equal justice be said of Gorky. Each embodied—and was regarded by contemporaries as embodying—crucial features of the historical moment they shared.* And they had more in common than Gorky is willing to admit here, including a profoundly dualistic attitude toward Russia, a lifelong stance of rebellion, a belief in the power of revolution, and a conviction that ordinary people need to be helped to realize their higher potential, to transform themselves from men into Men (the Russian word can apply to both genders).

In this piece, however, Gorky is interested only in underlining contrasts, undaunted by the risk of caricature. Hence his tendentious introduction, a ritual gesture at that faith in reason to which he clung, desperately and doggedly, all his life, though it is plainly of limited relevance to the memoir that follows, which

* For the larger implications of this pairing, see the concluding paragraphs of Boris Eikhenbaum's "Gorky as a Russian Writer," on pp. 278–79 below.

centers on Blok the man rather than on the poet or the poetry. Seen alongside Gorky's portraits of Tolstoy, Chekhov and Andreyev, this is the merest pencil sketch, but all the more vivid and suggestive for the honesty of its limitation.[1]

◀ • ▶

A. A. Blok

I sometimes think that Russian thought is sick from terror at itself: seeking to stand outside reason, it dislikes reason and fears it.

That wily serpent V. V. Rozanov laments in his *Solitaria:* "Oh, my melancholy experiments! Why did I need to know everything? Now I shall not die serenely, as I had hoped."

In Tolstoy's *Diary of My Youth* for 5 May 1851, we find the grim statement: "Consciousness is the greatest moral evil that can befall a human being."

Dostoyevsky says the same thing: "To be too conscious is a disease, an actual disease . . . Too much consciousness and even any consciousness is a disease. I insist on that."

The realist Pisemsky cried out in a letter to Melnikov-Pechersky: "Devil take the habit of thinking, that mange of the soul!"

Leonid Andreyev said: "There is in reason something of the spy, of the provocateur." And he conjectured: "It is quite possible that reason is a disguised version of that old witch conscience."

One could put together dozens of such aphorisms by Russian writers, all giving clear evidence of a mistrust of the power of reason. That is entirely in character for the people of a country whose life is arranged with an absolute minimum of reasonableness.

Curiously enough, P. F. Nikolayev, author of the book *Active Progress*—a man, one would have thought, unlikely to find this attitude congenial—wrote to me in 1906: "Knowledge increases one's needs; needs lead to dissatisfaction; a dissatisfied person is unhappy—which is what makes him valuable socially and sympathetic personally."

An absolutely incomprehensible, quasi-Buddhist idea.

All the same, even Montaigne sighed ruefully: "Why do we amass futile knowledge? Oh, what a sweet and soft pillow are ignorance and simplicity of heart for the fortunate few."

He explained the longevity of savages by their ignorance of science and religion, unaware that they had both in embryonic form. Montaigne, an epicurean, lived in an age of religious wars. He was cheerfully wise, finding the cannibalism of savages less repulsive than the tortures of the Inquisition.

Three hundred years later Lev Tolstoy said of him, "Montaigne is banal." Lev Tolstoy's thought, in form and content both, was that of a churchman. I don't think that dogmatism gave him any pleasure—or that the process of thinking gave Tolstoy the sort of enjoyment doubtless experienced by such philosophers as, say, Schopenhauer, watching with pleasure the development of their own thought. In my opinion thinking was, for Tolstoy, an accursed duty, and he must have been constantly mindful of Tertullian's words—words that express the despair of a doubt-stricken fanatic: "Thinking is evil."

It may well be, for dogmatists, that such fear of thought, and hatred of it, derive from the Bible: "It was Azazel who taught people to make swords and knives . . . taught them various arts . . . explained the course of the stars and the moon. And there appeared a great godlessness and corruption on earth, and the ways of men became crooked."*

All this came to mind after yesterday's unexpected conversation with Alexander Blok. We had left the World Literature office together and he had asked me what I thought about his "The Downfall of Humanism."†

* Gorky is citing (at second hand) the apocryphal *Book of Enoch*.

† World Literature was the publishing house organized on Gorky's initiative as a way of supporting—and, in the first place, feeding—the starving writers and literary intellectuals of Petrograd in the wake of the Bolshevik revolution and the ensuing civil war. Blok read his essay, "The Downfall of Humanism," at a staff meeting on 9 April 1919. For a vivid account of Blok in that context, see Zamiatin's essay "Alexander Blok" in Mirra Ginsburg, ed. and trans., *A Soviet Heretic: Essays by Yevgeny Zamyatin* (Chicago: University of Chicago Press, 1970), where one reads, inter alia:

A few days before, he had delivered a sort of lecture or short article on that subject. The article had struck me as unclear but full of tragic foreboding. Blok, as he read it, resembled the child in the fairy tale who gets lost in the wood: he feels the approach of monsters out of the dark and mumbles incantations in the hope of scaring them off. His hands shook as he turned the pages of his manuscript. I couldn't make out whether he was saddened or gladdened by the fall of humanism. He is not as supple or talented in prose as he is in verse, but he is a man of very deep and destructive feeling. In general a man of our "*décadence.*" I suspect that his beliefs are unclear to Blok himself; the words don't penetrate to the depth of the thought that is destroying this man along with everything he calls "the destruction of humanism."

Some of the ideas of the lecture struck me as insufficiently thought through, for example: "To civilize the masses is both impossible and unnecessary." "Discoveries are yielding place to inventions."

The nineteenth and twentieth centuries are so monstrously rich in inventions precisely because they have been a time of the most abundant and greatest discoveries of science. To say, then, that civilization is impossible and unnecessary for the Russian people is clearly Scythianism*—which

---

For three years after [an initial meeting in 1918] we were all locked up together in a steel projectile and, cooped up in darkness, whistled through space, no one knew where. In those last seconds-years before death, we had to do something, to settle down to some sort of a life in the hurtling missile. And so extravagant plans were hatched in the projectile: World Literature, the Union of Literary Workers, the Writers' Union, a theater. And all the writers, all those who had survived, were constantly bumping into each other in the cramped space—Gorky and Merezhkovsky, Blok and Kuprin, Muyzhel and Gumilyov, Chukovsky and Volynsky. . . .

In those days Gorky was in love with Blok—he always had to be in love with someone or something for an hour. "This is a man! Yes!" At the meetings of World Literature, Gorky listened to Blok as he listened to no one else. [205–6]

* Scythianism was a concept that flourished in Russia in the first two decades of the twentieth century. It saw Russians as both European and Asian, the latter element finding expression in energy and spontaneity, if also in savagery. Blok's poem *Scythians* (1918) celebrates the idea. The name was also adopted by a group of prominent writers and poets who published two volumes of an almanac under that title in 1917 and 1918.

I understand as a concession to the innate antigovernmental disposition of the Russian masses. But what does Blok need Scythianism for?

As tactfully as I could, I said all this to him. It's difficult to talk with him; I have the impression that he despises anyone who finds his world alien and incomprehensible—and I find that world incomprehensible. I have been sitting next to him at editorial meetings of World Literature twice a week lately, and I frequently make polemic interventions, criticizing translations that transgress against the spirit of the Russian language. But that does not bring us closer. Like almost everyone else on the editorial board, his attitude toward the work is formal and basically indifferent.

He said he was glad to see me freeing myself "from the intelligentsia habit of trying to solve the problems of social existence."

"I always felt," he told me, "that that wasn't genuine in you. Already [in your series of sketches] *The Town of Okurov* it's clear that you're disturbed by the 'childish questions'—the deepest and most terrible ones!"

He was wrong about that, but I didn't try to disabuse him; if he wants or needs to believe that, well, let him.

"Why don't you write about those questions?" he insisted.

I said that questions about the meaning of existence, about death and love, were strictly personal, intimate matters that concerned me alone. I don't like to trot them out in public, and if on rare occasions I do, I do it inadvertently—and always poorly and awkwardly.

"There is a special art to speaking about oneself," I told him, "and I don't possess it."

We turned into the Summer Garden and sat down on a bench. Blok's eyes were almost crazy. By the way they shone and by the quivering of his cold but tormented face I could see that there were things he desperately wanted to say and ask. Trying to rub out with his foot a shadow pattern the sun was making on the dirt, he reproached me:

"You hide yourself. You hide your ideas about the spirit and about truth. What for?"

And before I could answer he started talking about the Russian intelligentsia, condemning it in the most hackneyed terms—terms that were particularly inappropriate now, after the revolution.

I said that in my opinion a negative attitude toward the intelligentsia is a quintessentially intelligentsia attitude. A peasant could not have come up with it, knowing the intelligentsia only in the guise of the local doctor or the revered village teacher; nor could a worker who was obliged to a member of the intelligentsia for his political education. Such an attitude is both mistaken and harmful, not least because it saps the intelligentsia's respect for itself, for its historic and cultural work. Always, now and forever, our intelligentsia has played, is playing, and will play the role of the workhorse of history. By its tireless labor it has raised the proletariat to the height of a revolution unparalleled for the breadth and depth of the immediate tasks it has set itself.

He gazed morosely at the ground and seemed not to be listening, but when I stopped he began to speak again of the waverings of the intelligentsia in its attitude to "Bolshevism" and, incidentally, observed with justice: "Once we have called forth the spirit of destruction from the darkness, it is dishonest to say, 'We didn't do this, *they* did.' Bolshevism is the inevitable result of all the work done by the intelligentsia at its lecterns, in its editorial boards, and underground . . ."

A pleasant-looking lady greeted him affectionately; he responded drily, almost dismissively, and she retreated on unsteady little feet, smiling uncertainly. His eyes fixed on her receding figure, Blok asked: "What do you think about immortality, the possibility of immortality?"

He asked with some urgency and a stubborn look in his eyes. I said that perhaps Lammenais was right: since the amount of matter in the universe is limited, one must grant that its combinations will repeat themselves in the infinity of time an infinite number of times. From this point of view it is possible that in a few million years, on some dismal spring evening in Petersburg, Blok and Gorky will once again discuss immortality, sitting on a bench in the Summer Garden.

He said:

"You're joking, right?"

I was both astonished and a little irritated by his insistence, although I felt that his questioning arose not out of simple curiosity but, as it were, from a desire to extinguish and put finish to some unsettling and troublesome thought.

"I have no reason to consider the view of Lammenais to be less serious than any of the other views on this matter," I told him.

"All right, but what do you think—you personally?"

He even stamped his foot. Until this evening I had always felt him to be reserved and uncommunicative.

"I personally like to imagine a human being as an apparatus for turning so-called dead matter into psychic energy within himself, and that at some point in the immeasurably distant future he will turn the whole 'world' into pure psyche."*

"I don't understand. Is that a kind of pan-psychism?"

"No. For there will be nothing but thought; everything else will disappear, having turned into pure thought, which alone will exist, incarnating [*sic*] in itself all the thinking of mankind from the first glimmers to the moment of the final explosion of thought."

"I don't understand," Blok repeated, shaking his head.

I invited him to imagine the world as a constant process of the dissociation of matter. Matter, disintegrating, constantly gives off energy in the form of light, electromagnetic waves, Hertz waves, and so on—including, of course, the phenomena of radioactivity. Thought is the result of the dissociation of the atoms of the brain, which itself is created out of the elements of "dead," inorganic matter. In the physical brain of a man this material is constantly being transformed into psychic energy. I allow myself

* At one point, under the influence of the "God-building" theories of Alexander Bogdanov and Anatolii Lunacharsky, Gorky envisaged socialism as a result of the gradual conversion of matter into psychic energy, a kind of spiritual-psychic construction in which the Russian people would be elevated and refined through acquaintance with European culture and science.

to believe that some time all of the "matter" ingested by a person will be turned by his brain into a single energy: psychic energy. And it will find harmony in itself and will stand still in self-contemplation, in the contemplation of the infinitely various creative possibilities concealed in it.

"A gloomy fantasy," Blok said, and grinned. "It's nice to recall that the law of conservation of matter is against it."

"I on the other hand find it nice to think that laws created in laboratories do not always coincide with those laws of the universe that are still unknown to us. I firmly believe that if we were able to weigh our planet from time to time we would see that its weight is continually diminishing."

"All that's a bore," said Blok, shaking his head. "The matter is simpler, the point being that we have become too clever to believe in God, yet not strong enough to believe in ourselves. As a basis for life and faith there can only be God or oneself. Humanity? Can anyone really believe in the reasonableness of humanity after the last war, with new, inevitable, and even crueler wars in the offing? No, that fantasy of yours is chilling! But I think you were not serious."

He sighed.

"If we could just stop thinking altogether for even ten years, put out that treacherous will-o'-the-wisp that keeps luring us deeper into the world's night, and listen with our hearts to the world's harmony instead. Brains, brains . . . The brain is an unreliable organ, it is monstrously great, monstrously developed. Swollen, like a goiter."

He stopped, pressed his lips together, then said quietly:

"If we could halt all movement, let time stop . . ."

"It would stop if all forms of movement had the same speed imparted to them."

Blok looked at me askance, raising his eyebrows. Then quickly and confusingly he emitted a string of delirious words I could no longer follow; the impression was bizarre, as if he were casting off his rags and tatters.

He got up abruptly, extended his hand, and headed for the streetcar. His gait at first glance looked firm enough, but when you looked more carefully you saw that he was swaying uncertainly on his feet. And however well-dressed he was, you wanted to see him in something different, not looking like everyone else. The poet Gumilyov seems to be dressed like everyone else even when wearing the fur costume of a Lapplander or a Samoyed. But a Blok calls for unusual raiment.

I had just transcribed the interview with Blok when V., a sailor in the Baltic Fleet, came to pick up "some books that would be interesting." He loves science, expects it to provide a solution to the whole "muddle of life," and always speaks of it with joy and faith. That day, incidentally, he brought amazing news:

"I hear some really smart American has put together a stunningly simple machine—just a pipe, a wheel, and a handle. You turn the handle and it gives you everything—analysis, trigonometry, criticism, and the meaning of all the things that happen in life. The machine gives the answers—and it whistles!"

What particularly pleases me about that machine is the whistling.

In a restaurant one of the girls who work the Nevsky Prospect told me a story.

"Is that book of yours by the same Blok who's famous? I knew him too, but just once. It happened in the fall, very late one night, slush and fog all around, near midnight on the Duma clock and I'm worn out and ready to go home when all of a sudden, at the corner of Italian Street, a man comes up to me. He's dressed well enough, handsome fellow, with a haughty face, and I think to myself: must be a foreigner. We go on foot—not far to number 10 Caravan Street where there are rooms to let. I'm walking along, talking, and he's absolutely mum. I didn't like that, it's not usual, and anyway I like people to be polite. We get there, and I ask for tea. He rings but the servant doesn't come, so he goes out into the corridor and I'm so tired and cold I fall asleep sitting there on the couch. Later on I come to, and there he is sitting across from me with his head in his hands. He's leaning on the table and looking at me so fiercely. His eyes are scary. But I'm not even scared, I'm too ashamed, and I just think: 'My

God, he must be a musician!' He's curly-headed. 'Oh, sorry,' I say, 'I'll get undressed now.'

"But he gives me a nice smile and says: 'Don't bother.' He comes over to my couch, sits me on his knee, pats my head, and says: 'Go on, doze a little more.' And I go to sleep again, imagine! It's a scandal. I know it's wrong, but I can't help it. And he's rocking me so gently, and I feel so nice and cozy with him. I open my eyes and smile. And he smiles. I must have really gone to sleep then, because all of a sudden he's giving me a little shake and saying, 'Goodbye now, I've got to go.' And he puts twenty-five rubles on the table. 'Wait a minute,' I say, 'what are you doing?' You can imagine how embarrassed I was. I apologized. The whole thing was so ridiculous and odd. But he just gives a little laugh, squeezes my hand, even gives me a kiss. Then he leaves. And when I'm leaving, the servant says, 'You know who was with you? Blok, the poet. Have a look!' And he shows me his picture in a magazine, and I see that it's him all right. 'My God,' I think, 'what a weird thing!' "

And in fact a reflection of heartfelt sadness and hurt passed over that lively, pug-nosed face, its crafty eyes those of a homeless little dog. I gave the girl all the money I had and from that moment on I felt I understood Blok and that there was a bond between us.

I like that severe face of his, and that head of a Renaissance Florentine.

PART TWO

Gorky: *Fragments from My Diary* (Selections)

6

Introduction

Gorky began work on the items that were to make up his book *Fragments from My Diary. Reminiscences* soon after leaving Russia in 1921 for protracted expatriation in Germany and Italy. The project builds on his recently published memoirs of Tolstoy and Andreyev, taking its fragmentary structure from those works (and some of its impetus from the final volume of his autobiographical trilogy, *My Universities* [1923], on which he was working at the same time).

Many factors led him to produce these sketches from memory. Leaving Russia, he was writing finis to five years of unremitting activity, all of it a response in one way or another to the revolutionary cataclysm, and none of it literary. In a letter to Romain Rolland he declares his certainty that "nothing I write now will be read in Russia, for there is no talk there about love for people, and the necessity of such love is a matter of the gravest doubt. When you wish to make all of humanity happy at one fell swoop the individual rather gets in the way of the job."[1] In the same letter he adds: "Over in Russia the blizzards and the Communists are howling, snowdrifts cover the ground and word-drifts cover the people—excellent words, but they are like the snow, not simply because they are equally abundant but because they are cold. When fanaticism is cold, it is colder than the polar frost."

He wants to write about individuals, and he wants to write warmly, not from the stark black-and-white perspectives of politics but in a way that respects the enigma of individual character and in so doing frees him from categorizing and generalizing. Categories and generalizations can be, for a writer, forms of inhibition; the same is true of conventional narrative genres. Gorky is ready to abandon them all and see where his artistic unconscious—what we would call his heart and Russians would call his soul—may lead him.

It leads him to dredge up out of memory some dozens of the ten thousand people he claimed to have encountered, and they are all of such pronounced individuality as to be called eccentric. It is they in all their frequent grotesquerie who populate the Russia of his heart. They are by no means all lovable, but the territory they inhabit and constitute is. And it is vanished. Gorky's awareness that a different era has arrived, in his country's life and in his own, leads him to memorialize what he has seen. Originally he wanted to call the result "A Book of Russian People" or "A Book of Russian People As They Were." His final title eschews even that degree of implicit generalization in favor of an emphasis on the personal, direct, and immediate, on the presentation of ostensibly unreconstructed and unpolished material, emphasizing its being there for its own unaccountable sake. In the end he could not refrain from trying to explain what he had done, but it is significant that he does so only in the end; that is, after his unconscious process has run its course. That attempt at an explanation ("Instead of an Afterword") seems written as much for himself as for the reader; it is quite interesting, and entirely inadequate. Happily, post facto discovery of a purpose leaves the immediacy of the artistic achievement intact.

The initial impetus to write these pieces, then, is writerly. It is significant that the enthusiastic responses to them tended to speak of "a new Gorky." So, for that matter, did the author. He wrote his ex-partner, Maria Fyodorovna Andreyeva, when the book was in press: "Very moved, my friend, by your praise of the Fragments, very moved and sincerely grateful, although I must say that I personally don't regard them as being very important: it's just rubbish which I needed to get out of my soul and memory lest it interfere with my work. The Fragments have a much greater significance as lessons I am giving myself in 'penmanship' out of a desire to learn to write without extraneous words, in preparation for serious work. It's time for me to learn to write well, don't you think?"[2] One hopes that the first sentence is disingenuous, but he told others, too, what he says in the two following sentences, and he clearly meant it.*

The sketches draw on two of Gorky's legendary strengths, his memory and his skills as an impromptu storyteller. The critic and editor A. Voronsky joins many others in calling his memory "amazing." He had, Voronsky writes, "superb recall for the dates of minor events that had taken place forty or fifty years before; he remembered faces, the way people talked, the names of streets, the numbers of houses, who said what. When he would correct someone in conversation, he would amaze him with his precision. It is not by accident that he is one of the best portraitists in Russian literature; his memory was a major factor." As for his

---

* Cf. his remarks in a letter to Romain Rolland (dated Freiburg, 6 November 1923):
I am well aware of my shortcomings, the chief of which is . . . haste, the urge to tell what I have seen, what I know, and what most agitates me. Here the paradox that "it's not always useful for a man to know a lot" is fully applicable.

I suffer from an overload of impressions garnered from existence, a hypertrophied accumulation of facts, and I get too carried away by their external colorfulness, all of which makes me a storyteller rather than an explorer of the secrets of the human heart or the enigmas of life.

Anthropocentric with regard to man and anthropomorphic in depicting nature, I am still unable to express my true self with the requisite power and persuasiveness—that authentic self which bears the whole load of all my personal impressions.

When all is said and done, I think that if I were to write a critical article about Gorky it would amount to the most acerbic and pitiless critique. I assure you that I am far from posturing when I say this. I am least of all an admirer of Gorky, and if you want to know my ideal of a writer, it is daring and highly immodest: to write like Flaubert. I mean it.

(*M. Gor'kij i R. Rollan: Perepiska [1916–1936]* [Moscow: "Nasledie," 1995], 78.)

talk, testimony is similarly abundant that he was a mesmerizing storyteller, subtle and expressive. And in his oral accounts, Voronsky observes, "you were struck by the willfulness and refractoriness, the absurdities and rascalities [*ozorstvo*], the surprises and contradictions, the strivings, and the sheer unremittingness of all these things in the person he was telling about."[3]

Gorky had been reading Sherwood Anderson's *Winesburg, Ohio* with great enthusiasm—and making notes on it—just at the time he was working on these pieces, and while this is not the place to explore the connection, it is worth noting that he saw Anderson's collection of grotesques as "an utterly new thing in American literature." When Anderson was writing the stories that make up *Winesburg* he referred to them as "fragments." But Anderson's fragments are stories; Gorky's are something else.[4]

The diary they purport to come from never really existed, except metaphorically, which is to say that Gorky never kept a conventional diary. What he did do—as he had in putting together the Tolstoy memoir—was to draw on his prodigious memory, and on the little slips of paper on which, over the years, sporadically and unsystematically, he made notes which he then dropped into envelopes against possible future use. The people and events he writes about are all real; they are drawn from his experience in Nizhnii Novgorod and Arzamas from the 1890s into the early years of the new century, and in Petrograd during the years of war and revolution. The sketches themselves are not direct transcriptions, but they are not conventional memoirs either. Nor are they journalism. These polished fragments in fact constitute a new and hybrid literary genre—fragmentary, momentary, immediate in their effect. One critic called them the prose counterpart to *vers d'occasion* in poetry, but that, I think, is misleading, because there is in fact no occasion to which any of them are responding, no rationale for the appearance of any of them or for the grouping of them all. They are simply what Gorky comes up with when he drops his bucket into the well of memory.

His own uncertainty about them is one sign of their authenticity. A case in point is a passage from his archive, unpublished in his lifetime, dating from the period in which he was writing his *Fragments*. Referring to "a man I do not know," it reads: "I know nothing about this man and it is not clear to me how and why this need to think about him has arisen. This need persistently keeps me from writing anything else, stubbornly forcing me to imagine the life of a man whom I don't know and who is essentially uninteresting."[5]

This controlled surrender to his unconscious (which marks the fiction of the years 1922–25 as well) did not last long, but while it did it produced writing transcendent in its modesty and highly revealing personally—if not of Alexei Peshkov, then certainly of Maxim Gorky, whose hybrid nature it matched. Even after *Fragments* was published as a book Gorky wrote and published another five items in the Soviet magazine *Molodaja Gvardija* (The Young Guard) before turning away for good to the main project of his last years, the multivolume novel *Klim Samgin*. He equipped them with this introduction:

The longer I live, the more fascinating I find people.

I am saddened that I no longer have the time to write a book in which the lives of ten thousand Russian people would be shown in detail. I have no doubt that such a book would be more significant than Xenophon's *Anabasis*, for my ten thousand would make their retreat in at least two directions—a small part retreating from all that that exists in a person as a result of his animal nature, and the rest from all that derives from the logic of the history of culture worked out by the first group.

Ten thousand sharply etched portraits, and each of those individuals committed, one way or another, to trying to aggravate the maximum number of their fellow men in their own communities, in the course of which effort they display varying degrees of adroitness and meanness, shrewdness and fanaticism, even passion. Each of these individuals has his own way of speaking, his own favorite expressions; each is endowed with some portion of conceit, which makes him stupid in an original way; out of his large zoological stupidity each fashions a small reasoning faculty, at times amazingly acute; and each is talented in one way or another.

I have long been convinced that all people are talented, and Russians in particular. Yes, yes: Russians in particular—and that may be one of the reasons they do not know how to live.

In an endless chain there rise before me the dozens and hundreds of colorfully strange people I have encountered on my tortuous path toward oblivion—mine, and theirs.

The stupid and the clever, the base and the all-but-saintly, the unhappy in all their variations—all these people are dear to my heart; I have the impression that I understand them fairly well, and my heart is full of unflagging interest in them. Many whom I knew are already dead; I fear that there is no one besides me to tell about them as I would like to, and I am afraid that in the end it will be as if they had never existed.

And I simply cannot do it. It's not easy to invent ten thousand such people. That would require sketching in a fantastically distressing thousand-year history—and I personally would need another fifty years of life.

Using the word "invent" is not a slip; the point is precisely that these are all people who have been invented, and not entirely by me—in the last analysis, we are all constantly inventing each other. No, they are people who have invented themselves in order to make life more interesting, even if more complicated and more difficult.

I am utterly convinced that people, all people, aspire to a world in which, at last, not even one person would remain about whom nothing at all significant or amusing or at least nasty could be found to say. This surely is one reason that people are so ready and willing to lie and to slander each other.

I am particularly fond of people who are "unfinished," not especially "wise," a little crazy and "extreme"; whereas I find "sensible" people to be not of much interest. The man who is "finished," complete, like an umbrella, leaves me unmoved. It is, after all, my calling and my fate to be a teller of stories, and what is there to say about an umbrella except that it is useless in sunny weather?

A man who is something of a "crackpot" is not only more pleasing to me personally but more "believable" in general, more in keeping with the general tone of life, with the inexplicable and the fantastic—which make life so devilishly interesting.[6]

Considerations of space make possible only this sampling of Gorky's *Fragments*. A fuller, though incomplete and by now somewhat dated translation of the book by Moura Budberg appeared in 1924 and was republished as recently as 1975. In the Soviet period the book was published as a separate volume only in the original Russian-language Berlin edition of 1924. Inside the Soviet Union, while included in multivolume scholarly editions of his works, it seems never to have been printed separately, perhaps because of its radical departure from the stereotyped image of the "great proletarian writer."

7

The Town

This sketch introduces the volume.[7] It reflects Gorky's impressions from 1902, when he was exiled to Arzamas under police surveillance after being released from jail in Nizhnii (with Tolstoy's help). In May of that year he characterized the town in a letter: "A splendid town. Thirty-six churches—and not a single library. Down the streets, which are paved with enormous chunks of gray rock, walk pigs, policemen, and ordinary folks. They walk slowly with the look of creatures utterly devoid of any active intentions. Street life is on a high level: the locals beat their wives on the sidewalks."

◄•►

. . . I am sitting outside of town on the bare hills, the grass on them thin and patchy; around me I can barely make out the graves, trampled by the hooves of cattle and worn away by the wind. I sit by the wall of a toy-sized little brick box, covered with an iron roof. From a distance you might take it for a chapel, but up close it is more like a doghouse. Behinds its iron door chains are stored, along with lashes, knouts, and a few other instruments of torture once used to torment the people who are buried in these hills. They were left as a reminder to the town: *Do not rebel!*

But the townsfolk have already forgotten whose people were slaughtered here. Some say they were the Cossacks of Stepan Razin; others maintain they were the Mordovian and Chuvash followers of Emelyan Pugachev.

And only the old beggar Zatinshchikov, who is always drunk, says boastfully, "We rebelled under both of them . . ."

From the barren hilly field the town's houses, gray and low to the ground, look like piles of rubbish: here and there they are overgrown up to their roofs with thick dusty greenery. From these piles of gray litter you can see a dozen belltowers jutting out, and the watchtower of a firehouse; the white walls of churches sparkle in the sun, giving the impression of clean little linen patches on filthy rags.

Today is a holiday. Until noon the townspeople stood in the churches, until two they ate and drank, and now they are resting. The town is hushed. Not even the crying of the children is to be heard.

It is miserably hot. A gray-blue sky pours invisible molten lead over the earth. There is something impenetrable and dismal in that sky, as if the blindingly white sun had melted and was spreading across the heavens. The wretched, dried-out, and faded blades of grass on the graves do not stir. The ground crackles and flakes in the sun like a dried fish. To the left of the hills, beyond the invisible river, a haze streams over the naked fields: and in its midst the jug-eared belltower of the peasant settlement wobbles and sags—a hundred years ago that settlement belonged to the famous Saltychikha, whose name became famous for the refined tortures she visited on her enslaved serfs.

As for the city, it is covered by a cloud of some turbid yellowish dust. Perhaps it is the breathing of the sleeping population.

Strange people live in this city. The owner of the felting plant, a solid and intelligent enough man, has been reading Karamzin's *History of the Russian State* for more than three years and is into the ninth volume.

"A great work!" he says, stroking the leather binding fully. "A kingly book. You see right away that the writer was a brain. You pick it up on a winter evening and all your cares vanish. It's really nice. A book can give a man great solace! Providing, of course, that it's written from a sufficient height of reason . . ."

Once, smiling amiably and playing with his luxuriant beard, he made me a proposal:

"You want to have a look at something interesting? There's a doctor who lives in the house behind me, and a certain lady—not from around here, an out-of-towner—comes to see him. I watch them having a good time from my dormer: only the lower half of their window is curtained and you can see what they're up to in great detail. I even let a Tartar sell me a pair of second-hand binoculars, and once in a while I'll invite friends over for the fun of it. Some forms of licentiousness are highly stimulating . . ."

The barber Balyasin calls himself "the municipal tonsorialist." Tall and thin, he walks with his shoulders thrown back and his chest puffed out proudly. He has the head of a grass snake—small, with yellow eyes; his glance is at once friendly and mistrustful. The town considers him a clever man, and people go to Balyasin for treatment more readily than to the official doctor.

"Ours is a simple nature," say the townspeople. "Doctors are for educated folks."

The barber does cupping and lets blood; recently he cut away a callus for a patient and the patient died from blood poisoning.

Somebody joked, "There's zeal for you! They tell him to remove a callus and he removes the whole man . . ."

The thought of the tenuousness of existence gives Balyasin no peace.

"I think the scientists are having us on," he says. "They don't know anything exact about the way the sun moves. For instance, I look at the sun setting and I think, what if it doesn't come up tomorrow? If it doesn't come up, that's it—quitting-time! Say it gets caught on something, a comet for instance, it's go live in the dark for you! Or else it just stops on the other side of the earth and pops the lid of eternal darkness on us that way. You've got to assume that the sun has its own character like the rest of us. If that happened, we'd have to make bonfires out of the forests."

He guffaws, narrows his eyes, and goes on:

"That'd leave us with a fine sky—there'd be stars, but no sun or moon. Instead of the moon we'd have a black ball hanging up there, if it's true that the moon borrows its light from the sun. Live any way you want, there'd be no seeing anything. That would be fine for the thieves, but very unpleasant for people with other occupations. Am I right?"

Once he said as he trimmed my hair:

"Our people are used to everything, you can't scare them with anything, not fires, not anything. Some places get floods and earthquakes.
What do we get? Nothing! Not even cholera, even when everybody around
us had cholera. But a man longs for something unusual, something terrifying. Terror is good for the soul the way the bathhouse is for the body . . ."

The one-eyed man in charge of the town bathhouse (also known as the capster because he makes peaked caps out of old trousers) is somebody the town
doesn't like. They fear him. If they meet him on the street the townspeople
step aside apprehensively and look back at him like wolves, though now and
again someone will walk straight at the capster with his head lowered as if
planning to butt him. In that case it's the capster who gives way, and he is the
one who stares at the other one's back, narrowing his eyes and grinning.

"Why don't they like you?" I ask.

"I'm merciless," he boasts. "It's a knack I've developed. The minute
anybody does something wrong, I drag him off to court!"

The white of his eye is inflamed, criss-crossed with a network of tiny
veins, and in this network the reddish round pupil glitters proudly. The
capster is thickset, his arms are long, and he is bowlegged. He resembles a
spider.

"The fact is they don't appreciate me because I know my rights," he
explained as he rolled a cigarette of cheap tobacco. "Somebody else's sparrow flies into my garden, it's off to court! I was four months suing over a
rooster. The judge himself said to me, 'You,' he said, 'shouldn't have been
born human. By nature you're a horsefly!' I've even been beaten because I
don't show mercy, but beating me is not a smart move. Beating me is like
picking up a red-hot poker: you only get burned. When the beating's over,
I get to work and then—watch out . . . !'"

He gave a shrill whistle. He really is a busybody. The local judge is
deluged with his complaints and petitions. The capster is on a friendly
footing with the police; they say he likes to write denunciations and keeps
a register where he writes down the various transgressions of the townspeople.

I ask him: "What do you do that for?"

"Because I know my rights!" he answers.

Pushkaryov, bald and fat, is a metal worker and coppersmith, freethinker and atheist. Pursing his flabby lips, which curve strangely and are the color of the worms that surface in a rainstorm, he says in a deep, hoarse voice:

"God is an invention. There's nothing over us, just blue air. And all of our thoughts are made of blue air. We live blueness, we think blueness—there's the puzzle. The entire essence of my life and yours is very simple: first they existed and then they rotted."

He is literate and he's read a lot of novels. He particularly remembers one called *The Bloody Hand*.

"There's a French bishop in it who rebels and lays siege to the city of La Rochelle. And the man who opposes him is one Captain Lacuson, and the things that son of a bitch does! Your mouth actually waters when you read it. The sword is his instrument, and he never misses: one thrust and, voilà, another corpse! A really terrific fighter . . ."

Pushkaryov told me this story:

"I'm sitting one evening, just the way I am now. It's a holiday and I'm reading. Suddenly the counter for the local board—the statistician, in their lingo—shows up. 'I wish,' he says to me, 'to make your acquaintance.' 'Well,' I say, 'go on, make it.' Myself, I'm sitting with my side to him. He goes on about one thing and another, and I play dumb, I mutter and I keep staring at the wall. 'I hear you don't believe in God,' he says, 'is it true?' Well, that's when I let him have it! 'What are you talking about?' I say. 'You think that's permissible? You think we have churches, and priests, and monks for no reason—eh? What if I was to go to the police and tell them you've been trying to undermine my faith? *Eh?*' He got scared, I tell you. 'Sorry,' he says, 'I thought . . .' 'That's just it,' I tell him, 'you think about things you shouldn't. I don't need these thoughts of yours.' You should have seen him take off! Soon after that he shot himself. I don't like these functionaries, you can't trust them. They suck the peasant dry, that's what they live for. No place for these scientists to go? All right, fix them up in the local administration, tell 'em, 'Count!' And they go count. People don't care what they have to do, just so you keep raising their salary . . . ' "

Then there is the watchmaker Kortsov (nicknamed Jumping Flea)—a small hairy little man with long arms, a patriot and devotee of beauty.

"You won't find stars anywhere like our Russian stars!" he says, gazing up at the sky with eyes round and flat as buttons. "Or our spuds—best ones, for taste, in the whole world. Or take accordions: nobody's can touch the Russian! Locks! We've got plenty to outclass any America with."

He writes songs and, when he's been drinking, sings them himself. The lyrics are deliberately farfetched and absurd, but the song he sings oftener than the others goes like this:

> Gray is the bird, the titmouse
> Singing 'neath my window frame.
> In a day or two it will lay
> Its little egglet all the same.

> I will steal that little egg and
> Put it in the hoot-owl's bed.
> And whatever happens then
> Will happen also to my rowdy head.

> What does it mean, this nighttime dream,
> That has that owl, the bird of dark,
> Peck away at my poor skull—
> That owl, alone there in the park?

Kortsov sings his song to a cheerful, bouncy tune. As for that skull of his, it is perfectly round and totally bald, except for a fringe of reddish curls that runs from one ear to the other and overhangs the back of his neck.

He loves to rhapsodize over the beauties of nature, although the surroundings of the town are desolate, rising in barren hills, cut up by ravines, impoverished and ugly. But the watchmaker, standing on the banks of the river, polluted by the felt works, murky and foul-smelling, cries out in genuine ecstasy: "What beauty! Far and wide! Go wherever your fancy takes you! I could die of love for this beauty of ours!"

His yard is filthy, all overgrown with thistles and nettles, and strewn with bits of wood and iron; in the middle a large sofa sits decaying, clumps of hair sticking out of its seat. Indoors it's dusty and jumbled; hanging from the chains of the old grandfather clock instead of weights are pieces of lead pipe. Off in a corner his sick wife groans and grumbles, while her sister, a skinny and jaundiced old maid, bustles around with bared teeth in a pair of run-down men's boots, her skirt hitched up to her knees, baring her calves, which are covered with blue knots of varicose veins.

Kortsov has invented a lock that is loaded with three rifle shells and fires when the key is inserted. The lock weighs twelve pounds and resembles an elongated box. It seems to me that it ought to fire into the air and not at the person who goes to unlock it.

"No, it's meant to get him right in the kisser!" the inventor assures me.

The townspeople prize him for being an eccentric. And maybe they also like the fact that he is unlucky at cards and anyone can beat him. He enjoys flogging children and is said to have flogged his own son to death, but that doesn't stop those who know him from inviting Kortsov in as an expert at punishing the boys who despoil the local orchards and vegetable gardens.

Unhurried, his hands clasped behind his back, Yakov Lesnikov strolls around the town, tall and gaunt, with a beard that is long and narrow and a large, sad nose. Uncombed and dirty, he wears a long, loose robe resembling a monk's cassock, and perched on the tufts of his stiff and graying hair is a student's cap. His large watery eyes stare fixedly, as if the man were overcome with drowsiness but unable to sleep. Yawning constantly, he looks into the distance over the heads of the people he meets, and asks:

"So. How are things?"

The answers clearly are of no interest to him, and anyway he must know them in advance:

"So-so." "Not bad." "Can't complain."

He has a reputation as a womanizer and a great libertine. Kortsov said to me, not without pride:

"He even lived with a Spanish woman! These days, though, he wouldn't say no to a Mordovian . . ."

The rumor is that Lesnikov is the "illegitimate" son of some prominent person, a bishop or a governor. He has some acres of garden land and ponds which he rents to people in the settlement while he lives by himself in an apartment belonging to my neighbor, an ailing treasury functionary.

One evening he was lying on the grass in the garden, under a linden tree, drinking an iced beer, growling and yawning. His landlord, a skinny man with glasses and a sourly ingratiating manner, came up to him.

"How are things, Yasha?"

"Boring," Lesnikov said. "I'm trying to think what I should take up."

"It's too late for you to take up anything."

"Could be."

"You're a bit old."

"True."

Silence. Then Lesnikov observed in his unhurried way:

"It's really boring. Maybe what I should do is believe in God."

The functionary approved:

"Not a bad idea. At least you'd be going to church . . ."

And Lesnikov, yawning loudly, said: "That's the trouble . . ."

Zimin the dry-goods salesman, a sly peasant and a churchwarden, said to me:

"It's their mind that people suffer from, that's the main reason for this whole mess we're in. We have no simplicity. We've lost our simplicity. Our heart is honest but our mind is a crook! . . ."

I sit, gulping down the torrid air and recalling the words, the gestures, the faces of these people. I look at the town, wrapped in a hot shimmering haze. What need is there for a town like this and the people who inhabit it?

It was here in Arzamas that Leo Tolstoy first felt the horror of living. But can it be that that the town has existed since the time of Ivan the Terrible—and goes on existing—only for that?

I think there must be no other country where people talk so much, and think so incoherently and dissolutely, as people talk and think in Russia—especially in the provinces.

In Arzamas thoughts are accidental; they are like the birds tortured by little boys that sometimes fly, half-plucked and terrified, into dark rooms only to smash themselves to death against the impenetrable deception of the windowpanes, transparent as air. Futile, "blue" thoughts . . .

I observe these people and it seems to me that their life is above all stupid, and only then—and for that reason—filthy, dull, embitttered, and criminal. Talented people, but people fit only to tell anecdotes about.

From the river comes the sound of loud voices and splashing water—the boys have gone there to swim. But there are not many of them in town; most have gone into the forest or into the fields and ravines where it is cool. Blue smoke rises from the gardens: the housewives are up from their naps and lighting samovars in preparation for afternoon tea.

A girl's thin cry pierces the air:

"Oy, mama, oy, sweet mama, oy—not in the tummy, don't hit me in the tummy . . ."

And it is as if that cry fell straight into the earth.

The heat gets worse and worse. As if the sun had stopped. The earth breathes the dry dusty heat. The sky seems even more impenetrable—this dull impenetrability of the heavens is extremely unpleasant and even alarming. It makes you think that this may not be the same sky as everywhere else, but some special one, peculiar to this place, flat, condensed out of the labored breathing of the people of this strange town. Miragelike, the blue-gray distance wavers and streams, taking on the colors of glass that has scorched in the sun; it seems to be growing solider and advancing as a transparent but impenetrable wall toward the town.

Like little black dots the flies flicker senselessly, once again calling to mind the impenetrability of glass.

And the hot heavy silence keeps growing denser and heavier.
In the stillness a woman's languid, drowsy voice sounds liltingly:
"Tasya, you getting dressed?"
And a voice like hers, but lower, answers languorously:
"I am."
Silence. And then:
"Tasya, you putting on the sky-blue one . . . ?"
"Mmmm—sky-blue . . ."

8

The Spider

Yermolai Makov, an old man who dealt in "antiquities," was tall and thin
and straight as a post. He walked the earth like a soldier on parade, in-
specting everything with his huge bull's eyes, whose dull, grayish-blue
gleam suggested something morose and dim. I took him to be stupid, particularly because of one capricious and high-handed trait he had. He'd be
offering you a scrivener's inkwell, or a tavern-keeper's prize ladle, or some
ancient coin, and after bargaining hard and finally agreeing on the price, he
would suddenly say in a funereal voice:

"No, I don't want to."

"Why not?"

"I prefer not to."

"Then why did you waste a whole hour haggling?"

Silently he would shove the object into his bottomless coat pocket,
sigh, and leave without saying a word, as if deeply offended. But a day
later—sometimes just an hour later—he would show up without warning,
put the thing on the table, and say:

"Take it."

"So why wouldn't you sell it last time you were here?"

"I preferred not to."

He wasn't greedy for money; he gave a lot to beggars; and he was careless about his appearance, going around, winter and summer, in an old cotton coat, a heavy peaked cap, and worn-out boots. He was homeless,
traveling from one estate to another, from Nizhnii Novgorod to Murom,
from Murom to Suzdal, Rostov, Yaroslavl, then back to Nizhnii again,
where he always put up at Bubnov's filthy rooming house—a place popu-
lated by canary sellers, con men, detectives, and all sorts of seekers after

happiness who pursued it lying on decrepit sofas surrounded by clouds of tobacco smoke. Amid this human flotsam Makov stood out as a "popular" fellow and a good storyteller; his stories were always about how the old "nests of noblemen" were being destroyed and vanishing. He would talk about this lugubriously, with barely suppressed rancor, going out of his way to instance the frivolousness of present-day landowners.

"They chase wooden balls. They like to hit them with wooden clubs—it's a game they have. And they themselves are like those balls, rolling to and fro around the world without rhyme or reason."

One foggy night in autumn I found Makov on a steamship heading for Kazan. Feeling its way through the fog, its wheels scarcely turning, the ship was creeping downstream, its lights melting into the gray of fog and water, the foghorn sounding hoarsely, without letup; the whole dismal scene was like something out of a bad dream.

Makov was seated alone at the stern, as if hiding from someone.

We began to talk, and this is what he told me:

"For twenty-three years I've been living in constant terror and there's no way I can escape. And that terror, sir, is a very special one: *somebody else's soul has taken up residence in my flesh.* Yessir. I was thirty and I was involved with a female who was a witch—it's the truth and there's no other word for it. Her husband was a friend of mine. He was a good man but a sick one, and he was dying. And the night he died, while I laid there sleeping, that damned woman pulled my soul out of me and stuffed *his* soul into my flesh. That was an improvement for her because the husband treated her better than I did, may she rot in hell! As soon as he dies I notice it: *I'm not the same man I used to be.* I admit I never loved that woman—I was only fooling around. But now, all of a sudden, I see that my soul is being drawn to her. What's going on?! I don't like the woman—and I can't tear myself away from her. All my fine qualities have disappeared like smoke. Some mysterious sadness is weighing me down. I've become timid around her and I see that everything around is grayish like it was covered with ashes, but this woman has a face of fire! And it's playing with me, licking at me, drawing me into sin at night. That's when I figured it out: she'd switched souls on me and now I was living with somebody else's soul inside. And my own, my real one, the one God gave me—where was it? I was scared stiff . . ."

The foghorn blared apprehensively, its muffled sound dissipating in the mist. The boat, as if snagged on something, swung its stern around groaning, and the water gurgled under it, dark and oily as tar. The old man, leaning against the rail, shifted his legs in those heavy boots, and absurdly felt around himself in the darkness before going on in a low voice:

"I was scared stiff. I went up to the attic, made a noose, fastened it to the rafter . . . But the laundress spotted me and made a racket and they cut me down. And when I opened my eyes, there in front of me was the weirdest creature—a six-legged spider, about the size of a small goat, with a beard and horns and female tits. It had three eyes, two of them in its head and the third between its breasts, angled down, watching my feet. And wherever I go it follows after, all hairy, on its six legs, like a shadow from the moon, and nobody can see it except me, and—*here it is!* You don't see it, but it's here!"

Stretching his arm out to his left, Makov patted something in the air about a foot and a half above the deck. Then he wiped his hand on his knee, saying:

"It's wet."

"You mean you've been living like this, with the spider, for twenty years?" I asked.

"Twenty-three. You think I'm crazy? He's my guard, and now he's getting sickly, the spider is."

"Have you talked to a doctor about it?"

"Come on, my man, what could a doctor do? It's not some abscess you can cut out with a scalpel or eat out with carbolic acid or rub away with ointment. A doctor can't *see* the spider."

"Does the spider talk with you?"

Makov looked at me with astonishment and asked:

"You're joking, right? How could a spider talk? He's there to scare me, to keep me from being myself so I don't ruin someone else's soul— since it *is* someone else's soul inside me, sort of like stolen goods. Around ten years ago I decided to drown myself. I jumped off a barge. But he—the spider—grabbed hold of me, and grabbed hold of the side of the barge, and I just hung out over the side, dry as you please. Naturally I pretended I'd fallen overboard by accident. Later the sailors said it was my coat that caught on something and held me back. Sure! Right!"

Once again the old man stroked and patted the moist air.

"Some coat, eh?"

I didn't answer, not knowing what to say to a man who lived side by side with such a strange creation of his imagination and yet was not entirely crazy.

"I've wanted to talk to you about this thing for a long time," he said, quietly and beseechingly. "You talk straight about things. I trust you. Be so kind as to tell me: What's your opinion—is it God who sent this spider to guard me, or is it the Devil?"

"I don't know."

"You should think about it . . . My guess is that it's God that's guarding me and keeping someone else's soul in me. I figure he didn't want to assign an angel because I don't deserve an angel. But a spider, now—that's cleverer. It's scary, that's the main thing. I took the longest time getting used to it . . ."

Makov took off his cap, crossed himself, and said with quiet fervor:

"Great and benevolent is the Lord our God, Father of reason and shepherd of our souls."

. . . One moonlit night some months later, I ran into Makov in a desolate quarter of Nizhnii Novgorod. He was walking on the sidewalk and pressing himself against the fences as if making way for someone.

"What—is the spider still alive?"

The old man gave a knowing smile, leaned over, ran his hand through the air, and said affectionately:

"Right here . . ."

Three years after that I learned that in 1905 Makov had been robbed and murdered somewhere in the neighborhood of Balakhna.

9

The Executioner

Greshner, chief of the political investigation department of the Nizhnii Novgorod police, was a poet whose verses were published in conservative magazines and, I think, in *Niva* and *Rodina*.

I remember a few lines from them:

> Heartache comes crawling up from the floors
> And in through each one of the doors.
> It can cripple you, no doubt about it,
> Still, it's worse to be living without it.
>
> Without it I'd feel so alone,
> Like the earth without people or beasts . . .

He wrote an erotic poem in the album of a certain lady:

> There at the front door of the house
> A boy of six I see.
> I've met him somewhere else, before—
> Hold on there! Damn! It's me!

What followed was a string of similes and allegories not easy to summarize.

Greshner was shot by the nineteen-year-old Alexander Nikiforov, whose father Lev was a well-known Tolstoyan in his time and a man with a highly dramatic fate: he had four sons who perished one after the other. The oldest, a Social Democrat, worn out by years of jail and exile, died of heart disease; one doused himself with kerosene and burned himself to death; one poisoned himself; and the youngest, Sasha, was hanged for murdering Greshner. He killed him in broad daylight, on the street, virtually on the threshold of the Okhrana headquarters. Greshner was walking with a lady on his arm.

Sasha caught up with him and shouted, "Hey! Gendarme!"

And when Greshner turned around, Nikiforov shot him in the face and chest. They caught Sasha on the spot and sentenced him to death, but none of the criminals in the Nizhnii jail would agree to take on the odious task of serving as executioner. Then the police officer Poiré, who had worked as a cook for Governor Baranov, a braggart and a drunkard—he passed himself off as a brother of the famous caricaturist Caran d'Ache— prevailed on the fowler Grishka Merkurov to hang Sasha for twenty-five rubles.

Grishka was also a drunk, about thirty-five, tall, emaciated but sinewy; his jaw was like a horse's with clumps of dark hair sprouting from it; his sleepy eyes gazed dreamily out from under beetle brows. Once he'd hanged Nikiforov he bought himself a red scarf which he wrapped around his long neck with its enormous Adam's apple, stopped drinking vodka, and began coughing a particularly sonorous and imposing cough. His friends asked him:

"What's this, Grishka? You putting on airs?"

He explained:

"I've been hired to do secret work on behalf of the government."

But when he blurted out to somebody that he had hanged a man, his friends turned their backs on him, and even beat Grishka up. He then applied to officer Kevdin of the political investigation department for permission to wear the red tunic and the trousers with red stripes.

"So the civilians will understand who I am, and fear to lay their vile hands on me, and know that I am an eradicator of villains."

Kevdin inveigled him into certain other killings, and Grishka traveled to Moscow, where he hanged somebody and became convinced once and for all of his importance. But when he got back to Nizhnii he went to see

Doctor Smirnov, an oculist and violent right-winger, to complain that under the skin of his—Grishka's—chest, an "air bag" had inflated and was pulling him upward.

"The pull is so strong I can barely stay on the ground and have to hold on to something to keep from bobbing up and down and making people laugh. It happened right after I'd strung up some scoundrel: there was a thump in my chest and it started to puff up. And now it's got to the point where I can't even sleep at night. Whatever I do, I'm pulled up toward the ceiling! I pile all the clothes I have on top of me, I even put bricks in the sleeves and pockets to make me heavier. Nothing helps. Putting a table on my chest and stomach, tying my legs to the bed—none of it helps, I still drift up. Cut me open, I beg of you, and let the air out or very soon I'll be utterly incapable of locomotion on the ground."

The doctor advised him to go to the psychiatric hospital, but Grishka refused indignantly.

"The thing is in my chest, not my head . . ."

Shortly after that he fell off a roof, breaking his back and fracturing his skull. As he lay dying, he asked Doctor Nifont Dolgopolov:

"When they bury me—will there be music?"

Then, just a few minutes before he expired, he muttered with a sigh:

"Well, here I go, I'm rising up . . ."

10
People When They Think They're Alone

Today I observed a diminutive blond lady with the unformed face of a girl, wearing gray gloves and cream-colored stockings, standing on the Trinity Bridge and gripping the railing as if about to jump into the river, and noticed that she was sticking out her little red tongue at the moon. The sly old moon was stealing into the sky through a cloud of dirty smoke; it was very large and red-faced, like a drunkard. The lady was taunting it in all seriousness—vindictively even, or so it seemed to me.

That lady called to mind certain "oddities" that that have always, for as long as I can remember, disconcerted me. Seeing how a person behaves when he is by himself, I see that person as crazy—there is no other word for it.*

I first noticed this when I was still an adolescent. The English clown Rondale, walking down an empty corridor at the circus and passing a mirror, took off his top hat and bowed fully to his reflection. There was no one else in the corridor. I was sitting in an empty cistern above Rondale's head; he could not see me, nor had I heard his steps; as luck would have it, I had

---

* Gorky was not exempt from such oddities himself. "Once at Gorky's," Kornei Chukovsky writes, "I walked into a room to find him fussing with the stove and saying to himself: "My dear Alexei Maximovich, allow me to warn you that you are about to burn yourself."

And Valentina Khodasevich recalls how, during a visit to the Crimea, she espied Gorky on a terrace outside her room, sitting on a stool in the shadows and "talking with someone in a husky bass voice. Through a crack in the door I saw various small birds perched on a railing. Gorky was feeding them bread and talking to them, by turns politely and admonishingly, at times even administering reprimands. The birds would listen carefully, look around, answer by chirping or twittering and, if angered or frightened, would fly off and circle around before coming back again. Conversations of this kind could become quite earnest, even to the point of involving politics."

simply stuck my head out at the precise moment that the clown was bowing to himself. The astonishment I felt at seeing him do that was dark and unpleasant. Then I realized that a clown—and an Englishman at that—is a man whose trade or art is eccentricity . . .

But I have seen Anton Chekhov sitting in his garden and, trapping a sunbeam in his hat, try (and fail utterly) to put it on his head while keeping it inside the cap, and I have seen how this failure annoyed that catcher of sunbeams: his face became angrier and angrier. He ended by slapping the cap on his knee dejectedly, then jamming it sharply over his ears, irritatedly kicking his dog Tuzik aside, narrowing his eyes, glancing sideways up at the sky, and heading inside—when, seeing me on the porch, he said with a grin:

"Hello! Have you read Balmont's poem where he writes, 'The sun smells like grass'? That's stupid. In Russia the sun smells of Russian provincial soap, and here in the Crimea it smells of Tartar sweat . . ."

It was Chekhov too who tried long and diligently to stuff a thick red pencil into the tiny neck of an apothecary's vial. He was clearly seeking to violate some law of physics, and he was applying himself to that effort earnestly, with the stubborn persistence of a research scientist.

Leo Tolstoy once asked a lizard in a low voice:

"Are you happy, eh?"

The lizard was sunning itself on a rock in the bushes along the road to Diulber, and Tolstoy stood facing it with his hands stuck into his leather belt. And looking around carefully, that great man confessed to the lizard:

"*I'm* not . . ."

Professor M. M. Tikhvinsky, the chemist, sitting in my dining room, asked his reflection in a copper tray:

"How's life treating you, my boy?"

When the reflection did not answer, he inhaled sharply and began systematically trying to erase it with the palm of his hand, frowning all the while and twitching his nose, which resembled an embryonic trunk, unpleasantly.

I've been told that someone once caught the writer Leskov seated at a table where he raised a tuft of cotton and released it over a china bowl, then inclined his ear over it to hear whether it would make a sound when it landed on the china.

Father F. Vladimirsky stood a boot up in front of him and said commandingly:

"All right, walk!"

Silence.

"You can't?"

And with great dignity and conviction he concluded:

"That's the point! Without me you won't get anywhere!"

"What are you doing, Father Fyodor?" I asked as I entered the room.

Looking at me intently he explained:

"It's this boot! It's all worn down. They don't make boots the way they used to anymore . . ."

I have had frequent opportunity to observe how people laugh and cry when they are alone. One writer, completely sober (he was, in general, an extremely moderate drinker), wept as he whistled the barrel-organ tune to Lermontov's *Alone I Venture Out Upon the Highroad* . . .

He whistled badly because he was sniffling as he cried, like a woman, and his lips were trembling. From his eyes little teardrops slid slowly down, disappearing into the dark whiskers of his beard and mustache. He was crying in a hotel room, standing with his back to a window, his arms thrown out wide, making swimming motions (though not for exercise: the motions of his arms were slow, helpless, and unrhythmical).

But that is not particularly strange. Tears and laughter are expressions of moods we understand; there is nothing troubling about them. Nor are the solitary prayers of people at night, in the fields, the forest, the steppe, or at sea. A quite clear impression of madness, however, is produced by onanists; that too is natural, almost always repugnant, but sometimes extremely funny—and at the same time appalling.

A very unpleasant young lady in training to be a doctor, full of herself and inclined to boastfulness, had overdosed on Nietzsche, and though she flaunted a crude and naïve atheism, she used to masturbate in front of a reproduction of Kramskoi's painting, *Christ in the Wilderness.*

"Oh, come!" she would moan in a low and throaty voice. "Dear one, unhappy one, come now, come!"

She subsequently married a rich merchant, bore him two boys, then ran off with a circus strongman.

My neighbor in the Prince's Court Hotel, a landowner from Voronezh, came into my room one night by mistake, half-dressed, but quite sober. I lay on the bed. The light was out, but the room was flooded with moonlight, and through a hole in the curtain I saw a dry face with a smile on it and heard the whispered dialogue of a man with himself:

"Who's that?"

"It's me."

"This isn't your room."

"Oh, sorry!"

"That's all right."

He fell silent, surveyed the room, looked into the mirror to smooth his mustache, and began to sing in a low voice:

"You're in the wrong place, ace! How come, you bum?"

At this point he should have left, but he took a book from the table, stood it up like a roof, and looking at the street, said loudly and clearly, as if reproaching someone:

"It's bright as day; but this day was a dark one. And a rotten one! Go figure! . . ."

Then he left on tiptoe, his arms out wide for balance, and taking great care to close the door behind him without making any noise.

There is nothing remarkable in a child's trying to lift a drawing from a book with his fingers, but it is strange to see a learned man, a professor, engaged in such an effort, looking around and listening to see whether anyone was approaching.

He was evidently convinced that a printed drawing could be lifted off the paper it was on and hidden in a person's vest pocket. A couple of times he found himself succeeding—he took something off the page of the book and, holding it with two fingers, like a coin, tried to shove it into the pocket. But each time, after looking at his fingers, he would frown, study the drawing in the light, and start again doggedly trying to loosen the printed image from the page—but it still didn't work. Hurling the book aside, he left abruptly, stamping his feet in anger.

I looked through the whole book very carefully. It was a technical work in German, illustrated with photographs of different electric motors and their parts; there was not a single drawing pasted into it, and it is a well-known fact that you can't just lift the print off a page with your fingers and stuff it into your pocket. The professor probably knew that too, even though he was a humanist and not a technician.

It's not rare to see women talking to themselves while they play solitaire or apply makeup, but I watched for a full five minutes while an educated woman, eating chocolate candies by herself, spoke to each one of them as she picked it up with tongs:

"I'm going to eat you!"

She would eat it and ask:

"Well, didn't I?"

And then, again:

"I'm going to eat you!"

"Well, didn't I?"

She did this sitting in an armchair next to a window; it was about five o'clock on a summer afternoon, and from the street the dust and noise of a great city forced their way into the room. The woman's face was serious, and her grayish-blue eyes remained fixed on the box in her lap.

In a theater lobby a beautiful brunette who had arrived late and was adjusting her hair in front of a mirror asked someone sternly and in a fairly loud voice:

"So we've got to die?"

There was no one but me in the lobby; I too had arrived late but she hadn't seen me; I hope that if she had, she would not have confronted me with that rather inopportune question.

I have been the observer of many such "oddities." Here is one more:

The poet Alexander Blok, standing on the stairway of the World Literature publishing house, was writing something in pencil in the margin of a book when suddenly, with a respectful gesture, he pressed against the railing to make room for someone, though there was no one there that I could see. I was standing on the next landing up, and when Blok's eyes, which were smiling as they followed the invisible someone who had passed him on the way up, met my own, which must have looked astonished, he dropped his pencil, bent over to pick it up, and asked: "Am I late?"

11

A Good Laugh

Funny things happen in war, too. For instance, five of us go into the forest for firewood when all of a sudden a shell from the Jerries lands—BAM! I'm knocked into the crater, covered with dirt, stones raining down on me. When I come to, I lie there and think: "Well, this is it! You've had it! You've kicked the bucket, Semyon!" But I come to a little more, I wipe my eyes, and—no buddies! The trees are all torn to pieces and I see that guts are hanging on some of the twigs. And I burst out laughing! I mean, it's hilarious—guts draped on the twigs. Later it struck me as a little heavy. I mean, they were people too, my buddies, more or less like me, whatever you say. And all of a sudden not one of them left, like they'd never been. . . . Just the same, at the beginning, what a laugh I had!

━ ◆ ━

We come to this little village? It has—count 'em!—three huts in it. In front of one an old lady is sitting. Close by, a cow is walking around. We say, "Grandma, whose livestock might this be? Not yours, by any chance?" She starts to cry, she wails, she gets down on her knees, ek-cetera. "My grand-children," she says, "are sitting in the cellar and will die . . ." We tell her, "Don't yell, we'll leave you a receipt." There was a kid from Kostroma with us, from our company, a thief all his life, and he's the one who writes out the receipt: "This old lady has lived ninety years and plans on living an-other ninety but she won't make it." And the son of a bitch signs it, "The Lord God."

We hand her the receipt, take the cow, and leave. But we're laughing so hard we can barely walk. So we stop and just roar till the tears come.

12

The Gardener

1917: February

Splattering mud on the walls of buildings and on pedestrians, motorcars race down the street, rattling and roaring. Soldiers and sailors are packed tight in them, the steel needles of their bayonets looking like the bristles of gigantic enraged hedgehogs. From time to time the dry crackling of rifle shots can be heard. The revolution has started and the Russian people are in motion, rushing around as if trying to catch hold of freedom, as if freedom were to be found somewhere outside of themselves. In the Alexander Gardens a man who looks to be about fifty is working alone; heavyset and awkward, he is calmly raking leaves and litter from the pathways and flowerbeds and shoveling away the half-melted snow. The frantic activity around him plainly holds no interest for him; he seems not to hear the roar of car horns, the shouts, songs, and shots, or to see the red flags. Watching him I keep waiting to see him raise his head and look at the people hurrying around him, or at the trucks glinting with bayonets. But he stays bent over, working doggedly, like a mole—and, apparently, as blind as one.

March

Down the street and along the paths of the Alexander Gardens, heading for the House of the People, hundreds—no, thousands—of soldiers are marching slowly, some dragging machine guns like iron piglets behind them. It is an endless machine gun regiment from Oranienbaum; rumor has it that it numbers upwards of ten thousand men who have no place to go and have been wandering the city since morning looking for shelter. The civilians fear them; the soldiers are tired, hungry, and surly. Several of them have now plunked down and stretched out on the edge of a big round flowerbed after dropping their machine guns, rifles, and knapsacks into it. The gar-

208

dener, a broom in his hand, walks slowly up to them and admonishes them in an angry voice:

"Hey you, what kind of a place is this to stretch out? Can't you see we're going to be planting flowers here? You blind or something? This place is for kids. Up with you now, move on!"

And the angry armed men move off obediently.

July 6th

Soldiers in metal helmets have been called in from the front and are surrounding the Peter and Paul Fortress; unhurriedly they walk along the wooden paving blocks through the garden, dragging their machine guns and carrying their rifles carelessly. From time to time one or another of them calls cheerfully to the civilians: "Better clear out, there's going to be shooting!"

The civilians would like to watch the fighting. Silently and stealthily they follow after the soldiers, hiding behind trees and stretching their necks out, straining to see what's happening up ahead.

In the flowerbeds of the Alexander Gardens the flowers are blooming as the gardener walks the paths. He wears a clean apron, carries a shovel, and barks at the spectators and the soldiers as if they were sheep:

"Watch where you're going! Get off the grass there! Road not big enough for you or what?"

A bearded peasant, in a soldier's uniform, ironheaded, cradling his rifle in the crook of his arm, tells the gardener:

"Watch it, pops, you could get yourself shot . . ."

"Never mind, sharpshooter, just keep moving off!"

"We're at war, friend."

"*You're* at war. I've got my own job."

"True enough. Got anything to smoke?"

Taking a pouch out of his pocket, the gardener grumbles for all to hear.

"You're walking where you're not supposed to walk!"

"We're at war!"

"Whatever . . . Fighting's simple enough, but I'm here by myself! Anyway, you should clean your rifle, it's got rust spots . . ."

There is a piercing whistle and the soldier, who hasn't had time to light up, runs between the trees while the gardener, spitting in his direction, calls out:

"What the hell are you doing? Can't you see there are paths? . . ."

Autumn

The gardener walks down the allée with a ladder on his shoulder and shears in his hand. He is pruning the trees. He has lost weight and shriveled up; his clothes hang on him like a sail clinging to the mast on a windless day. The shears as they bite through the bare branches make a loud and angry click.

Looking at him, it struck me that no earthquake and no flood could keep this man from doing his job. And if it turned out that the trumpets of the archangels when they announced the end of the world and the imminence of the Last Judgment did not shine brightly enough, this man would surely tell the archangels in a stern and businesslike way, "You need to polish those trumpets . . ."

13

Instead of an Afterword

It is strange the way opinions sometimes coincide: In 1901, in the town of Arzamas, the archpriest Fyodor Vladimirsky declared:

"Every people possesses a spiritual vision, a vision of aims and goals. Certain thinkers call this trait 'the instinct of the nation,' but as I understand it an instinct raises the question of how to live, whereas I am speaking of a vague uneasiness of mind and spirit about the question of what one should live *for*. So, for instance, although the setting of practical goals is not much developed in us Russians because we haven't yet built up our culture to a height from which we might see where the history of mankind would have us go, all the same, I think that it is precisely we who are fated to torment ourselves with the question, 'What should one live for?' At the moment we are living blindly and noisily, groping our way, but for all that we are already people with a little something of our own, people with a plus."

Five years after that, in Boston, the philosopher and pragmatist William James was saying:

"The current events in Russia have heightened interest in that country but have made me understand it even less. When I read the Russian authors I am confronted with people who are irritatingly interesting, but I can hardly say that I understand them. In Europe and America I see people who have done something and, basing themselves on what they already know how to do, strive to increase the sum of the materially and spiritually useful. The people of your country, by contrast, strike me as creatures who feel no need to accept reality, finding it illegitimate and even distasteful. I see the Russian mind analyzing intensely, seeking, rebelling. What I do not see is the goal of the analysis; I do not see what exactly they are seeking beneath the phenomena of reality. One gets the impression that the Russian considers himself called upon to try to locate, discover, and record whatever is unpleasant and negative. Two books in particular have astonished me—Tolstoy's *Resurrection* and Dostoyevsky's *Karamazovs.* It seems to me that they both portray people from another planet, where everything is different and better. They have landed on our earth by accident and are annoyed, even insulted, by that. You see something childish in them, something naïve, and you feel the stubbornness of an honest alchemist who believes himself able to discover 'the cause of all causes.' You are a very interesting people, but you seem to be working in vain, like a machine that is idling. It may be of course that you are destined to astound the world with something quite unexpected."*

It is amid such people that I have spent half a century.

I hope that this book makes it sufficiently clear that I have not shrunk from writing the truth when that is what I wanted to do. But in my view truth is not everything, nor is it as necessary for people as they think. When I have felt that one or another truth only assaults the soul without carrying any lesson, only humiliates a person without explaining him to me, it goes without saying that I have preferred not to write about that truth.

For there are more than a few truths which one should forget. These truths are born of falsehood and have all the properties of that most pernicious of lies which, distorting our relations with each other, has made life a filthy and senseless hell. What good is there in mentioning what must and should vanish? He who simply and solely registers and records the evil of life has got himself a poor occupation.

I was tempted to call this collection "A Book About the Russian People as They Were."

But I decided that that would sound too categorical. And I was not clear in my own mind: would I want these people to be other than what they are? Alien as nationalism, patriotism, and other such diseases of spiri-

---

* Gorky met William James in August 1906 during his trip to the United States. He refers in a letter to a lecture by James which may have contained the sentiments he cites. Or he may have heard them directly from James in conversation.

tual vision are to me, I do nonetheless see the Russian people as exceptionally, fantastically talented and original. In Russia even the fools are stupid
in an original way, and the lazy are downright geniuses. I am sure that in
their ingenuity, their capacity for the most amazing escapades, the intricacy
of their thinking and feeling, the Russian people constitute supremely re-
warding material for an artist.

I believe that when this astonishing people has suffered its way past
everything that now weighs it down and confuses it from within; when it
begins to work with a full awareness of the cultural and what might be
called the religious significance of the sort of labor that makes the whole
world one; then it will live a fabulously heroic life and will have much to
teach this exhausted and crime-maddened world of ours.

14

Appendix
Gorky on Gorky

Introspection was never Gorky's forte; a doer by nature, he was impatient with the merely personal. And of course the biography, which he was so concerned not to "spoil," was so much more than the life (inner or outer) of the man, Alexei Peshkov; it was, as Gorky all but admitted and as countless commentators have insisted, a complex phenomenon with a life of its own.

But that very fact makes one want to know—even after we understand that Peshkov achieved his selfhood by transcending it—who was there beneath the legend, behind the mask. And however doomed the curiosity may be, however right Freud may have been to insist that "biographical truth does not exist," the quest for some approximation to it will inevitably continue.

For all his principled diffidence, his more than ten thousand published letters offer some important clues, particularly such post-Soviet collections as those to his long-term companion, Moura Budberg, and his fellow writer Romain Rolland.[8] But even in those cases illumination comes often from inferences gleaned in reading the letters of his correspondents.

It is, of course, largely from inference that we derive a sense of the man behind (or before, in the sense of prior to) the writing in the memoirs and sketches that make up this book.

All the more interesting, then, are the entries he made in that unconventional "diary" of his, consisting of labeled envelopes into which he would drop little slips of paper containing jottings about the people and things he had seen, read, and thought.

In 1969 the contents of these envelopes were published. The editors acknowledge "how extremely restrained the writer is in recording his personal feelings and emotions," but stress the value of this material in the way it crystallizes "a particular and very substantial part of his experience as man and as writer."[9]

The envelope labeled "On the Personal" is exceptional for the way Gorky takes an outside, analytical view of himself. Most of the thirty-nine items in it were noted down in the late 1920s as he contemplated his approaching sixtieth birthday in 1928. They may not be definitive, but being written for himself alone, and being at the same time connected in so many ways with so much in the present volume, they have a strong claim on our attention. Here is a selection from them.

◄ • ►

I very early came to know people and while still young I began to invent Man, in order to satisfy my thirst for beauty. Wise men—those tireless creators of error—convinced me that I had done a poor job of inventing a consolation for myself. Then I went among people again and, understandably, turned once again to Man. (*Beginning of the 1830s*)[10]

My memory, both visual and auditory, is highly developed, but indifferent and even antagonistic to other people's ideas. In the sphere of ideas, I find those of other people suspect; it is my habit and preference to wring ideas out of my personal experience . . . If my ideas coincide with those of others, that is natural, for there are not many ideas. . . . I have probably seen and experienced more than I should have, hence the haste and carelessness of my work. In general I am much less talented than that M. G. whom the critics sometimes praise excessively. (*1920–1929*) [194–95]

■

I never believed it when people told me I was talented. It is quite possible that I don't even now, having been regarded for thirty years as a talented person. I think my only talent is an ability to see, aroused by a constant thirst for seeing. I never tire of that, but it's a bad thing that I have ceased to be surprised at anything. And perhaps even worse is the fact that I do not know how to think about myself. I never learned; I lacked the leisure. (*1922–1928*) [196]

■

There are days when everything seems disgusting—everything: flowers, chairs, people, the sun. And the man is disgusting, this one, the one who is writing, myself. Disgusting in his feeling of powerlessness to master himself.

If I am clever enough to live a few more years, a very lonely and difficult old age will sneak up on me. (*12 February 1926*) [197]

■

Sometimes I feel an urge to write a critical article about Gorky as artist. I am convinced that it would be the most malicious and the most instructive article ever written about him. (*1925–1928*) [197]

■

At the time I was drawn to people who were solitary, eccentric, "individuals with peculiarities"; that was entirely natural for a man who, already possessing quite a motley and odd store of impressions, landed in intelligentsia circles that had been wonderfully if somewhat monotonously ironed flat by the heavy ideas of love for the people and reverence for the people. My experience did not fit into these ideas without distortion and without some loss for me. And, to this day, it doesn't. (*Early June, 1926*) [193]

■

About Myself

I do not belong to the tribe of the persecuted and as a consequence have never felt the need to persecute anyone.

I cannot boast of having suffered seriously, since from childhood I have felt a repulsion for that vocation, of which Russians are particularly fond.

I have to say that there have been times—not many, not many!—when I complained (to whom I can't remember) about the hardness of my life. But I seem to have done that for the same reason that people sometimes take a street they don't like to get to their destination, or as guests, out of politeness, eat food they don't feel like eating, or laugh when something is not funny.

I am very polite. At times it seems to me that I have lived my whole life with excessive politeness. . . .

I think that the best of what I have done has been poorly motivated. From which it does not follow that in the best cases I have acted unconsciously. No, I have acted so as to cause the least harm to others, and have always considered that to be in my own interest.

(1926–1929), [199]

■

Thirty-five or so years ago, when the life I had lived seemed to me full of insoluble riddles, I thought: the madness of the brave—there is the wisdom of life. They are wrong to consider that romanticism. *(1927)* [200]

■

Talent is a catalyst.

Experience, direct and from books.

When they call me "great" I feel like a boy that other boys are teasing, the way they tease a cripple for being lame, a one-eyed person for being one-eyed.

As a writer I am not "great"; I am simply a good worker.

(1928) [201]

■

As I see it, I have had a large store of love—and real love—for people, but I have expended it generously, never asking whether any given person was worthy of the love in question. I admit that my love included a large share of pity, which may not be very flattering for the individuals involved. I saw clearly that they were living badly but that that fact did not trouble them as much as I would have liked. Better put: I felt uneasy around them. In the end I became conscious of the need to help everyone, in all ways possible, to live better. And this consciousness came not from my mind, but rather from my whole being. Nonetheless, I don't mean to say that I am kind. I think that I was irritated with fish who lived patiently in water that wasn't salty enough for them, being myself a bird that lives on fish and finds them not tasty enough.

Fifty, or two hundred, or maybe a thousand times I have been asked: "So how, when all is said and done, do you feel about the world?"

And I have had my countless contradictions pointed out to me (and frequently even termed criminal).

I think that now, having lived sixty years and being no longer, most likely, capable of doing well what I most love to do, I can devote some time to the useless task of self-scrutiny. (*1928*) [201]

■

[What Lenin called] my fish eyes see an enormous lot of what is terrible and what is base. I am sometimes tempted to think that no one before me ever observed so many stupid horrors, so much base lying and senseless evil. I could boast—most sorrowfully—of that knowledge.[11]

■

I think I have never possessed much faith in the durability of mutual sympathies, friendship, etc. But I have known how to arouse sympathy for myself—when I wished to. . . .

My mind convinces me with irresistible clarity now that I've lived for sixty years that it is ludicrous to entertain certain lyrical feelings. And yet they do not disappear. I pounce on each new person with an eagerness that, most likely, is taken by many of them as an expression of "homesickness for Russia" and as the garrulousness of the old. But I know very well that this is not so. No. More and more I am overwhelmed and agitated by pity for each individual, no matter who he may be. And the pity is most acute for people who are talented and honest. It is unbearably difficult for them, and will only keep getting more so. Probably never before has there been a time when being an honest person meant being a superfluous man to such a horrifying degree as nowadays. (*March 1928*) [202]

∎

I never felt reality to be stable and never bowed down to it, even if one or another phenomenon aroused joy in me.

There were not, to be sure, many such phenomena; more often than not, things offended me, but did not weaken me, rather stimulating an awareness of the necessity of changing reality.

To what I saw today I always added something, both deliberately and instinctively, from tomorrow. That is the source of my romanticism. Plato. Renan. (*1930*) [203]

∎

I see that for many people I am more and more unpleasant, and actually hateful for some. I understand that in the interests of maximally clear relations, it is necessary to intensify hatred. (*1930–36*) [203]

∎

For me culture is something dearer and more intimate than it is for you. For you it's a habit of yours, something into which you were born and as necessary as trousers. (*1924*) [270] [*Addressee unknown*]

∎

PART THREE

Others on Gorky

15

Khodasevich
"Gorky"

Vladislav Khodasevich (1886–1939), hailed by Vladimir Nabokov as "the greatest Russian poet of our time," was also a critic, historian of literature, biographer, and—as this article shows—an extraordinarily gifted memoirist. Eighteen years Gorky's junior and his polar opposite in temperament and esthetic views, he shared with Gorky a reverence for Russian literature and, during the time of their close association, an active concern for its future which found expression in their work together editing the journal *Beseda* (Colloquy). Conceived as a bimonthly meeting ground for Russian writers in emigration and in Soviet Russia, as well as for noted non-Russian writers, the journal (which was published in Berlin at irregular intervals between 1923 and 1925) foundered over Soviet refusals to allow more than token quantities of each issue into the country. In all, only seven numbers appeared.[1]

As Khodasevich makes clear, however, his relations with Gorky were principally "informal and personal" rather than "official or literary." Khodasevich was a frequent visitor at Gorky's Petersburg apartment beginning in 1920. In 1921, under pressure from Lenin, Gorky left Russia for Western Europe; Khodasevich followed in 1922, and over the next three years there were extended periods when they saw each other almost every day—seven months in the German town of Saarow, four months in Prague and Marienbad, and six months when Khodasevich (and his partner Nina Berberova) lived as part of Gorky's household in Sorrento (October 1924 to April 1925).

(This singular household deserves a word of explanation. Formed already in Petrograd in the period of the 1917 revolutions, and then reassembled in Sorrento in 1924, it was described by one early member as "something like a commune." The Petrograd apartment had eleven rooms, of which Gorky occupied four small ones. The rest—as in traditional Russian country estates—housed between half a dozen and a dozen regulars, some there for more or less extended stays, others permanent members. They were a motley group that would never have lived together were it not for chance and the fact that Gorky seems to have feared solitude [despite his constant complaints about its absence]. Some performed household tasks, others did not. They all stood in for family, and in Sorrento for the first time they actually included Gorky's son and daughter-in-law. Such living arrangements, with "the great proletarian writer" in the role of Russian patriarch, were, needless to say, as anomalous in emigration as they had been in revolutionary Petrograd. The acute critic and historian of Russian literature D. S. Mirsky, who had been living as an émigré in London, visited Gorky in Sorrento in January 1928 and wrote him afterward: "I feel I've been not in Sorrento but in Russia . . . There is surely no other man who could bear Russia within himself the way you do . . ."[2])

The closeness between Gorky and Khodasevich in this period was a complex and unlikely one, fueled on both sides by respect and curiosity. In producing this account of it, Khodasevich manages to do for Gorky what Gorky did in his memoir of Tolstoy: strip away the clichés ("the great proletarian writer," "St. Leo") to convey an exceptionally vivid and persuasive (because concrete, complex, and contradictory) sense of the remarkable individual behind the reputation. Just as there is no better portrait of Tolstoy the man than Gorky's, there is no better portrait of Gorky the man than Khodasevich's, written in 1936 upon Gorky's death and published in Paris the following year.[3]

"Gorky"

I have a clear recollection of Gorky's first books and all the hullabaloo surrounding the emergence of this "hobo writer"; I was present at one of the
first performances of *The Lower Depths* [in late 1902], and, under the influence of his *Song of the Falcon,* once wrote a pretentious prose poem of my
own. But I was quite young then. Later, in the spring of 1908, my friend
Nina Petrovskaya visited Gorky on Capri and saw a copy of my first book
of poems on his desk. Gorky asked her about me, because he read everything and was interested in everybody. However, it was years before we
had any direct contact. My literary life was spent among people who were
alien to Gorky and to whom he was just as alien.

In 1916 [the critic] Kornei Chukovsky came to Moscow and told me
that a new publishing house, Parus (The Sail), had just started up in Petersburg with plans to put out children's books. He asked me whether I
knew any young artists who might be hired to do illustrations. I named two
or three people in Moscow and gave him the address of my niece, who was
then living in Petersburg. The Sail took her on board; she met Gorky in its
offices and quickly became a regular visitor to his always bustling, perpetually crowded apartment.

In the fall of 1918, when Gorky was organizing the famous World Literature publishing house, I was summoned to Petersburg and offered the job of
managing its Moscow branch. After accepting the offer, I felt I ought to meet
Gorky personally. He came out to greet me looking like a learned Chinaman
in a red silk robe and motley skullcap; he had prominent cheekbones, large
glasses perched on the tip of his nose, and a book in his hands. To my astonishment, he showed no interest in talking about the publishing house. I got
the impression that in this business his name served only as window dressing.

I stayed on in Petersburg for a week and a half. The city was dead
and oppressive. Occasional streetcars crawled lazily down the streets past
boarded-up stores. The unheated buildings reeked of preserved fish.
There was no electricity. But in Gorky's dining room on Kronverksky
Prospect there was a large kerosene lamp, and every evening people

gathered around it. A. N. Tikhonov was there, and Z. I. Grzhebin, who ran things at World Literature. Chaliapin would arrive noisily, cursing the Bolsheviks. Once Krasin* appeared—in a tailcoat, from some "diplomatic" dinner—though I can't imagine what diplomacy could have been in process at that time. Maria Fyodorovna Andreyeva† would come out to greet the guests with her secretary, P. P. Kriuchkov‡. The wife of one of the members of the imperial family would appear; her husband lay sick in the recesses of Gorky's apartment, in a room with a large portrait of Gorky painted by my niece. When asked whether I might come in, he held out his feverish hand to me, while a bulldog that had been wrapped in a blanket to keep him from attacking growled and struggled next to the bed.

In the dining room the talk was all about the famine and the civil war. Drumming on the table with his fingers and gazing over the head of his interlocutor, Gorky said: "Yes, they're bad; things are bad"—and it was not clear for whom things were bad and whom he sympathized with. In general

---

* L. B. Krasin (1870–1926), commissar of foreign trade in the earlier postrevolutionary years, later ambassador to Great Britain and then to France.

† Andreyeva (1868–1953), an actress who played major roles in several of Gorky's plays, was in effect his second wife—"in effect" since he had never divorced his first wife, Ekaterina Pavlovna Peshkova, from whom he parted in 1904. It was Andreyeva's presence as his companion in New York in April 1906 that led to a public scandal, prompting William Dean Howells to cancel a dinner in the Russian writer's honor and Mark Twain to withdraw his previously expressed support for Gorky's anti-tsarist fundraising. After the revolution Andreyeva held a variety of administrative and political posts.

‡ Petr Petrovich Kriuchkov (1889–1938) was at this time Andreyeva's secretary in the Petersburg Theatrical Administration and, Khodasevich recalls, living in her half of Gorky's apartment. When Gorky went abroad in 1921, Khodasevich writes, Andreyeva soon followed, bringing Kriuchkov with her, "to keep an eye on [Gorky's] political behavior and his expenditures." She used her influence to get Kriuchkov named head of the Mezhdunarodnaia Kniga publishing enterprise, so that he "almost automatically became Gorky's publisher and the go-between in his dealings with Soviet magazines and publishers." Thus he became "the chief source and overseer of [Gorky's] finances." (Khodasevich, "O smerti Gor'kogo," in *Nekropol.' Literatura i vlast.' Pis'ma B.A. Sadovskomu* [Moscow: SS, 1996], 211–12.) In 1932, when Gorky decided to move back to the Soviet Union for good, Kriuchkov became his secretary—and, by all indications, the agent of Yagoda, head of the GPU. After Gorky's death he was charged with conspiring to assassinate Gorky and executed.

he tried to cut these conversations short. Then people would sit down to play lotto, and the game would go on for a long time. And then, through the foul Petersburg night, to the crackling of distant gunfire, my niece and I would return to our lodgings in Bolshaya Monetnaya street.

Soon after, Gorky came to Moscow. The All-Russian Union of Writers had been recently formed, and I was charged with inviting Gorky to join. He agreed on the spot and signed an application to which, according to the bylaws, two members of the administration had to add their recommendation. These were duly signed by [the poet] Iu. K. Baltrushaitis and myself. This amusing document can probably be found in the union's archive, if the latter has survived.

In the summer of 1920 a calamity befell me. It was discovered that one of the medical commissions that examined men called up for the war had been taking bribes. Several of the doctors were shot, and everyone they had exempted from service was reexamined. I wound up among these unfortunates, all of whom the new commission—too terrified even to consider any evidence to the contrary—now certified as fit for service. I was given two days' notice, after which I was to leave the sanatorium directly for Pskov, and from there into combat. By chance Gorky turned up in Moscow. He instructed me to write Lenin a letter which he himself then took to the Kremlin. I was examined yet again—and, of course, exempted. As he was leaving, Gorky said: "You'd better move to Petersburg. Here a person has to serve, but there he can still write."

I took his advice and in the middle of November settled in Petersburg. By this time Gorky's apartment had become extremely crowded. Gorky's new secretary, Maria Ignatievna Benkendorf (later Baroness Budberg),*

---

* Budberg (1892–1974), known as Moura, was Gorky's secretary, translator, and lover from this point until his return to the Soviet Union. Generally believed to have been a double agent (for British as well as Soviet intelligence), she was a strong and colorful woman who had been romantically involved with the British diplomat Bruce Lockhart before she met Gorky, as she was with H. G. Wells afterward. See Nina Berberova, *Moura: The Dangerous Life of the Baroness Budberg*, trans. Marian Schwartz and Richard Sylvester (New York: New York Review Books, 2005), an abbreviated version of her *Železnaia ženščina* (New York: Russica, 1981).

was living there, and so were a little medical student nicknamed The Mole-
cule (a wonderful girl, the orphaned daughter of some old acquaintances
of Gorky's), the painter Ivan Nikolayevich Rakitsky, and, finally, my niece
and her husband. It was the presence of the last two that determined once
and for all the nature of my relationship with Gorky, which, rather than official or literary, was wholly informal and personal. Of course literary matters figured at the time and afterward, but they were always secondary; it
could hardly have been otherwise, given the difference in our ages and our
literary opinions.

A crush of people filled the apartment from early morning to late at
night. Each of the people who lived there had visitors, and Gorky himself
was positively besieged by them. They came on business from the House
of Art, the House of Writers, the House of Scholars, World Literature.
Writers and scholars from Petersburg and from out of town kept arriving;
workers and sailors came, seeking protection from Zinoviev, the all-
powerful commissar of the Northern Region*; actors came, along with
artists, speculators, former dignitaries, and high-society ladies. They asked
him to intercede for people who had been arrested, to arrange for rations,
apartments, clothing, medicines, cooking oil, railroad tickets, official trips,
tobacco, writing paper, ink, dentures for the old and milk for the
newborn—in short, for everything that couldn't be gotten without influence. Gorky heard them all out and wrote innumerable letters of recommendation. Only once did I see him refuse anyone. That was when the
clown Delvari insisted that Gorky be the godfather of his future son. Gorky
came out to him all red in the face and coughing, pumped his hand for a
long time, and finally said: "I've thought over your request. I'm really very
flattered, you know. All the same, I really am awfully sorry, you know. But
I can't. It just won't work, don't ask me why. You must forgive me." And
with a wave of his arm, he bolted from the room in embarrassment.

* Grigory Yevseyevich Zinoviev (1883–1936) was head of the Comintern (1919–26),
Politburo member, and Party boss of Petrograd, where he showed unremitting emnity
toward Gorky. He perished in the first of the great purges of the 1930s.

My place was a great distance from Gorky's. It was exhausting to walk those streets at night, and not without its dangers from muggers. For that reason I often stayed the night, sleeping on an ottoman in the dining room. In late evening the bustle would die down; then the family would gather for tea. I became the latest listener to those reminiscences of which Gorky was particularly fond and which he always trotted out when he wanted to charm a newcomer. In time I came to see that there was a limited number of these and that, though they sounded like improvisations, they got repeated word for word from year to year. Many times I have come across accounts by casual visitors to Gorky, and laughed each time when I came across the stereotyped phrase: "Alexei Maximovich's thoughts can turn suddenly to the past, and then he involuntarily surrenders to the power of his memories." Be that as it may, these sham improvisations were splendidly done. I listened to them with pleasure, puzzled as to why his other listeners were winking to each other and wandering off, one after another, to their rooms. I confess that later on I did the same thing myself, but in those early times I loved the late-night hours when Gorky and I would stay on, just the two of us, by the cold samovar. It was in those hours that we gradually grew close.

Gorky's relations with Zinoviev were bad, and worsening by the day. Things reached a point where Zinoviev ordered searches of Gorky's apartment and threatened to arrest certain people who were close to him. But communists hostile to Zinoviev did sometimes gather at Gorky's, too, their gatherings camouflaged as inconsequential drinking sessions by having others present as well. I happened to attend one of them in the spring of 1921. Lashevich, Ionov, and Zorin were there. At the end of dinner a fairly tall, well-built, blue-eyed young man in a well-fitting soldier's blouse left the other end of the table and sat down next to me. He said a lot of flattering things and quoted my poems from memory. We parted friends. The next day I learned that that had been Bakayev.*

The hostility between Gorky and Zinoviev (which was to play an

---

* Deputy chairman of the Petrograd Soviet. The other three were lower-level government officials.

important role in my life as well) ended by forcing Gorky, in the fall of 1921, to leave not only Petersburg but Soviet Russia. He went to Germany. In July of 1922 personal circumstances led me there also. I lived for a while in Berlin, but in October Gorky persuaded me to move to the little town of Saarow, near Fürstenwald. He lived in the sanatorium there, and I in a little hotel next to the station. We met each day, sometimes as many as two or three times. In the spring of 1923 I moved into the same sanatorium. This Saarow routine broke off in the summer, when Gorky and his family moved to the vicinity of Freiburg. I think this may have been for political reasons, though officially it was all explained as having to do with his illness.

We parted. In the fall I traveled to Freiburg for a few days and then, in November, to Prague. Shortly after that Gorky, too, came to Prague, putting up at the Hotel Beranek, where I was staying. However, we were both drawn to more out-of-the-way places, and at the beginning of December we moved to empty, snowbound Marienbad. At that time we were both applying for visas to Italy. Mine came through in March of 1924, and since I was almost out of money I hastened to leave without waiting for Gorky. After spending a week in Venice and three weeks or so in Rome, I left Rome on April 13; Gorky was due to arrive that evening. Financial matters forced me to stay in Paris till August, and then in Ireland. Finally, at the beginning of October, we met up with each other in Sorrento, where we lived under the same roof until April 18, 1925. After that I never saw him again.

In all, my acquaintance with Gorky lasted seven years. If I tally the months I lived as a member of his household, they amount to about a year and a half—which gives me grounds for thinking that I knew him well and that I know a good deal about him. It is not my purpose here to record everything I remember, both because that would take up too much space and because I would have to touch too closely on matters involving people who are still living. That last consideration forces me, incidentally, to avoid almost entirely an important aspect of Gorky's life: I mean the whole area of his political views, relations, and actions. I cannot say all that I know and think at this moment, and to speak by innuendo would be unworthy. So I offer only a cursory sketch, comprised of a few observations and thoughts which I believe may be of some help in understanding Gorky as a person. I even make bold to suppose that these observations might prove helpful for the understanding of that side of his life and activity which I do not intend to go into here.

■

The greater part of my association with Gorky took place in a more or less rural setting, where the basic character of a man is not obscured by the exigencies of urban living. For that reason I will begin by speaking of the most external features of his life, his daily habits.

His day began early. He got up around eight in the morning and, after drinking coffee and swallowing two raw eggs, worked without a break until one in the afternoon. Dinner was usually at 1 and, with after-dinner conversation, took about an hour and a half. After that people would start trying to drag Gorky out for a walk, which he would do his best to get out of. After the walk he hurried to his work table again, and stayed there until about seven in the evening. The table was always large and spacious, with his writing instruments arranged in perfect order. Alexei Maximovich was a lover of good paper, different colored pencils, new pens and holders (he never used a fountain pen). At hand also was a supply of cigarettes and a motley collection of mouthpieces, red, yellow, and green. He smoked a great deal.

The hours between the walk and supper were mostly given over to correspondence and to the reading of the countless manuscripts that kept arriving. All letters, except for the most absurd, he answered immediately. All the manuscripts and books, sometimes in several volumes, he read with astonishing attention, setting forth his opinions in the most detailed letters to their authors. On the manuscripts he not only made marginal comments but also carefully corrected misspellings with a red pencil and added punctuation. He treated books the same way: with the vain stubbornness of the most diligent proofreader he corrected all their misprints. Sometimes he would do the same with newspapers—and then throw them away.

Supper was served around seven; then tea and general conversation, which oftener than not was followed by card playing, either 501 (in the words of the poet Derzhavin, "penny ante and nothing back") or bridge. In the latter case what occurred, strictly speaking, was his slapping down of the cards, because Gorky didn't have—and could not have had—the foggiest idea of the game: he was absolutely without mathematical skills or any memory for cards. Playing—or more often throwing down—the thirteenth trick, he would sometimes ask, timidly and gloomily: "Excuse me, what were trumps?"

This would prompt loud laughter, to which he would respond by taking umbrage and getting angry. He also got angry at constantly losing, and that might just be the reason he liked bridge better than other games. His partners were a different story. They came up with all kinds of excuses for not playing, until at length it became necessary to formalize the obligation: when bridge was played, they took turns.

Around midnight he would go to his room, put on his red dressing gown, and either write or read in bed, which was always simple and neat, hospital-like. He slept little and spent a good ten hours a day—sometimes more—working. He didn't like lazy people; he had a right not to.

Over the course of his life he read a colossal number of books and remembered everything in them. His memory was astounding. Sometimes in discussing a question he would begin spouting quotations and statistical data. When asked how he knew those things, he would shrug his shoulders in surprise:

"What do you mean? How could anyone not know? There was an article about it in *The Messenger of Europe* for 1887, the October issue."

He took every scientific article as gospel; on the other hand, he was mistrustful of fiction, since he suspected all fiction writers of distorting reality. Regarding literature as in part something like a reference book on matters of daily life, he became positively furious whenever he found some inaccuracy in the depiction of quotidian facts. When Nazhivin's three-volume novel about Rasputin came, he picked up a pencil and sat down to read. I made fun of him, but he labored honestly for some three days. Finally he declared that the book was disgusting. Why? It turns out that the heroes of Nazhivin's novel, living in Nizhnii Novgorod, go off to have dinner on a steamship that has come from Astrakhan. At first I couldn't see what had upset him. I said that I myself had had occasion to dine on Volga steamships tied up at the pier. "But that's before a trip, not after!" he shouted. "After a trip the buffet doesn't operate! You've got to know those things!"

He died from inflammation of the lungs. There was undoubtedly a connection between his final illness and the tuberculosis he contracted in youth. But the tuberculosis had been treated a good forty years before, and if there were reminders of it in his cough, bronchitis, and pleurisies, it was nevertheless not as serious as commentators constantly made it out to be, or as the public thought. In general he was strong and energetic; it is not by mere luck that he lived to sixty-eight. The legend of his serious illness was something he had long since learned to use any time he didn't want to make a trip or, conversely, if he needed to go somewhere. On the pretext of sudden illness he would decline to participate in various meetings or to receive unwelcome visitors. But at home, with his intimates, he didn't like speaking about illness even when it was real. Physical pain he bore with remarkable courage. In Marienbad when he had teeth extracted he refused any anesthetic and never once complained. One time, back in Petersburg, he had been traveling on a packed streetcar, standing on the bottom step. A soldier jumped on while the streetcar was moving at full speed and landed hard on Gorky's foot with his iron-shod heel, shattering the little toe. Gorky didn't even go to a doctor, but for the better part of the next three years he would periodically give himself over to a strange evening activity, pulling shards of bone out of the wound with his own hand.

■

For over thirty years rumors about the luxurious life of Maxim Gorky have circulated in Russian society. I can't speak about the time before I knew him, but I can state categorically that in the years of my closeness to him any talk of luxury of any sort would have been preposterous. All those old wives' tales about the villas Gorky owned and the near-orgies that went on in them are a lie, and a ridiculous one, sparked by literary envy and spread out of political enmity. The man in the street was not only ready to believe this gossip but refused to let it go. Its persistence has been astonishing, an irritant that people seem to have hung onto and cherished like an emotional wound—for the thought of Gorky's luxurious way of life offended a lot of them. Journalists have returned to the theme every time they have had occasion to write about Gorky. In 1927–28 I pointed out several times to the late A. A. Yablonovsky that he shouldn't write about the fairytale villa on Capri, if only because Gorky was living in Sorrento, because it was already fifteen years since he had set foot on Capri, and because in fact he had been given his Italian visa on the express condition that he not live on Capri. Yablonovsky listened, nodded, and shortly thereafter started up with the old story again because he didn't like destroying popular illusions.

It is true that in recent years the villa in Sorrento has sometimes replaced the one on Capri, but even more luxury has been imputed to the life imagined as taking place in it, and that has called forth even greater indignation. At this point I must make a public confession: this ill-starred villa was rented not only with my help, but even at my insistence. When he came to Sorrento in the spring of 1924, Gorky had settled into a large, uncomfortable, run-down villa which, being slated for reconstruction, was let to him only until December. It was there that I found him. As the time to move out approached, the search for a new haven began. Since it gets quite cold in Sorrento in winter, the idea was to move to the southern slope of the peninsula, in the vicinity of Amalfi. There a villa was found which they were on the point of taking. Maxim, Gorky's son from his first marriage, went to look at it one more time and, having nothing else to do, I went with him. The villa turned out to be standing on a tiny ledge of rock; beneath its southern facade was a sheer drop of some hundred yards, straight into the sea; the northern facade was separated only by a narrow strip of road from an enormous rock that not only jutted out at right angles, but overhung the road as well. This rock was constantly crumbling, as is the whole Amalfi shoreline. Seven months before, the villa we were thinking of moving into still stood at the western edge of a little village which had been literally crushed by the last landslide and carried off into the sea. I remembered this well because at the time it happened I had been in Rome. About a hundred people died in the catastrophe. Army engineers had dug out those who had been buried alive; the king himself paid a visit. By some miracle the villa survived, hanging over the newly formed precipice so that now its eastern facade too looked into an abyss whose bottom remained strewn with chunks of trees, brick and iron. I announced to Maxim that I valued my life and that I would not live there. Maxim knit his brows: there were no other villas available. We drove to Amalfi, and as we were returning some two hours later we were obliged to stop a kilometer from "our" villa. The road was being cleared: while we'd been having our lunch another landslide had occurred.

There was nothing for it but to rent Il Sorito, the villa that was fated to become Gorky's last refuge in Italy. It was not in Sorrento proper but a kilometer and a half outside it, on the Capo di Sorrento. Elegant to look at and beautifully situated, with a marvelous view of the whole bay—Naples, Vesuvius, Castellamare—it had serious shortcomings on the inside: there was very little furniture, and it was cold. We moved in on November 16 and froze terribly all winter, stoking the few fireplaces with damp olive branches. But it had the advantage of being cheap; the rent was six thousand lira a year, which at the time was equivalent to five thousand francs. On the top floor was a dining room, Gorky's room (bedroom and study together), the room of his secretary, Baroness M. I. Budberg, the room of N. N. Berberova, my room, and one more, a small one, for guests. Downstairs, on both sides of a little hall, were two more rooms, one of them occupied by Maxim and his wife, the other by I. N. Rakitsky, a painter, a sickly and uncommonly sweet man; back in Petersburg, in 1918, while serving as a soldier, he had come to Gorky's to warm up because he was ill— and more or less accidentally remained in the house year after year. To this core population must be added my niece, who lived in Il Sorito all of January and afterward would occasionally visit from Rome, and also E. P. Peshkova, Gorky's first wife, who would come from Moscow for two weeks at a time. Sometimes people staying nearby in the Hotel Minerva would call: the writer Andrei Sobol, who had arrived from Moscow to recover after a suicide attempt; Professor Starkov with his family (from Prague); and [the writer and art critic] P. P. Muratov. Sometimes the two young ladies who owned the villa and kept a part of the lower story for themselves would drop in for evening tea.

Life was different on the two floors. The top floor was where work got done; on the lower one (which Alexei Maximovich called the nursery) people played. Maxim was then close to thirty, but his behavior made him seem closer to thirteen. With his wife, a very pretty and kind woman whose nickname in the house was Timosha, he would occasionally have disagreeements of an entirely innocent kind. Timosha had a talent for painting. Maxim himself liked to draw things. It would happen that both of them might need the same pencil or eraser at the same moment.

"That's my pencil!"

"No, it's mine!"

"No, it's mine!"

Hearing the noise, Rakitsky would appear, followed through the doorway by clouds of smoke—he never aired out his room because fresh air gave him headaches. "Fresh air is poison for the organism," he would say. Standing in the smoke, he would shout:

"Maxim, give the pencil back to Timosha this minute!"

"But I need it!"

"Give it back to her this minute; you're older so you should let her have it!"

Maxim hands over the pencil and leaves, pouting. But in five minutes he has forgotten the whole thing and is whistling and dancing.

He was a fine fellow, cheerful and easy to get along with. He liked the Bolsheviks a lot, not out of conviction but because he'd grown up among them and they had always pampered him. He called Lenin "Vladimir Ilyich" and Dzerzhinsky "Felix Edmundovich," but it would have been more in character if he had called them Uncle Volodya and Uncle Felix. He dreamed of going back to the USSR because they'd promised to give him an automobile there; it was the object of his passionate daydreams, and sometimes even of his dreams at night. For the time being he took care of his motorcycle, collected stamps, read detective novels, and went to the movies—which, on his return, he would recapitulate scene by scene, imitating his favorite actors, especially the comedians. He himself had a re-markable talent for buffoonery, and if ever he had needed to work he could have made a first-class professional clown. But he had never done anything in his life. Viktor Shklovsky* nicknamed him the Soviet prince. He was the apple of Gorky's eye, but the love Gorky felt for him was an animal sort of love, arising from his concern that Maxim be alive, well, and happy.

Sometimes Maxim would put one or two of us in the sidecar of his mo-torcycle and we would drive around the neighborhood or simply into Sor-rento to drink coffee. Once we all went to the movies. On Christmas Eve in the children's half of the house there was a tree with gifts; I got a deck of cards for solitaire, and Alexei Maximovich got long underwear. About once a month, when things had become very dull, Maxim would buy two bottles of Asti, a bottle of orange liqueur, and some candy—and invite everyone to his room in the evening. They would dance to phonograph records, Maxim would clown, there would be charades followed by group singing. If Alexei Maximovich got stubborn and refused to go sleep, after a while they would start singing "The Sun Rises and Sets." At first he would implore them, "Stop it, you devils!"—and then he'd get to his feet and slink upstairs.

To be sure, this tranquil routine did get diversified every Saturday. In the morning someone would be sent to the Hotel Minerva to order seven baths, and from about three until dinner time, at regular intervals, people would be crossing the road to and from the hotel, carrying bathrobes, tow-els, and implements for scrubbing. At supper they would inquire of each other how their baths had been, consume a ravioli soup that our ladies had prepared, and praise the efficient patroness of the Minerva, Signora Cac-cacce, whose name Alexei Maximovich insisted on treating as a Russian adverb.[†]

When I got to Paris I was informed that Gorky lived on Capri and spent his time in something close to orgies.

■

* Viktor Borisovich Shklovsky (1893–1984), brilliant critic and theoretician of litera-ture, an emigrant in the early 1920s, subsequently returned to the Soviet Union.

† Evidently associating it with the Russian verb *kakat,* '"to shit."

Only by living in his house could you get a true notion of how famous he was all over the world. Not a single one of the Russian writers I have met could compare with him in this regard. He received an enormous number of letters in all languages. Wherever he appeared, strangers would come up to him asking for his autograph. Interviewers besieged him. In the hotels where he was staying newspaper reporters would book rooms for two or three days just to get a glimpse of him in the garden or at the table d'hôte. Fame brought him a lot of money; he earned close to ten thousand dollars a year, of which he spent only a tiny portion on himself. His tastes in food, drink, and clothing were far from fancy. Besides cigarettes, a glass of vermouth at the corner cafe on the only square in Sorrento, or a cab home from town, I can't think of a single expenditure of a personal nature. But the circle of people permanently dependent on him was very large—some fifteen individuals in Russia and abroad at the very least. They came from the most varied strata of society, all the way up to titled émigrés, and their relations to him were highly varied: the spectrum ran from blood relatives and in-laws to people he had never set eyes on. Whole families lived lives at his expense that were much more free and easy than his. Besides the regular pensioners there were many casual ones—including, incidentally, some émigré writers who from time to time applied to him for help.

No one was ever refused. Gorky handed out money without considering the real need of the applicant or what the money would be used for. The money might never reach its final destination; Gorky would pretend not to notice. Nor was this all. Certain individuals in his entourage, making use of his name and situation, engaged in the most reprehensible activities, even including extortion. Those same individuals, at times fiercely hostile to each other because of Gorky's money, kept a keen eye out to ensure that Gorky's public behavior remained sufficiently profitable, and tried, through concerted efforts and friendly pressure, to guide that behavior. Occasionally Gorky would rebel, but he always ended by giving in. The reasons for that were in part the simplest psychological ones: habit, attachment, a desire to be left alone to work. But the chief reason—the most important one, of which he himself was probably unaware—had a particular and very important source: that exceptionally tangled attitude to truth and falsehood which showed itself very early and exercised a decisive influence both on his works and on his life as a whole.

He grew up and lived for a long time amid all sorts of vile behavior. The people he saw were sometimes its perpetrators, sometimes its victims, but most often they were both. It is natural that he should have been led (partly through reading) to dream of different and better people. Later he learned to detect the rudiments of different and better people in some of those around him. By mentally cleansing these rudiments of the savagery, crudity, spite, and dirt that clung to them, and developing them in his writing, he came up with the half-real, half-imaginary type of noble hobo who was essentially a cousin of the noble brigand celebrated in romantic literature.

He received his initial literary education among people who saw the meaning of literature only in the accuracy of its descriptive detail and social observation. In Gorky's own view his hero could carry social significance— and hence literary legitimacy—only against the background of reality and as an integral part of it. So Gorky began placing his not-very-real heroes against a background of particularly realistic settings. For the public and for himself he had to pretend to be a chronicler of everyday events. He himself half-believed in that half-truth all his life.

Philosophizing and speaking through his characters, Gorky endowed them in the highest degree with the dream of a better life—the dream, that is, of finding a moral-social truth that might cast its radiance over everything and arrange everything for the good of humanity. In the beginning Gorky's heroes didn't yet know what that truth consisted of—any more than he did himself. For a time he sought and failed to find it in religion. In the first years of the century he saw (or was taught to see) an earnest of it in social progress, understood according to Marx. And if he didn't manage to make himself a genuine, disciplined Marxist either then or later, he nonetheless adopted Marxism as his official faith, or as a working hypothesis on which he sought to base his work as an artist.

These are my recollections of Gorky, not an article about his works. Still, before returning to my principal subject, I need to pause over what is quite possibly the best thing he ever wrote and certainly one that is central to his work—his play *The Lower Depths.*

Its basic theme is truth and falsehood. Its chief protagonist is the wanderer Luka, "the wily old man," who appears in order to captivate the denizens of the "lower depths" with the comforting lie that somewhere there actually exists a realm of righteousness. In his presence living is easier—and dying, too; when he disappears, life again turns evil and frightening.

Luka has put Marxist critics to a lot of trouble trying to convince their readers that he is a pernicious personality who infects the have-nots with dreams that distract them from reality and from the only thing that could procure for them a better future—the class struggle. In a way the Marxists are right: Luka, with his faith in the improvement of society through the improvement of the individual, must in fact seem pernicious from their point of view. Gorky foresaw this and so, as a corrective, juxtaposed to Luka the character of Satin, who personifies the awakening of proletarian consciousness. It is Satin who, so to speak, voices the play's intended message. "Lies are the religion of slaves and masters; truth is the god of the free man," he proclaims. But if we look at the play more closely, we notice immediately that the figure of Satin is pallid by comparison with the figure of Luka; it has been created without love.

Gorky's positive hero is a less successful figure than the negative one because Gorky endowed the former with his official ideology, and infused the latter with his own instinctive feeling of love and pity for people. It is remarkable that, in anticipation of the accusations that were later to be leveled against Luka, Gorky should have made Satin and no one else his defender. When the other characters of the play curse Luka, Satin shouts at them: "Silence! You're all animals! Fools! Enough about the old man! . . . The old man is not a charlatan . . . I understand the old man . . . Yes! He was lying . . . But it was out of pity for you, devil take you! There are many people who lie out of pity for their fellows . . . There are lies that console, lies that reconcile." It is even more noteworthy that Satin ascribes his own awakening to the influence of Luka: "The old man? He is a clever one! He has acted on me like acid on an old and filthy coin . . . Let's drink to his health!"

The famous phrase—"Man, that is glorious! That has a proud ring!"—is also put in the mouth of Satin. But the author for his part was aware that it had a most bitter ring as well. Running through his whole life is a piercing note of pity for man, whose fate seemed to him hopeless. The one salvation he could see for man lay in creative energy, which involves by definition the constant overcoming of reality by hope. He had no very high estimate of man's ability to make his hopes come true, but the very capacity for dreaming, the gift of dreaming, set him to trembling with rapture. To create any sort of dream capable of captivating humanity was in his eyes a true sign of genius, and he regarded the promotion of such a dream as a profoundly humane thing.

> Gentlemen! If the world cannot find
> The way to holy truth,
> Then honor to the madman who
> Brings to mankind a golden dream.

These rather weak but quite expressive verses pronounced by one of the characters of *The Lower Depths* amount to a kind of motto defining Gorky's whole life as a writer, as a public figure, and as an individual. Gorky was fated to live in an age when the "golden dream" came down to a dream of social revolution as panacea for all human suffering. He subscribed to this myth and became its spokesman not because he believed so firmly in revolution but because he believed in the saving power of the dream as such. In another time he would have defended other beliefs and other hopes just as passionately. He passed through the Russian liberation movement, and then through the revolution, as a fomentor and upholder of the dream—as Luka, the wily wanderer. From his early story, written in 1893, about the lofty siskin "who lied" and that lowly "lover of truth," the woodpecker, his life and work alike testify to a sentimental love for all kinds of lies and a stubborn, persistent dislike for truth. "I hate the truth most sincerely and unshakably," he wrote to E. D. Kuskova in 1929.* I can close my eyes and see him bristling, his face angry, the vein in his neck bulging, as he pens those words.

■

On 13 July 1924 he wrote me from Sorrento: "It's the season of festivals here—fireworks, processions, music and 'popular rejoicing' just about every day. 'While back in Russia . . . ?' I ask myself. And then—forgive me!—I am overcome with such a mixture of envy, pain, nausea, etc., that I want to weep and howl with rage."

He adored Italian festivities with their music, flags, and the crackle of fireworks. In the evenings he would go out on the balcony and summon everyone to see the rockets and Roman candles flashing around the bay. Rubbing his hands in excitement, he would cry out: "That's at the Torre Annunciata! And that one's near Herculaneum! And that one over there's in Naples! Lord, lord, lord, look at them go!"

The fact is that this "great realist" truly liked only what embellishes reality, or distracts from it, or takes no account of it, or simply supplies something that is not to be found in it. I have heard not a few writers express pride in the fact that Gorky wept as he listened to their works. Actually, they had nothing special to be proud of, since I can't think of anything he did *not* cry over—except, of course, for the sheerest nonsense. Not infrequently it would happen that, after reflecting a little on what had made him cry, he himself would disparage it—but his first reaction was almost always tearful.

---

* Ekaterina Dmitrievna Kuskova (1869–1958) was a Socialist activist and friend of Gorky's from the early 1890s in Nizhnii Novgorod. Exiled in 1922, she lived in Berlin, Prague, and Geneva. The letter Khodasevich cites was written from Sorrento and dated 22 January 1929. The passage in question reads: "I most sincerely and unshakably hate the truth, 99 percent of which is an abomination and a lie. You probably know that when I was in Russia [in 1928] I spoke out . . . against 'self-criticism,' against the deafening and blinding of people with the foul and poisonous dust of everyday truth. I did not, of course, succeed. But that doesn't diminish my ardor; I know that that truth is harmful for the 150 million-strong Russian people, and that people need a different truth, one that would raise instead of lowering the level of their energy for work and creation." (Ek. Kuskova, "Tragedija Maksima Gor'kogo," *Novyj Žurnal* 28 [1954]: 241.)

What shook and moved him was not so much the quality of what he read as the mere presence of creativity, of something that had been imagined, called into being, and written down. Mayakovsky once announced in print that he was ready to sell a waistcoat Maxim Gorky had wept on for a song; that was a base thing to do, because it amounted to sneering at the best and purest impulse of Gorky's soul. He was not ashamed of crying over his own writings too: the second half of every story he read me was invariably drowned in sobs, snuffling, and the wiping of his fogged-up glasses.

He was particularly partial to young beginning writers; their hopes for the future and dreams of fame pleased him. He was reluctant to discourage even those who were outright bad and plainly hopeless; he thought it blasphemous to destroy illusions of any sort. The main thing was that with a beginning writer—again, even the most unpromising—he was cherishing a dream of his own, happy to be keeping the writer company in his self-deception. Remarkably enough, he treated established writers quite differently. The truly outstanding ones he liked (for example, Bunin, whom he understood) or tried to make himself like (for example, Blok, whom he basically did not understand but whose significance he could not help but feel). On the other hand, he had little liking for authors who were already out of swaddling clothes and had managed to acquire a certain position but had failed to prove really first-rate. He seemed to be angry at them because you could no longer dream of how they might take flight, become remarkable or even great. He was particularly annoyed in the case of these middling writers by their self-importance, Olympian pose, and sense of their own significance—traits which in fact characterize them more often than they do genuinely outstanding writers.

He liked all people of creative temperament, anyone who brought (or merely dreamed of bringing) something new into the world. The content and quality of that innovation was of secondary importance; his imagination was equally stirred by poets and scholars, devisers of impracticable schemes, and inventors (up to and including inventors of perpetual motion machines). Related to this tendency was a positive fondness, ardent and tinged with glee, for people who violated or sought to violate the established order of the world. The range of this fondness may even have been broader, extending from those who purported to transgress the laws of nature (that is, magicians and card sharps) to those who worked to bring about the profoundest social transformations. This is not to say that a fairground buffoon and a great revolutionary had the same value in his eyes; but it is clear to me that, while regarding them differently with his mind, he loved them both with one and the same part of his soul. It is no accident that in *The Lower Depths* he did not hesitate to make Satin, his positive hero and the spokesman for a new social truth, a card sharp.

He liked anyone, absolutely anyone, who brings an element of rebellion, or just of mischief into the world—up to and including compulsive arsonists, about whom he wrote a lot and could talk for hours on end. He himself had a bit of the arsonist in him. Never once after lighting a cigarette did I see him put out the match: he invariably left it burning. It was a favorite and daily habit of his after dinner or at evening tea, when the ashtray was full enough of cigarette butts, matches and papers, to imperceptibly edge a lighted match into it. Then he would try to distract the attention of those present while slyly glancing over his shoulder at the bonfire that was erupting. These little family conflagrations, as I once proposed to call them, seemed to hold some wicked and joyful symbolism for him. He regarded attempts to split the atom with great respect, saying often that if they succeeded, then, for example, from a stone picked up in the road it would be possible to extract a quantity of energy sufficient for interplanetary travel. But he said it somehow lackadaisically, as if reciting from a textbook and only, it seemed, in order to add at the end, his face now animated and cheerful, that "some fine day these experiments, hmmm, well, you understand, may lead to the destruction of our universe. That would be some little fire!" And he'd make a clucking noise with his tongue.

From arsonists through the magnificent Corsican bandits (whom he had not managed to know), his love descended to counterfeiters—of whom there are so many in Italy. Gorky talked about them in detail and even paid a visit to one of their patriarchs in Alessio. After counterfeiters came adven-

turers, swindlers, and thieves of every kind and condition. Some managed
to hang around him all his life. He bore their tricks, which occasionally cast
a shadow on him, with a tolerance bordering on encouragement. I can't recall a single instance when he exposed one of them or expressed the slightest displeasure. A certain Rodé, formerly the owner of a famous café
chantant, invented a whole revolutionary biography for himself. I once
heard him go on solemnly about his "long years of revolutionary work."
Gorky adored him and made him manager of the House of Scholars, which
distributed provisions for the scholars, writers, artists, and actors of Petersburg.* Once when I let myself refer, offhandedly and punningly, to the
House of Scholars as "the Rodé Beneficial Institution," Gorky was peevish
with me for several days.

Petty crooks and cadgers gravitated to him every time he went out on
the street. What he liked in their line of work, just as he did in the work of
magicians, was the interweaving of truth and deception. He lent himself to
their tricks with evident pleasure and would stand there beaming while a
street boy or tradesman tried to palm off some rubbish on him. He particularly appreciated impudence in such affairs, most likely because he saw it as
connected with rebelliousness and mischief. He himself was not above

---

* Anatolii Sergeyevich Rodé (d. 1930) was director of the House of Scholars, which
opened in Petrograd on January 31, 1920. Before the revolution he owned a cabaret called
the Villa Rodé, which featured a Gypsy chorus and private rooms. Viktor Shklovsky offers
this portrait of Rodé in his memoirs of Gorky: "Rodé is a character from a café chantant. . . .
How did Rodé wind up with Gorky? Rodé knew a lot of things, and was a skilled conversa-
tionalist. If you said to Rodé, 'Bring me a rope!' he would call an assistant and say something like: 'Bring me twine #13.' The fact that ropes had numbers and that a culture of ropes
existed astonished Gorky, and Rodé assumed a place among Gorky's necessities." (*Sbornik
statej i vospominanij o M. Gor'kom.* [M-L, 1928], 383.) Chukovsky describes in his diary a
visit to Rodé on 30 April 1921: "To Rodé. A giant, all paunches and chins. Oily black eyes.
At first he shouted, Come back on Tuesday, but then, when he found out that I was leaving
tomorrow, kindly received me and even vouchsafed a conversation. Actually, it was more a
hymn than a conversation—a hymn in praise of one energetic, noble, susceptible, self-
denying person—and that person was Rodé himself.' " (Rossijskaja Akademija Nauk, In-t
mirovoj literatury im. A.M. Gor'kogo, *Neizvestnyj Gor'kij (k 125-letiju so dnja roždenija)*
[= *Gor'kij i ego epoxa, Materialy i issledovanija,* vyp. 3], [Moscow: "Nasledie," 1994], 127.)

trying his hand at the same sort of thing in his domestic circle. For fun we came up with the idea of publishing the *Sorrento Pravda* (Truth), a manuscript newspaper that would parody certain Soviet and émigré newspapers. (We produced three or four issues.) The staff consisted of Gorky, Berberova, and myself. Rakitsky was the illustrator, Maxim the typist. We also elected Maxim editor in view of his extreme literary incompetence. From the start Gorky tried to fool him in any way he could, submitting excerpts from his old writings and pretending that they were unpublished. For him that was the chief pleasure, whereas for Maxim it was catching him at these tricks. In view of his senseless expenditures, the household took away all his money, leaving only small change for out-of-pocket expenses. One day he ran into my room beaming, doing a little dance, rubbing his hands together, and looking for all the world like an apprentice out on a spree.

"Hey!" he announced. "Look at this! I swiped ten lira from Marya Ignatievna! On to Sorrento!"

We walked to Sorrento, had a vermouth there, and came back with a driver we knew who, taking the ill-gotten ten-lira note from the hand of Alexei Maximovich, instead of giving him seven lira in change, lashed his horse and galloped away, cracking the whip, looking back at us, and roaring with laughter. Gorky's eyes grew wide with delight, his eyebrows went up, he laughed, slapping his sides, and was unspeakably happy for the rest of the day.

∎

He never refused his money or good offices to anyone who asked for them. But there was one peculiarity in his charity: the more bitterly the supplicant complained, the more discouraged he was, the cooler Gorky would feel toward him—and not because he required of people firmness or restraint. His demands went much farther: he could not bear depression and demanded that a person hope, no matter what. And in this could be seen his peculiar and stubborn egoism: *in exchange for his kindness he demanded for himself the right to fantasize* a better future for the person he was assisting. And if the petitioner's despair got in the way of such fantasizing, Gorky would grow angry, his help would be reluctant, and his vexation plain to see.

The stubborn admirer and creator of uplifting illusions, he regarded all disillusionment, all low truths, as manifestations of a metaphysically evil principle. A destroyed illusion, like a corpse, triggered squeamishness and terror in him, as if he sensed in it something unclean. This terror, accompanied by animosity, was also evoked in him by anyone guilty of destroying illusions or undermining a good feeling based on a dream—by any disturber of an elevated or festive mood. In the fall of 1920 H. G. Wells came to Petersburg.* At a dinner in his honor Gorky, among others, spoke of the prospects which the young dictatorship of the proletariat was opening to science and art. Suddenly [the writer and journalist] A. V. Amfiteatrov, whom Gorky regarded warmly, stood up and said something that went counter to the preceding speeches.† From that day on Gorky hated him— and not at all because the writer had spoken out against the Soviet regime, but because he had turned out to be the destroyer of a holiday atmosphere, a *trouble-fête.* In *The Lower Depths,* at the very end of the last act, everyone is singing in chorus. Suddenly the door opens and the Baron cries from the threshold: "Hey . . . you! Come over here! In the vacant lot over there . . . The Actor has hanged himself!" In the silence that follows Satin answers

* Wells was in Petersburg in October 1920. He describes his impressions in his book *Russia in the Shadows* (1921).

† Yuri Annenkov cites Amfiteatrov's "nearly hysterical" words:

" 'You,' he said, addressing Wells, 'have eaten cutlets and pastries here— rather primitive ones, to be sure, but you of course did not know that these cutlets and pastries, prepared in your honor, are for us something more attractive and more exciting than our meeting with you, something more seductive than your cigar! It's true that you see us dressed respectably; as you may observe, there is even one tuxedo here. But you surely cannot have realized that many of us—and perhaps those who are most worthy to shake your hand—are absent simply for lack of a decent jacket, and that of those here present not a single one could bring himself to unbutton his waistcoat in your presence, since all he has underneath are filthy rags that used to be called, if I recall correctly, 'undergarments.' "

(Ju. P. Annenkov, "Maksim Gor'kij," *Dnevnik moix vstrech: Tsikl tragedij,* reprinted in *Maksim Gor'kij: Pro et Contra* [Sankt-Peterburg, 1997], 163–64.)

him softly: "Damn. He's spoiled the song, the fool!" With this the curtain falls. It's not clear whom Satin is blaming—the Actor who hanged himself so inopportunely, or the Baron who brought the news of it. Most likely both, because both are guilty of *spoiling the song*.

There you have the whole of Gorky. He felt no compunction, in life any more than in art, about being angry with the bearers of bad news. I once said to him, "You, Alexei Maximovich, are like [Pushkin's] Tsar Saltan:

> In his wrath he started raving
> And ordered that the messenger be hanged.*

He answered, frowning: "A wise tsar. Bringers of bad tidings should be executed."

Perhaps he recalled that conversation of ours when, replying to the "low truths" of Kuskova, he voiced a furious wish that she die as soon as possible.

■

One thing he would never allow himself was to be the messenger of failure or misfortune. If silence was impossible, he preferred to lie, believing sincerely that he was acting humanely.

Baroness Varvara Ivanovna Ikskul was one of those fascinating women capable of charming old and young, rich and poor, celebrities and ordinary people. Among her admirers were foreign sovereigns and Russian revolutionaries. In her salon, which once was famous in Petersburg, she brought together people of the most various parties and positions. It is said that on one occasion she received in her sitting room the fierce minister of internal affairs while sheltering in the depths of her apartment a man the police were seeking. She maintained good relations with the Empress Alexandra Fyodorovna until the very last days of the monarchy. Supporters and enemies alike of Rasputin considered her their own. Needless to say, the revo-

---

* Khodasevich's misquotation. The second line should read: "And wanted to hang the messenger."

lution ruined her. She managed to get quarters in the House of Arts, where I was her frequent guest. Gorky, who, like many others, had received favors from her in the past, asked me about her several times, and I mentioned the fact to her. Once she said: "Ask Alexei Maximovich whether he can't arrange for me to be allowed to go abroad." Gorky answered that this would not be difficult. He instructed Varvara Ivanovna to fill out a form, draft a petition, and enclose photographs. Soon afterward he went to Moscow. This was in the spring of 1921. It's easy to imagine with what impatience Varvara Ivanovna awaited his return. At length he came back, and I went to see him that same day. He announced to me that permission had been granted but that the passport would be ready only "late this afternoon," and that in about two days A. N. Tikhonov would be bringing it. Varvara Ivanovna thanked me with tears I am ashamed to recall. She took steps to sell off some of her possessions; the rest she gave away. Each day I tried to phone Tikhonov. No sooner had he arrived than I went to see him and learned with astonishment that Alexei Maximovich hadn't asked him to do anything, that he was hearing about this matter for the first time. It would not be interesting if I tried to describe my attempts to get an explanation from Gorky, and in any case I don't recall the details. The point is that at first he spoke about "misunderstandings" and promised to make everything right; then he deflected conversations on the subject; and finally he himself went abroad. Varvara Ivanovna, without waiting for a passport, managed to flee—in the winter, with a young boy as guide, across the frozen Gulf of Finland, and from Finland to Paris, where she died in February 1928. A few months after she fled I was in Moscow and learned at the foreign ministry that Gorky had in fact presented her petition but received a categorical denial on the spot.

The point here is not that he was unwilling to admit his powerlessness with the authorities: at the time Gorky even took pleasure in telling about that powerlessness. Knowing Gorky, I have no doubt that he simply wanted to keep up hope in the petitioner as long as possible, and—who knows?—he may also have been using the illusion to comfort himself as well as her. Such "internal theater" would have been entirely in character;

in fact, I know several plays that he staged in that theater. I'll tell here about one of them—the most striking one, in which the creation of a happy illusion passed over into outright cruelty.

Living in Petersburg in the first years of the Soviet regime, Gorky maintained relations with many members of the imperial family. And so it was that on one occasion he sent for Princess Paley, the widow of Grand Duke Pavel Alexandrovich, and announced to her that her son, the young poet Prince Paley, had not been shot but was alive in Ekaterinoslav, and had just sent a letter along with some verses from that city. It is not hard to imagine the mother's astonishment and joy. To her misfortune, she found it all the easier to believe Gorky in view of a coincidence which Gorky himself had not foreseen: the Paley family had some close friends in Ekaterinoslav, and it would have been natural for a young man who escaped execution to take refuge with them. Eventually Princess Paley of course did find out that he had been killed, and thus Gorky's consolatory deception became a source of renewed suffering when she was forced to experience the news of her son's death a second time.

I don't remember what prompted it, but in 1923 he told me this story himself—with some distress (which nonetheless struck me as inadequate). I asked him: "But were there in fact a letter and verses?"

"There were."

"Then why didn't she ask you to show them to her?"

"Indeed she did. But I'd stuck them somewhere and couldn't find them."

I didn't conceal from Gorky how upsetting I found this story, but I could not get him to say what had actually happened. He only threw up his hands, clearly sorry that he had mentioned the matter.

A few months later he gave himself away. He'd gone to Freiburg, and in one of his letters he wrote: "It turns out that the poet Paley is alive, so I did have a certain justification for misleading Countess (sic!) Paley (sic!). I am sending you the verses of said poet, just received; they look bad."

After reading the poems, which were utterly inept, and after making some inquiries, I realized what had happened. Both then (in Petersburg)

and now (in Europe), Gorky had received a letter and poems from the proletarian poet Paley, a worker by birth. Gorky may not have known or remembered him. But neither by content nor form nor orthography nor even
handwriting could the verses of this Paley by any stretch of the imagination
have been taken as the work of the Grand Duke's son. I never saw the letters, but they clearly could have provided even fewer grounds for a good-
faith mistake. Gorky had deliberately deluded himself; by mislaying the
letters and poems he had not only kept them from Princess Paley but, first
and most importantly, from himself, because he had taken it on himself to
stage a devilish tragicomedy for the consolation of an unhappy mother.

Aside from the fact that it would be hard to account for this story in
any other way, I have no doubts about my explanation because I have been
privy to other incidents of precisely the same character.

■

His attitude toward lies and liars was, one might say, careful and solicitous. I never saw him unmask anyone or expose a lie—even the most brazen or
transparent. He was credulous, to be sure—but over and above that he pretended to be credulous. Partly he hated to embarrass the liars, but the main
thing was that he considered it his duty to respect a flight of fancy or a dream
or an illusion, even when it manifested itself in the most pitiable or repugnant
way. I had many occasions to see his delight at being taken in. Therefore it
took no great effort to deceive him, or even to make him the accomplice of a
deception.

Often enough he himself had occasion to tell an untruth. He did this
with astonishing ease, as if sure that no one could or would want to catch
him in the lie. Here is one incident, characteristic in that respect and in the
fact that the lie arose out of a desire to strike a pose—not so much in my
eyes as in his own. I believe in general that most of the time the principal
object of his deceptions was himself.

On 8 November 1923 he wrote me:

Here is shocking news. [The émigré journal] *Nakanune* has published "Michelangelo's Painting of La Gioconda," while in Russia

Nadezhda Krupskaya and a certain M. Speransky have prohibited the reading of Plato, Kant, Schopenhauer, Vl[adimir] Soloviev, Taine, Ruskin, Nietzsche, L. Tolstoy, Leskov, Yasinsky (!), and many similar heretics. And they have added: "The religious section should contain only anti-religious books." All this appears to be* not hearsay but printed in a book entitled *Index to the Removal of Anti-Artistic and Counterrevolutionary Literature from Libraries Serving the Mass Reader.*

I have written in the words "appears to be," for I still cannot force myself to credit this spiritual vampirism, nor will I believe it until I see the *Index.*

My first reaction was to draft a statement to Moscow renouncing my Russian citizenship. What else can I do in the event that this atrocity turns out to be true?

If only you knew, dear V. F., how desperately difficult and painful this is for me!

The only true thing in this letter is that it was "difficult and painful" for him. Learning about the removal of the books, he felt it his duty to protest sharply against this "spiritual vampirism." He even entertained a fantasy about how this protest would take the form of a declaration renouncing his Soviet citizenship. He may even have begun writing such a declaration, but of course he knew that he would never send it, that all this was only "internal theater." And so he resorted to the most naïve lie imaginable: first he wrote me about the appearance of the *Index* as a fait accompli, and then he inserted the words "appears to be" and pretended that the matter needed verifying and that he even "couldn't make [him]self believe" in the existence of the *Index.* Meanwhile he can have had no doubts whatever, because *he had had a copy of that little white volume for quite some time.* Two months before this letter, on 14 September 1923, in Berlin, I visited the

---

* "The words 'appears to be' are inserted above the line" (Khodasevich's note). Four years later Gorky denied, in a letter to Romain Rolland, that any such action had been taken.

publishing house Epokha and met Baroness M. I. Budberg there. The manager of the publishing house, S. G. Sumsky, in my presence handed her that *Index* to give to Alexei Maximovich. That same day Maria Ignatievna and I went to Freiburg together. Immediately on our arrival the *Index* was handed over to Gorky and there was a good deal of talk about it during my three-day stay in Freiburg. But Gorky had forgotten these conversations, along with the fact that I had seen the *Index* in his hands—and now here he was, assuring me in the most nonchalant way that he hadn't yet seen the book and even had doubts about its existence. What is further remarkable in all this is his telling me the whole story about his intention to send a declaration to Moscow for no reason other than the desire to act a part for my benefit, and particularly—I repeat—for his own.

If you caught him in some deviation from the truth he would try to justify himself—helplessly and with embarrassment—more or less as the Baron does in *The Lower Depths*. When the Tartar cries out, "Ha! He's stuck a card in his sleeve!" the Baron answers in embarrassment, "Where would you have me stick it, in your nose?" In such cases he would sometimes have the look of a man unbearably bored in the company of people who do not know how to appreciate him. The exposure of a trivial lie evoked in him the same weary annoyance as the destruction of an exalted fantasy, and reestablishing the truth struck him as the drab and vulgar triumph of prose over poetry. Not for nothing is the champion of truth in *The Lower Depths* Bubnov—a talentless, crude, and tedious character whose very name seems to come from the verb meaning "to drone on" [*bubnit'*].

■

"There are people who are merely people, and there are others who are human beings," the elder Luka says, plainly expressing in this less than crystal-clear formula a clear enough idea of the author's. The point is that "human beings" should be printed with capital letters. Gorky deeply honored "Human Beings," which is to say, heroes, creators, promoters of the progress he worshipped. As for people—mere people, with unremarkable faces and modest biographies—he despised them and called them philistines. He did acknowledge, however, that they too might show a

striving—if not to be better than they were in fact, then at least to seem to
be. As Luka puts it, "People have drab little souls, and they all want to add
a touch of rouge." Gorky looked on that kind of touching-up with genuine,
heartfelt sympathy and considered it his duty not only to support in people
an exalted sense of themselves, but also—as far as possible—to foster such
a sense in them. He evidently thought that self-delusion of that kind could
open a door to, or help along, the process of an individual's overcoming
the philistine in himself. For that reason he liked to serve as a sort of mirror in which each person could see himself more exalted, more noble,
more intelligent, and more talented than in fact he was. Of course the
greater the discrepancy between the reflection and the reality, the more
people were grateful to him, and this was one of the reasons so many
found him charming.

He himself was no exception to the law he had established. There was
a discrepancy between his actual image and the imaginary, so to speak,
ideal one. However, it is quite curious—and highly significant—that in this
case he followed not so much his own imagination as another, collective
one. He often recalled how in the early 1900s, in the period of his initial
and unexpected fame, one small provincial publisher of so-called "books
for the people"—that is, of folk tales, manuals of dream interpretation,
songbooks—tried to persuade him to write an autobiography in that vein,
predicting enormous sales, and big money for the author. "Your life,
Alexei Maximovich, is pure gold," he said. Gorky used to laugh as he related this. Meanwhile, if not then, at least later, and if not in the pulp format
then all the same in a form close to that, the biography of Gorky the untu-
tored genius, Gorky the stormy petrel, Gorky the sufferer and progressive
fighter for the proletariat gradually came into being on its own and took
root in the minds of certain strata of society. There is no denying that all
these heroic features were actually present in his life story, which was by
any standard an unusual one, but fate had not traced them nearly as starkly,
clearly, or strikingly as they came to appear in his ideal or official biography. And so, though I would by no means wish to say that Gorky believed
or was necessarily determined to believe in the latter, still, borne along by

circumstances, fame, and pressure from those around him, he accepted it, and ended by adopting it once and for all, along with his "official" outlook. And once he had done that he became, to a considerable degree, its slave. He felt it his duty to appear before humanity, before "the masses," in that image and pose which those masses expected and demanded from him in exchange for their love. Often—too often—he had occasion to experience himself as a kind of mass illusion, a part of that "golden dream" which, once it existed, he, Gorky, no longer had the right to demolish. Surely the enormous shadow he cast must have pleased him by its size and sharp outlines. But I am not sure that he really liked it. I can in any case attest that it often caused him distress. A great many times, doing something he didn't really want to do or something that went counter to his conscience—or, conversely, refraining from something he wanted to do or that his conscience prompted him to do—he would say glumly, grimacing and shrugging his shoulders in vexation: "I can't, it would spoil the biography." Or: "No help for it, I've got to—it's either that or spoil the biography."

■

For the provincial Alexei Peshkov who received a poor boy's schooling in Nizhnii Novgorod to have become the world-famous writer Maxim Gorky is an enormous achievement, however one may estimate Gorky's talent. It would seem that an awareness of his accomplishment, especially when combined with that constant concern for his "biography," must inevitably have had a pernicious effect on him. But that was not the case. Unlike so many others, he didn't chase after fame or worry about hanging on to it; he did not fear criticism any more than he felt joy at being praised by fools or ignoramuses; he was not on the lookout for confirmations of his fame—perhaps because it was genuine; he was not conceited, nor did he, like many celebrities, play the spoiled child. I have never seen anyone who carried his fame with more skill and nobility than Gorky.

He was exceptionally modest, even on those occasions when he felt satisfied with what he had done. This modesty was unfeigned. It came chiefly from a reverence for literature, and also from a certain diffidence. Having acquired his rather elementary esthetic concepts once and for all (roughly speaking, those that dominated the '70s and '80s), he made a sharp distinction between content and form in his own writings. The content seemed to him unassailable enough because it rested on firmly held social views. But when it came to form, he did not feel himself so well equipped. Comparing himself with his favorite writers, or even with masters he didn't like (for example, Dostoyevsky and Gogol), he found in them a suppleness, complexity, elegance, and subtlety that he himself did not command—as he confessed more than once. I have already mentioned that he would often read his stories aloud with tears in his eyes. But when that emotional excitement had subsided, he would ask for reactions, hear them out gratefully, and, turning a deaf ear to praise, pay attention only to the criticisms. Many times he would defend himself and argue, but just as often he would give in, and once he'd done that, he would invariably make changes and corrections. Thus I convinced him to re-do some things in his "Story About Cockroaches" and completely rewrite the last section of his novel *The Artamonov Business.* There was, though, one area in which he knew he was helpless—and it caused him the most real suffering.

"Tell me, what do you think of my verses? Are they very bad?"

"They're bad, Alexei Maximovich."

"Pity. It's a terrible pity. All my life I've dreamed of writing at least one good poem."

He looked up with his melancholy, faded eyes, and fished out a handkerchief to wipe them.

I was constantly surprised and moved by the winningly human inconsistency with which this most consistent hater of truth suddenly became a lover of truth as soon as his own writings were in question. Then he not only did not wish to be deluded; quite the contrary: he staunchly sought the truth. Once he declared that [the critic] Iu. I. Aikhenvald, who was still alive, had unfairly attacked his new stories as a way of settling political and personal scores. I replied that that was impossible because, while disagreeing with Aikhenvald about many things, I knew him as a critic to be eminently fairminded. This conversation took place at the end of 1923 in Marienbad. At that time Gorky and I were editing the magazine *Beseda* together. The argument reached the point where I, as a kind of wager, proposed that we publish two stories of Gorky's in the next number, one to be signed with his real name, the other with a pseudonym, and see what would happen. In the fourth number of *Beseda* we published "The Story of a Hero" over Gorky's name, and next to it another, called "The Story of a Certain Romance," over the pen name Vasily Sizov. In a few days we received the issue of the Berlin newspaper *Rul,'* in which Sizov was taken to task if anything more than Gorky—and Gorky said to me with real, unfeigned joy: "It's clear that you were right. That's very good, you know. I mean, what's good is not that he attacks me but the fact that I was clearly wrong about him."

Nearly a year later, when we were already in Sorrento, a strange thing happened involving that same story. Andrei Sobol, who had just arrived from Moscow, asked to read all the issues of *Beseda* (which was not being allowed into Soviet Russia). About three days later he brought the magazines back. Dinner was ending, but everyone was still at the table. Sobol began to state his opinions. He praised various things published in *Beseda,* among them Gorky's stories—and suddenly blurted out: "But you made a mistake publishing that fellow Sizov. It's awful rubbish."

I don't remember what Gorky answered, or whether he answered anything, and I can't say what kind of expression he had on his face because I looked away. Before going to sleep I dropped in to Gorky's room for some reason. He was already in bed and said to me from behind the screen: "Don't even think about explaining things to Sobol. We'd be as embarrassed for each other as two naked nuns."

■

Before sending my reminiscences of [the poet] Valery Briusov to the offices of *Sovremennye Zapiski,* I read them to Gorky. When I'd finished there was a brief silence. Then he said:

"It's cruel what you've written—but superb. When I die, write something, please, about me."

"All right, Alexei Maximovich."

"You won't forget?"
"I won't."
    Paris, 1936

◄•►

Four years after Gorky's death, in 1940, Khodasevich published another piece, concentrating on Gorky's relations with Moscow from the time he left Russia in 1921 to his ultimate return a decade later. The crux of Khodasevich's argument is "the eternal, unshakeable ambivalence of his attitudes toward everything connected with the Soviet regime." His conclusion, offered as his "personal opinion about the internal reasons for G's vacillations with regard to the Soviet government," is worth quoting in full:

> Whatever may have been the grounds for Gorky's leaving Russia in 1921, the fundamental reason was in any case the same as for many of us. He had pictured the revolution as a humane thing, bringing freedom. The Bolsheviks gave it quite a different character. Realizing his powerlessness to change anything in that fact, he left, and came close to breaking entirely with the Soviet government—but only so close as a man who holds a revolver to his head, knowing all the same that he will not fire, comes to committing suicide. There is no question but what Mara [Moura Budberg], E. P. Peshkova, and others whom I have not mentioned here in the interests of brevity all contributed considerably to his reconciliation with the regime. But it would have happened even without them, for the reasons lay in Gorky himself. He was one of the most stubborn people I have ever known, but at the same time one of the least steadfast. A great admirer of dreams and of the ennobling deception, which because of the primitive nature of his thinking he never knew how to distinguish from ordinary, often vulgar lying, at some point he adopted his own "ideal" image—partly genuine,

partly imaginary—as the bard of the revolution and the proletariat. And although the revolution itself turned out not to be as he had imagined it, the thought of the possible loss of that image—of "spoiling the biography," was unbearable to him. Money, automobiles, houses—these were things that those around him needed. He himself needed something different. In the last analysis, he sold himself—not for money, but, for his own sake and that of others, in order to preserve the principal illusion of his life. By turns digging in his heels and rebelling, he knew all the same that he would not hold out but would rush back to the USSR, because whatever the revolution there was like, it alone could guarantee him fame as a great proletarian writer and leader while he lived, and a place for his ashes in the Kremlin wall when he was dead. In return for all this the revolution demanded of him what it demands of everyone—not honest service but slavishness and flattery. He became a slave and a flatterer. From being a writer and a friend of writers, he was put in a position that turned him into their supervisor. That too he accepted. One could make a long list of the other things he accepted. To put it simply, he turned into the extreme opposite of that lofty image that he had made his peace with the Soviet regime in order to preserve. Whether he was aware of how tragic this was I cannot say. Probably he was and was not, and probably to the extent that he was he tried to conceal it from himself and others with the help of new illusions, new elevating deceptions of the kind that he so loved and that destroyed him in the end.[4]

16

Zamiatin

"M. Gorky"

O ne of the most brilliant and original writers of the early Soviet period, Evgeny Zamiatin (1884–1937) is best known outside Russia as the author of *We* (1920), a dystopian satire whose influence can be seen in Aldous Huxley's *Brave New World* and George Orwell's *1984*. His many stories, essays, and plays, though less known, are in no way no less remarkable.[1] His belief in writing as heresy inevitably got Zamiatin into trouble with Soviet censors and literary authorities. By the late 1920s he had to relinquish his post as leader of the All-Russian Union of Writers; soon after, his works were banned and he found himself forced to write a letter to Stalin requesting permission to emigrate. After Gorky interceded on his behalf, permission was granted, and in 1931 Zamiatin and his wife left for the West. In 1932 they took up residence in Paris, and lived there in poverty until his death five years later—just months, as it turned out, after completing this memoir. [2]

◀ • ▶

"M. Gorky"

They lived together, Gorky and Peshkov. Fate bound them together, intimately and inextricably. They resembled each other strongly, and yet they were not quite identical. At times they argued and quarreled with each other, only to reconcile and go on living together. Their paths diverged only recently: in June of 1936 Alexei Peshkov died, while Maxim Gorky went on living. That man with the most ordinary of Russian workingmen's faces and with the modest name of Peshkov was the same man who chose for himself the pseudonym Gorky.

I knew them both. But I see no need to speak of the writer Gorky; his books speak best about him. I want to reminisce here about the man with a great heart and a great biography.

There are many remarkable writers who lack biographies and pass through life only as superbly gifted observers. Anton Chekhov, Gorky's contemporary and one of the subtlest masters of the Russian word, was one such. But Gorky could never remain simply a spectator; he was forever inserting himself into the very thick of events. He wanted to act. He was charged with the sort of energy that needed an outlet beyond the pages of a book, that had to spill over into life. His life was itself a book, a novel—and a fascinating one.

The background against which the opening chapters of that novel unfold is extraordinarily picturesque, and at the same time, I would suggest, symbolic.

On the high bank of a river: the crenellated walls of an ancient Kremlin, the golden crosses and domes of countless churches. Below, close to the water, endless warehouses, barns, wharves, stores. It is here that each summer a famous Russian fair would take place, accompanied by Homeric drinking and the making of millions; here Asiatic robes could be seen mingling with the frock coats of Russian merchants. And finally, on the facing bank, a piece of Europe: a forest of smokestacks, the fiery maws of blast furnaces, the iron hulls of ships.

This city, where Russia of the sixteenth century and Russia of the twentieth century live side by side, is Nizhnii Novgorod, Gorky's birthplace. The river on whose bank it grew is the Volga, home of the legendary Russian rebels Stenka Razin and Emelyan Pugachev, and subject of so many songs of the Russian barge-haulers. Gorky's primary tie is with the Volga; his grandfather was a Volga boatman.

The grandfather was a Russian version of the American type called a "self-made man." Having begun life as a barge-hauler, he finished it as the owner of three brickworks and several buildings. It was in the house of this miserly and stern old man that Gorky lived as a child. His childhood was brief: at the age of eight the boy was apprenticed to a shoemaker—thrown into the murky river of life and forced to fend for himself as best he could. Such was the system of education his grandfather had chosen for him.

From that point on it was a dizzying series of locales, adventures, professions, in a way that connects Gorky with Jack London and even, if you will, with François Villon (translated to the twentieth century and a Russian setting). Gorky the cook's assistant on a ship; Gorky the icon seller (what an irony!); Gorky the ragman; Gorky the baker; Gorky the stevedore; Gorky the fisherman. On the Volga and the Caspian Sea, in Astrakhan, the Zhigulev Mountains, the Mozdoksk steppe, Kazan. And later: the Don, Ukraine, Bessarabia, the Danube, the Black Sea, the Crimea, the Kuban, the Caucasus. All of the above on foot, in the company of picturesque homeless wanderers, sleeping by bonfires on the steppe, or in abandoned huts under overturned rowboats. How many events, meetings, friendships, fights, confessions in the night! What material for the future writer, and what a school for the future revolutionary!

His initiation into the order of revolutionaries came from Russian students for whom at that time rebellion was as sacred a tradition and as essential a characteristic as the blue student caps they wore. The "initiation" took place in Kazan. It was there that Gorky met up with one professional revolutionary. That led to a classic "going to the people": Gorky goes off to a village and works there as a sales clerk in a grocery shop. But of course both "sales clerk" and "employer" were only conspiratorial masks for the spreading of propaganda among the peasants. The target of the propaganda was evidently chosen unsuccessfully: one dark night the peasants set fire to the hut of the conspirators, who barely managed to save themselves. It may well be that night which was the origin of Gorky's antipathy for the Russian village and the Russian peasant and determined Gorky's turn to the city and the urban proletariat.

A few years later this romantic hobo published a book of stories, confronting his astonished reader not only with the hitherto unknown world of the tramps, but with the entire system of anarchist philosophy espoused by these stepsons of society. "The member of the housepainters' guild Alexei Peshkov," as his passport identified him, had turned into Maxim Gorky. He immediately became one of the most popular writers in Russia, particularly among the left-wing youth and the intelligentsia.

It seemed that now he could afford to forget about risky adventures and rest comfortably on his laurels. But his restless boat-hauler's blood was too hot to allow that: the same year that saw publication of the book by the writer Gorky saw the revolutionary Peshkov arrested by the police and dispatched "to the scene of the crime," to Tiflis, where he was confined in the Metekhsky fortress. The confinement did not last long. Gorky was released— but only in order to find himself in a Nizhnii Novgorod jail soon after, and exiled from there to a remote village.

Given the oppositional mood of the Russian intelligentsia at that time, these misadventures of Peshkov only fed the inordinately rapid growth of Gorky's fame. At just over thirty he was elected to the Imperial Academy of Sciences.* A revolutionary and former tramp, and member of the Imperial Academy? That was unheard of, scandalous. The elections were set aside by order of the emperor, Nicholas II, who noted on the Academy's report, "More than original!"

There is no denying His Majesty a certain amount of foresight: a few years later, in 1905, during the first Russian revolution, Gorky wound up in an isolation cell in the famous Peter and Paul Fortress. To lock up an academician in solitary confinement would, of course, have been slightly embarrassing.

The next chapters in the novel of Gorky's life are set abroad. He became a political émigré, cut off from Russia and from the Volga he so loved.

---

* In February 1902 Gorky was elected as an honorary academician in the area of belles lettres, an honor previously accorded to Tolstoy and Chekhov, among numerous other contemporaries—as it had been to Pushkin and Gogol in their time. When the election was vacated on the grounds that Gorky was under indictment for revolutionary agitation, Chekhov and Korolenko renounced their memberships in protest.

The opportunity to return to his country came only shortly before the revolution of 1917.*

For almost two years during the war I lived in England, where I had been sent as an engineer for the building of icebreakers that had been ordered by the Russian government. I returned to Petersburg only in the fall of 1917, and it was then that I met Gorky for the first time. Thus it happened that I met Gorky and the revolution simultaneously. For that reason the image of Gorky invariably arises in my memory connected with the new, post-revolutionary Russia.

A little white room—the office of the editor of the magazine *Annals* [*Letopis'*]. An autumn evening in Petersburg. Sporadic shooting out on the streets. This accompaniment is evidently something the editor is used to; it does not in the least interfere with the lively conversation.

The editor is Gorky, but the theme of the conversation is by no means literary; the question of my story is settled: Gorky likes it and has already sent it to the printer. What he wants to talk about is the icebreakers I built, and the technology, and my lectures on ship design. "Damn! I really envy you. I'll die a mathematical illiterate. It's a pity!"

An autodidact who in all his life spent only half a year in school, Gorky never ceased to study all his life. He knew a great deal. And his attitude toward things he didn't know was touching, childlike in its deference. I have had occasion to observe that trait in him many times.

The shots outside were getting closer, and I found myself recalling aloud the raids of German zeppelins and airplanes on England—and the measures the English used against them. Another thing that was new to Gorky, something he hadn't known—and, of course, should have known. But the secretary kept looking in the door with letters and galley proofs. "Look," Gorky proposed, "if you can wait just a little, we could go to my place for supper, eh?"

He lived on the top floor of an enormous Petersburg apartment house.

---

* Gorky in fact returned to Russia in 1913.

From its windows you could see, not far off to the right, the gray walls and golden spire of the Peter and Paul Fortress . . .

There were two hosts, Gorky and his second wife, M. F. Andreyeva, a former actress of the Moscow Art Theater. But around the table sat about a dozen guests. Some of them, as I learned afterward to my astonishment, had been living as "guests" in Gorky's house for years—as had been the way in the houses of Russian provincial gentry.

When Gorky had to do with a new person who for one reason or another interested him, he could be as bewitching as any woman. Not much was required: all he needed to do was to start telling of his adventures and the people he had met. He was a superb storyteller. The people he was talking about came to life and sat down at the table with us; you could see them and hear them. I was later to meet some of these people in a book of Gorky's, and it seemed to me that Peshkov had told of them better that evening than Gorky had in his book.

Three or four weeks later the occasional rifle shots that had been the accompaniment to my first meeting with Gorky turned into the chatter of machine guns and the dull booming of cannons. There was fighting on the streets of Petersburg. It was the October Revolution. Russia was like a huge ship, torn from the shore by a storm and carried off into the unknown. No one, including its new captains, knew whether the ship would shatter into smithereens or put in to some new continent.

One morning, sitting in Gorky's book-lined study, I told him of an idea for a fantastic novel that had come to me during those days. The setting was a spaceship on an interplanetary mission. When it is not far from its goal there is an accident, the space ship begins to fall. But the fall will last a year and a half! In the beginning my characters are, naturally, in a panic, but how will they behave once that passes? "Shall I tell you?" Gorky asked, twitching his mustache slyly. "Within a week, as if nothing had happened, they will start shaving and writing books and in general acting as if they had at least another twenty years to live. And really, that's the way. We've got to believe that we won't be shattered, otherwise all is lost."

And he believed.

Gorky the writer was sacrificed. For several years he turned into a sort of unofficial minister of culture, the organizer of public works projects for the derailed and starving intelligentsia. These projects were like the construction of a new Tower of Babel. They were meant to last for decades—the World Literature publishing house for the publication in Russian translation of the classics of all times and peoples; the Committee for Historical Plays to produce nothing less than stage versions of all the major events of world history; the House of the Arts to unite the practitioners of all the arts; the Scholars' House to unite all scholars and scientists.

In the capital, where there was no longer bread or electricity or streetcars, surrounded by destruction and catastrophe, these undertakings looked at best to be utopian. But Gorky believed in them ("We've got to believe"), and managed to infect the skeptical inhabitants of Petersburg with his own faith. Learned academicians, poets, professors, translators, and playwrights began to work in the institutions Gorky had created, with ever greater enthusiasm.

I found myself among the leadership groups of three or four of these institutions, of which Gorky was always the president. At that time I had to meet with him very often, and I remember how many times I found myself wondering in bemusement how many hours that man had in each of his days. How did he—half-wasted away with tuberculosis and constantly coughing through his cigarette-stained mustache—find the strength for all this activity? I once put the question to him. With a mysterious look he led me to the buffet, where he took out a dark little vial and explained that this was an extract from the miracle-working Chinese ginseng root, brought to him by an admirer from Manchuria. But I believe it would be more accurate to say that the real ginseng was his faith.

Another thing that sticks in my memory is the calm confidence with which he presided over meetings of professors and academicians. It would never have occurred to a casual observer that this man who cited names and dates with such ease—his memory was exceptional—was a former tramp and an autodidact. The only thing that set him apart from the others was his (to put it mildly) original way of pronouncing foreign names and words: he did not know a single foreign language.

One of Gorky's ideas at that time was to publish one hundred volumes of the best works by Russian writers, beginning with Chekhov. I mention this comparatively modest undertaking because it gave me the chance to witness something very curious: Gorky as critic of Gorky.

In those days there was no shortage of sycophants around Gorky. One of them, at a meeting of the editorial board of "The Hundred Volumes," began ecstatically reeling off the titles of Gorky's works, drenching each one of them with the sauce of compliments. Gorky looked down and tugged angrily at his mustache. When the speaker named his famous poem in prose, "Song of the Stormy Petrel"—an early work— Gorky interrupted: "You must be joking. I don't even like to think about that piece. It's a very weak piece." When several of Gorky's plays had been named, again with compliments, he cut in once more: "Sorry, gentlemen, but the author you're talking about is a bad playwright. There is one exception, *The Lower Depths,* but in my opinion all the rest is worthless."

Much later I happened to witness another incident of the same sort but entirely comic. Among Gorky's guests was a rather forward young "proletarian" writer. Gorky asked him what he was working on. The guest answered that he'd been about to start a novel in three volumes, but then thought better of it: "In our dynamic time only idiots write three-volume novels." Gorky replied icily: "Yes. You know, they say Gorky is also working on the third volume of his *Klim Samgin* . . ."

The young writer was ready to sink into the ground. But behind Gorky's jocular tone you could sense the pained awareness of his failure with that huge last novel of his.

Of all the things Gorky wrote after the revolution, perhaps the best were his remarkable recollections of Leo Tolstoy. They are particularly memorable for me because they opened a door into Gorky's inner world, into those mental apartments to which one is loath to admit strangers.

A literary evening had been arranged in Petersburg; its highlight was a reading by Gorky of his not-yet-published recollections of Tolstoy. He stood on the stage, tall, thin, stoop-shouldered; the reading glasses aged him by ten years. From my seat in the first row I could see his every movement. When in reading he approached the end of his memoirs, something very strange started to happen. It was as if he could no longer see through his glasses. He began to stammer and halt. Then he pulled off his glasses and you could see the tears rolling down his face. He sobbed aloud, muttered, "Forgive me," and walked off the stage into an adjoining room. This Gorky was not the writer and not the old revolutionary, but simply a man unable to speak calmly about the death of another man.

I know that there are many in Russia—and especially in Petersburg— who recall Gorky the man with gratitude. Dozens of people are indebted to him for their lives and freedom.

Everybody knew that Gorky and Lenin were close friends and that he was well acquainted with other leaders of the revolution. And when the revolution turned to terror, Gorky was the last channel of appeal and the last hope, and the wives and mothers of those arrested came to him. He wrote letters, swore over the phone, and in the most serious cases traveled himself to Moscow to see Lenin. Sometimes his intervention failed. On one occasion I was obliged to seek his help for an acquaintance of mine who had landed in the hands of the secret police. When he returned from Moscow, puffing angrily on his cigarette, Gorky told how Lenin had reprimanded him, saying: "It's time you knew that politics is a dirty business in general, and that it's better for you not to mix in to these stories."

But Gorky kept on "mixing in."

It is my impression that the policy of terror was one of the principal reasons for Gorky's temporary split with the Bolsheviks and for his departure abroad.

It so happened that shortly before he left I found myself on the same train from Moscow to Petersburg with Gorky. It was night, the rest of the passengers were already sleeping. The two of us stood together in the corridor for a long time, watching the sparks fly by in the darkness, and talking about the great Russian poet Gumilyov, who had been shot several months earlier. This was a man both politically and literarily alien to Gorky, but Gorky had nonetheless done everything he could to save him. As he told it, he had already obtained a promise in Moscow that Gumilyov's life would be spared, but the Petersburg authorities had caught wind of that and hastened to carry out the sentence on the spot. I never saw Gorky so upset as he was that night.

About a year and a half later, in a remote Russian village where I was spending the summer, I chanced to see an issue of the provincial Communist newspaper with a headline in big black letters: "Gorky is Dead!" The headline was the work of some journalistic wit; the article was about the "political death" of Gorky, who had published abroad some protest at the trial of the Socialist Revolutionaries (a Russian party that adhered to the Second International) then going on in Moscow.

That was the high point of Gorky's falling out with the Bolsheviks. And not only with them but also with himself, because alongside "Peshkov," a man with an almost feminine softness of heart, there plainly dwelt within him a Bolshevik.

When the revolution turned from ruthless destruction to the building of a new life, Gorky returned to Russia. What had led to his leaving in the first place was evidently forgotten. When I tried to look inside him and find out what "Peshkov" now thought (or rather, felt), the answer I got was: "*They* have very lofty goals. And for me that justifies everything."

In a recent article about some new Russian novels (in *Marianne*) I mentioned Gorky and called him "Le pape de la Littérature soviétique." A curious typographical error turned "pape" into "pope"—the word for an Orthodox priest. By a strange coincidence this error virtually repeated what Gorky used jokingly to say about himself. He called himself a "literary archpriest."

I think that with this joke Gorky defined most accurately his position in Soviet literature. There were of course not a few authors who presented themselves to Gorky in order "to kiss the pope's slipper." Such devout pilgrims bored Gorky, and he always hastened to see them out the door. "He looks at me as if I were some jackass decked out in a uniform and medals," he fumed about one such visitor. But for the majority of writers who came to him he was not a man with literary medals but simply a man; they came not to Gorky but to Peshkov.

I witnessed the beginning and development of Gorky's friendship with the group of young Petersburg writers who called themselves the Serapion Brothers; I, too, was very close to them. This group came into being in the Petersburg House of Arts, where in the early revolutionary period Gorky succeeded in organizing a kind of literary university (in which I was one of the lecturers). When several talented writers emerged from among the auditors of this university, Gorky felt like a happy father; he took care of them like a brood hen with her chicks. Even later, when these chicks had matured and become something like classics of the new Soviet prose, Gorky preserved his very touching relationship with them.

Most curious is the fact that this whole group of writers was, literarily speaking, more "left" than Gorky; it sought new forms, and sought them in areas far from the realism of Gorky—which made their attitude toward him all the more telling: it was love pure and simple for the man himself.

For this group, as for all Soviet writers who were not Communists but only fellow travelers, the most difficult period was in the years from 1927 to 1932. Soviet literature fell under the command—there is no other word for it—of the organization of "proletarian writers" (in Soviet jargon, RAPP). Their chief talent was party membership and a purely military decisiveness. These energetic young people took on themselves the task of "reeducating" all the other writers. Nothing good, needless to say, came of this. Some of those being reeducated fell silent; in the works of others false notes began to be heard, of a kind that grated even on the most undemanding ear. Anecdotes about the censor multiplied; among the fellow travelers dissatisfaction grew.

When we would meet I often had occasion to speak about these things with Gorky. He would smoke and chew his mustache, saying nothing.

Then he would stop me, saying: "Wait a minute, I've got to write this story down."

The importance of those "notes" became clear to me only much later, in 1932. In April of that year, to everyone's surprise, a genuine literary revolution occurred: a government decree branded RAPP's activities "a hindrance to the development of Soviet literature," and the organization was disbanded. Gorky alone showed no surprise. I am utterly certain that it was he who had prepared that act, and done it like a highly skilled diplomat.

At this time he was living not in Petersburg but in Moscow. There the house of the millionaire Riabushinsky had been put at his disposal, though he used it only at intervals; most of his time was spent at his dacha a hundred kilometers from Moscow. Stalin's own dacha was nearby, and the leader took to visiting his "neighbor" Gorky more and more often. Closeted over a bottle of wine, the "neighbors"—one with his invariable pipe, the other with his cigarette—would talk for hours . . .

I think I will not be mistaken if I suggest that the correction of many "excesses" in government policy and a gradual softening of the dictatorship's rule resulted from these friendly conversations. This is a role of Gorky's whose recognition and assessment can come only in the future.*

I will not go into the hows and whys of it here, but I came to see that I would be better off going abroad for a time. In those years it was no easy thing for a writer with my "heretical" reputation to obtain a passport for foreign travel. I sought Gorky's intervention. He argued that I should wait until spring (of 1931): "Things are going to change, you'll see." In the

---

* Zamiatin's optimism in this case has not been borne out by the documents published since the fall of the Soviet Union. Gorky may well have tried to get Stalin to moderate some of his policies, but the record also shows him to have supported many harsh and illiberal ones in his last years, and it seems clear that Stalin consistently and successfully used him for his own purposes. Writing from France in 1936, Zamiatin could not have known that Gorky had been living under what amounted to house arrest, his movements limited and his visitors screened. (Gorky had in fact confided to a visitor the previous year: "It's as if they've put up a fence around me—a line I cannot cross. They've surrounded me. . . . Not backward, not forward! This is something unprecedented!")

spring nothing changed. And so Gorky, somewhat reluctantly, agreed to obtain permission for me to go abroad.

One day Gorky's secretary phoned with an invitation to come to Gorky's dacha that evening for dinner. I remember well that exceptionally hot day and the thunderstorm—a tropical downpour—in Moscow. Gorky's car plowed through a wall of water, carrying me and several others who had been invited to his place.

The dinner was a "literary" one; there were some twenty people at the table. In the beginning Gorky sat there tired and silent. Everyone was drinking wine, but he had a glass of water in front of him: wine was forbidden him. After a while he rebelled and poured himself a glass of wine, followed by another and another, and became his old self.

When the storm ended I went out onto the enormous stone terrace of the dacha. Gorky followed immediately and said: "Your passport is arranged. But you could, if you wanted, return the passport and stay." I said that I would be going. Gorky frowned and went back to his guests in the dining room.

It was already late. Some of the guests would be staying over at the dacha; others, myself included, were returning to Moscow. In parting, Gorky said: "When will we see each other again? If not in Moscow, then perhaps in Italy? If I'm there, you must come to see me! In any case, till we meet again, eh?"

That was the last time I saw Gorky.

Our paths, however, were to cross one more time, in a purely literary way and quite recently. A month or so before his death a film company in Paris decided to make a film of his famous play *The Lower Depths,* from my scenario.[3] Gorky was informed about this and answered that he was pleased at my involvement, would like to see the adaptation, and would be waiting for the manuscript.

By the time the manuscript was ready for mailing, there was no reason to send it: the addressee had departed this world.

1936

17

Eikhenbaum
"Gorky as a Russian Writer"

Boris Mikhailovich Eikhenbaum (1886–1959), a leading historian, theoretician, and critic of Russian literature (and the preeminent interpreter of Tolstoy in his generation), wrote this piece for a Leningrad conference devoted to Gorky in December 1927, shortly before the writer's first return to Russia from his seven-year expatriation in Germany and Italy. At this time Eikhenbaum was turning away from text-centered study to the larger questions of literature's functioning in society—and to the ways in which the writer's "behavior" and public image join (and may even on occasion outweigh) his texts themselves in the public's sense of him. The great Russian writers of the nineteenth century had sometimes sought, and sometimes simply had attributed to them, a role in society that went beyond the creation of literary art, though the art invariably remained the ground of their fame. But in Gorky's case primacy of the writing was not always easy to discern. He quickly became not simply a public figure but, in the full modern sense of the word, a celebrity—both in his country and in the wider world—though it must immediately be added that, in a characteristic Russian gesture, he reinvested that celebrity in taking on the most serious political and social roles.

It is this new model of the Russian writer—amounting in its uniqueness to a kind of sport or mutation—which Eikhenbaum sets out to trace and explain in his short but exemplary article. [1]

◄•►

"Gorky as a Russian Writer"

Leo Tolstoy not only marks the end of a whole period of Russian literature that began in the 1840s; he also represents at its fullest the figure of the Russian writer in the nineteenth century. Yasnaya Polyana was the last haven of that powerful dynasty. Tolstoy's flight from it [in the last days of his life] was not only a private act but a social one—a renunciation of his own power in the presentiment of a new age, an age of wars and revolutions.

Russian literature had already begun to lose its earlier, exclusively high position by the 1870s. Tolstoy had preserved his power by turning away from the periodicals with their editorial pettinesses and polemics to make of his Yasnaya Polyana an impregnable literary fortress, and of himself a literary magnate, independent of editors, publishers, and the whole literary marketplace. This was the last effort of the Russian writer to hang onto his significance as spiritual and intellectual leader.

Beyond the confines of this fortress the Russian writer was turning into a journalist, a reporter, a filler of orders. Russian literature was becoming overgrown with "the press." Writing was becoming a more widespread activity, a mass profession serving the various tastes and needs of society. Quality in culture was turning into quantity, a constant and inevitable law of history. . . .

If in 1845 [Russia's leading critic] Belinsky had been obliged to accept and approve the appearance of second-rate fiction as something needed for the sake of its broad accessibility, by the end of the 1870s critics were beginning to speak of something else—of the way the reading public was expanding, the way the "cheap press" was taking on importance, and of literature's obligation to meet the new demands of the book market. As a leading journal wrote in 1877, "The Russian reader has simply been spoiled by Russian literature, and Russian literature in turn has been spoiled by its history, which was centered exclusively on developing the more or less 'higher' forms of writing."

The time when one could speak of our literature as a monolithic thing (in contrast to that of Western Europe, where "boulevard literature" and magazines of the most diverse kinds had long existed) was clearly coming

to an end. It was no longer a matter of creating literature "for easy reading,"
as in the 1840s, but of the differentiation and stratification of literature in
response to a whole spectrum of indicators, purposes, and appetites. The
very notion of being a writer became vague once anyone with nothing more
definite to do could set up as a writer.

That was the literary situation in the 1880s and 1890s, in the midst of
which Maxim Gorky's appearance was at once the most sensational and the
most characteristic event.

2

Gorky learned literature on the run and entered it with a boldness instilled
in him by nature itself.* His appearance in the ranks of the Russian writing
intelligentsia was no simple or ordinary fact. His very pseudonym, "Maxim
Gorky [literally, Maxim the Bitter], which now sounds no worse than any
other in the 1890s, carried a special sense, a sense of a challenge, daring
and defying tradition. Nor was this merely a pseudonym. It was the gesture
of a new man who had arrived as an emissary from the anonymous masses,
from the unruly Volga region. This pseudonym announced a new voice, a
new tone, a man whose appearance in literature was capable of producing
panic—or at least scandal.

And so it was. Maxim Gorky's success in the beginning was not so
much literary as social.† An intruder had appeared in Russian literature, an
autodidact, not a member of the intelligentsia, someone fitting none of the

---

* In the first published version Eikhenbaum wrote "the age"; in his book, *Moj
vremennik*, it becomes "nature"—and then, in a copy he gave a friend, he substituted
"history."

† Yuri Tynianov points to another aspect of the social nature of Gorky's initial success: "The Russian provincial cities lived from the appearance of one Gorky story to another. People suddenly began to read and talk about him who had never read anything
before, and in the far corners of the country some even learned to read and write just to be
able to read him. Literature had changed because its meaning had changed: a new reader
had come to expect direct and immediate answers to the question of how to live." Jurij
Tynjanov, "Aleksej Maksimovič Gor'kij," *Literaturnyj sovremennik*, no. 6 (1938): 171.

familiar labels or categories. What was important was less that he wrote about tramps and hoboes than that he himself had lived in that environment and come out of it. What was important was that he had seen, known, and done things that no Russian writer had seen, known, or done before him. Behind his stories, from the beginning, loomed the legend of his life. Postcards with his picture sold like hotcakes; this man with a working-man's simple face, wearing a simple blouse, did not look like any Russian writer. He could hardly make his way down a street; everyone wanted to gawk at him. Tolstoy was not alone in having a special, "ethnographic interest" in him; so too did the public. It was hardly accidental that his literary successes were accompanied by all sorts of scandals (like the confrontation with the public in the Moscow Art Theater). Nor was it by chance that false Gorkys began turning up in various cities, or that reporters dogged him everywhere. He was inspected and studied like something exotic. This was fame, no question about it; but it was a risky sort of fame, created by the crowd's curiosity about a new variety of Russian writer. By itself fame did not open the way into real literature, which was the business of the so-called intelligentsia. And the intelligentsia had reasons for keeping its distance from this newcomer.

Within Russia's writing intelligentsia two layers existed at the time. The top one comprised a closed literary group that came to be called "decadents," and later "symbolists." Hostile to the civic tradition, this group, basing itself in philosophy and religion, set about developing a new poetry, renewing forgotten esthetic traditions, and seeking to save literature from "the press," from topicality; this was an "aristocratic" group, preferring the forms of patronage to those of paid professional work. From the other layer, catering precisely to the civic-minded, there emerged a group of new prose writers, sharing no particular set of literary principles, basing itself chiefly on journalism and working on old and tired material—an intermediate group, though a worthy enough one.

But the law of historical contrast required something brash and unexpected; the top layer needed to be opposed not by an intermediate layer but by a bottom one. Lofty and complex philosophical poetry needed to be opposed by "bad" literature, strong by virtue of its naïvete, banality, and accessibility. What was needed at this moment, in other words, was not so much a new literature as such, but rather a new version of the writer, a new version of the writer's fate.

3

Gorky became a celebrity before he had time to turn around and look at Russian literature or consider how he looked in it. It was as if history had shoved him into the ranks of Russian writers for reasons of its own (taking the risk on itself). He began by diligently describing nature and portraying hoboes of genius—and this turned out to be not simply "colorful," but precisely what was needed. On the ruins of prose and verse Gorky began speaking in a semi-poetic way about the sea, about prostitutes, about people who had sunk to the bottom, in a way that was verbose and exaggerated, with embellishments and metaphors and a garish lyricism. And that kind of "romanticism" proved to be just what people wanted. In the 1870s all this had been described dutifully and ethnographically—as in the novel by one P. Zarubin, *The Dark and Bright Sides of Russian Life* (1872), where the author warns readers that "the present composition does not, in the strict sense, have the customary form of a novel," and that in it he will be showing the Russian in a petit-bourgeois setting—"as public figure, as family man, as merchant and tradesman on the Volga, and, finally, as autodidact and independent thinker." Gorky developed this last point of Zarubin's program and made the déclassé, petit-bourgeois tramp into a romantic hero.

Now that he had won fame, Gorky began to reflect on his fate as a writer. The sensation he had caused was waning, but his work had only begun. Fame had been so strange and sudden in coming that he was now forced to consider his future behavior, because in a fate like his a great deal necessarily depended on behavior. He needed to learn not only how to write, but how to be a writer. There were many who tutored him in how to write. But there was no one from whom he might learn how to be a writer with "a fate" except Tolstoy.

Accordingly, Gorky now begins to follow Tolstoy with a watchful eye, as if seeking to ferret out some secret of his. He both admires and unmasks, surprised and pleased at what he sees and discovers; Tolstoy is a sly old man, a wizard who speaks listlessly of God, a mischief-maker who peppers his speech with indecent words. And yet—he is a great man, not least by virtue of his fate and his behavior. Gorky inspects him from all sides and in various situations, he studies his gestures, his hands, his fingers. Warily he keeps track of Tolstoy's attitude toward him and notes resentfully: "His interest in me is an ethnographic interest. In his eyes I am only a specimen of a tribe he knows little about."

And so Gorky is no longer the rebel come to insult "the Russian intelligentsia" and its literature. His concern is with the problem of his own self-preservation as a writer. He becomes a member of the intelligentsia himself, sharing its social ideals and its fortunes in the struggle for them. The legends are replaced by long autobiographical novels. People have become accustomed to Gorky, and it seems that they will soon turn their attention elsewhere.

History, however, really did have designs on him, and his observation of Tolstoy had not been in vain: a time came when everything began to depend on "behavior." The intelligentsia of that upper stratum which had created "symbolism" found itself crushed and helpless; for it, the revolution was a tragic surprise and meant the collapse of its whole cause. The revolution frightened Gorky insofar as it threatened to sweep away the very ideals he so cherished of public life and culture, but it contained no tragedy for him. He had never been infected by those bacilli which were infecting others who had passed through "decadence" and known the temptations of mystic dreams and leanings over abysses. Less complex, less intellectual, strong in the sensation of being connected with the dark mass of the Russian people, proud to believe in man and in reason, Gorky wound up serving as *a stand-in for the Russian intelligentsia,* its representative and advocate before the harsh tribunal of the revolution.

And so, at the height of this new phase of his behavior comes the meeting with Blok, who is already on the brink of perishing and who, as if from the beyond, judges Gorky—and in his person the Russian intelligentsia. After his *Reminiscences of Tolstoy,* the most remarkable of Gorky's works is his *Fragments from My Diary,* and within it the pages about Blok. They barely understood each other. To Gorky, Blok sounded delirious, while Blok's problem was not so much understanding Gorky as believing him: "You're hiding. You're hiding your thoughts about spirit, about truth. What for?" Blok in those days was already possessed by wrath and an urge for death and destruction, while Gorky knew just one thing—Man—and was therefore possessed by an urge for self-preservation. This was a conversation between two cultures, if not two breeds. And the defeated one is judging the victorious one. Blok is tormented by the question of consciousness: "We have become too clever to believe in God, yet not strong enough to believe in ourselves. As a basis for life and faith there are only God or oneself. Humanity? Can anyone really believe in the reasonableness of humanity after the last war, with new, inevitable, and even crueller wars in the offing?" And Gorky? He outlines for Blok the notion that inert matter becomes psychic energy and will eventually turn the whole world into sheer psyche. "I don't understand," Blok says again, gloomily. And so it transpires that Gorky is defending the Russian intelligentsia while Blok reviles it . . .

Yes, history had its designs on Gorky. The zeal for self-preservation, even if unconscious, even if dogmatic, even if somewhat disingenuous ("You're hiding"), turned out to be what was needed. The tragic consciousness that was Blok's strength leads inevitably to ruin—and the more heroic it is, the more surely it does so. But there are periods in history when people are needed who do not so much think about truth as believe in the rationality of humankind and see the future not as a tragic dead end but as the apotheosis of reason. If truth is single, then Blok is its crazy knight and Gorky its faithful servant.

18

Adamovich

"Maxim Gorky"

Georgy Viktorovich Adamovich (1894-1972) left the Soviet Union in 1922; from 1923 on he lived in Paris, where his articles and reviews in the Russian-language press quickly established him as one of the most influential émigré critics of the interwar period. It is from the point of view of a Russian living abroad and contemplating Gorky's apparently unqualified embrace of Stalin's regime that Adamovich writes, with a directness, a balance (refusing to reduce Gorky to the sum of his weaknesses), an independence, and a literary acumen that make this obituary a document of lasting value.[1]

◄ • ►

"Maxim Gorky"

It would be natural enough to entitle these remarks "In Memory of Gorky," but there is something that gets in the way of that. The phrase suggests graveside reverence, and it would hard for us to do reverence at Gorky's grave with full sincerity or unclouded gratitude—impossible, in fact. Of course one may bow to an enemy. To say "Gorky is our class enemy" might seem to explain everything, but in fact it explains nothing. Whatever else may have persisted in the emigration, one finds very little "class" hostility, "class" intolerance, "class" zeal; we have long since been open to all sorts of reconciliations and forgettings. But in this case it is not a matter of forgetting; it is a matter of pain, deep and sharp. Gorky, to put it rhetorically, is an open wound for us. If we had not been so attached to him, if he had meant less to us, there would be no wound. Forgetting oftener than not arises from indifference, and in this case we are not yet indifferent. We can forget nothing.

People will say, "That means you have cut yourself off definitively from Russia . . ." And it is true that there, in Russia, an apotheosis, a posthumous triumph of an unprecedented kind is taking place. The masses of the people are grieving over the passing of a writer from the people, and a people's regime is rendering him honors in the name of the whole people. But who will be deceived by this deification? There are surely many there who share our misgivings. This is not mere supposition; we know it for a fact.

At this point of course, no one has the right to judge Gorky. We do, however, have a right to declare that he always pretended—and pretended with cause—to an authority that was not only specifically artistic but moral as well; that he stood on the very brink of spiritual greatness, only to suffer, in his final years, a terrible downfall . . . With his intelligence and his sensitivity, he must have understood that. He must have sensed that the game was lost, that in any case its outcome was hardly what he had aimed at.

Was he a great writer? The most demanding and competent minds of Gorky's generation disputed such a characterization, and they dispute it to this day. The following generation approached Gorky differently. From their vantage point what was most significant about him came into focus; namely, the presence of an exceptional nature, an original and generous personality. That generation refused to apply purely esthetic criteria in evaluating Gorky, and I believe they were right to do so. What is important in Gorky is the wellspring, the deep source of the writing. Behind his every line you feel the man, with whose advent something changed in the world, and whether that line is good or bad in itself, it is all the same more valuable than any impeccable but impersonal exercise could be. But a qualification is immediately necessary: Gorky seems to flaunt his singularity; he hypnotizes us with it, and perhaps leads us astray. Some writers (like Chekhov) are diffident about their own power or originality, while others go out of their way to flaunt it. Gorky of course belonged to the second type, as Mayakovsky did in poetry. How far the reality matched the impression is not entirely clear. Mistakes are possible.

But it is precisely his external image as a writer that led to his immediate and dizzying success. In the nineties Russia was despondent from "stagnation," from quiet and calm; the only significant spiritual fact in those years—the preaching of Tolstoy—was powerless to change that mood. Some simpler and coarser nourishment was needed, a nourishment designed for readers of a different emotional age group—and it was into that lull, so charged with "stormy" forebodings, that Gorky burst with his fables about falcons and stormy petrels—the man everyone had been waiting for. What did he bring along with him? No one could say for sure—but that was hardly the point. Did it really matter whether his home-grown, instinctive Nietzscheanism was mixed with anarchism or Marxism? At the time such nuances were hardly of crucial importance. There was, on the one hand, the "yoke of oppression," and on the other hand everything that sought to do away with it; on the one hand "arbitrary power," on the other everything that struggled against it. The distinction was not always straightforwardly political; more frequently it followed a winding path that separated any sort of light from any sort of darkness. Whatever was talented, fresh, and new was part of the forces of light, among whom Gorky was accepted as a trailblazer and a leader.

Gorky's early works have aged badly and, apart from two or three stories and one or two plays, they are now unreadable. It is interesting that Gorky grew as an artist just at the time he was being solemnly pronounced a has-been as a writer*—a time when, having lost some of his previous zeal, he had replaced his earlier creative self-intoxication with sober creative concentration. It was as if he had come down off his stilts and planted his feet on the ground.

In *The Town of Okurov,* in *Childhood* and other autobiographical narratives; in a long list of beautiful stories, some of them simply unforgettable, such as "The Mumbly-Jumblies" [*"Strasti-mordasti"*] or "About Cockroaches," we encounter a multitude of sharply drawn characters. Are these images authentic? Not entirely. They are rather silhouettes, sketches,

* Reference is to D. Filosofov's much-discussed article of 1907, "The End of Gorky."

arranged into an uncommonly picturesque "panorama." Their animation is somewhat superficial, and the liveliness of the author's hand makes one wonder whether Gorky is not by the nature of his gift a master of the sketch (and whether he doesn't do violence to that gift when he tries to be a poet). The doubt is legitimate enough, but it vanishes the more you read of him. The author of *My Universities* has a theme and a general conception which he follows; he has, in other words, what makes a writer a poet. The characters he has created form a mass and, taken together, raise the question of the position of man in the world, an agonizing and tragic question that at times is presented in a narrowly historical-national framework (Russia and Russian conditions at the beginning of the twentieth century), and at other times transcends that framework to stand forth in all its timelessness and boundlessness. This alone is what accounts for the passionate, worldwide sympathy that Gorky's writing elicited. The "mass" reader, as so often happens, saw and felt the importance of his contribution to the spiritual life of the age better than did the professional evaluators.

But Gorky's gift is undermined at its very core. He was a writer with two souls, as Chukovsky observed long ago, and in his struggle both came to be weakened. His rationalism in any case clipped the wings of the poet in him.

Art—and literature as one branch of it—has in its purest specimens always been unaccountable. If it has posed questions, they have been only the kind that are not susceptible of practical solution. Gorky, conceiving his projects as a true poet and confronting his theme at a very deep level, will then proceed to offer answers that are acceptable and accessible to all: culture, progress, the reordering of human relations, even courtesy, even neatness or punctuality . . . The answers are fine in themselves. For Russia in particular they are doubly good and relevant. But if these answers are elevated to the status of an artistic motif, the artistry immediately turns shallow—for, worthy as these concepts are, it is not of them that the human soul dreams, nor to them that it aspires in its moments of greatest intensity. In Gorky social concern was always very strong. One might well think that he deliberately and consciously impoverished himself by not making a place in his created world for those aspirations and drives that can never be quenched; this is to say that, being moved by sympathy for people, he found all his humane notions, true or not, compelling him to subordinate the dangerous powers of poetry to the principles of rationality and utility. But the point is precisely that Gorky's creation is least of all "humane," and in this his duality shows most clearly. However softhearted or even sentimental Gorky may have been in daily life, in his writing he is fierce and cruel. Inspiration strikes him only in the face of evil, and no other Russian writer has left a gallery of types to rival the Gorky gallery, which is one to make the heart sink. There is no light in Gorky's creation. Nor does it contain much eroticism; it is a world closed in on itself and in the grip of some intractable aridity.

In Russian literature Gorky is close to the writer he most hated—Dostoyevsky. This claim is only seemingly paradoxical. It is not justified merely by the "taste for suffering" characteristic of both poets; it is justified most of all by the way their characters are deracinated, divorced from the land—and by the elemental aloneness that is the result. The dry and melancholy aftertaste of the work is mitigated in Dostoyevsky's case by his eschatological insights and yearnings, and in Gorky's by his faith in the power of reason. That is not enough, however, to get rid of the aftertaste entirely. The attitude toward nature, incidentally, is a telling one. Dostoyevsky scarcely noticed nature. Gorky not infrequently deigns to describe it, but his attitude is unwaveringly hostile. Nature is an enemy; he rings constant variations on that theme. In this sense he breaks the most profound poetic traditions and is immeasurably far from Tolstoy's intuition, or from Goethe, with whom "the waves of the sea spoke." Where they approached the world—which is to say, nature—as proprietors, well disposed to it, he approached it as a conqueror, his heart forever poisoned with fear and suspicion. A random stylistic trifle: Gorky's famous phrase, "the sea laughed." That phrase troubled Tolstoy; it irritated him—and not only because Tolstoy was a stylist from a different school, but also because his grasp of nature was too accurate and too organic. If Gorky had truly felt nature, he would have forgone literary coquettishness. The sea doesn't "laugh," which means that something different needed to be said. The phrasing gives Gorky away.

All this, taken together, gives Gorky's books a tinge of "intentionality," to use Dostoyevsky's brilliant word for the city of St. Petersburg. In fairness to Gorky it must be noted that such "intentionality" has been in the air in our time and is one of the things that make him genuinely contemporary. He would be even more "representative" of modern literature were it not for his psychological anticuriosity—but here, evidently, that dark enigmatic hatred of Gorky's for the truth takes over; this is something he has spoken of for years, and no less insistently than about his hostility toward nature (see, for a particularly vivid example, his correspondence with Leonid Andreyev). Gorky is a realist, but the only real object of realism—the human psyche—is of no interest to him, and he rejects any "digging" or "poking" around in it. He recognizes individuality only in action, but what is behind the action, or above it, he shows no interest in knowing. It may be that a lot of this is to be explained in terms of his social and pedagogical pursuit of control and discipline, which I have already mentioned. But there is something else at work here as well: his mistrust of the individual soul and his difficulty in believing that digging around in the dirt—*any* dirt—can lead at length to the light.

It may well be that this tragic, stifling, issueless atmosphere that hangs over Gorky's creation is what kept him from producing the great book he always dreamed of. Flashes of the earlier, portraitistic manner can be found right up to his last years, but the two broad canvases he attempted—*The Artamonov Business* and *The Life of Klim Samgin*—are clear failures. This is particularly true of *Klim Samgin,* the novel that Gorky certainly realized would be his final work. As a picture of mores *Klim Samgin* is vivid enough, and it is useful in portraying the moods of the prerevolutionary Russian intelligentsia. But it is sadly indicative that, after so much searching and questioning—and in a time when those searchings and questionings were being put to such terrible tests—Gorky, in his old age, should have produced a book that was merely "useful." A writer's last works constitute a kind of key; though they may be weaker than his earlier ones, they nonetheless reflect his mind, heart, and conscience with particular clarity.

Gorky did not retain the attention he once aroused. Passionate sympathy has turned, little by little, into an indifference which, according to many accounts, is especially strong over there, in Russia. It is growing everywhere, and is unlikely to change in the future.

But that is not what distances us from Gorky. What creates the distance is his position in Russia in recent years, and what he has been doing there—the whole horrifying, never-to-be-forgotten perversion of the idea of the artist as teacher and the poet as moralist. I need not explain what I am referring to. Everyone knows.

Respect for Gorky, I repeat, requires us to believe that he was aware of his downfall. Hatred for the truth could not keep him from seeing and understanding it this time. Comparison with the fate of other major Russian writers must have led him to uncomfortable and sorrowful thoughts. There was no other "patent of nobility" available to him. Whoever maintains that everything in Gorky's fate was as it had to be, natural, and even splendid, does his memory a great disservice.

Afterword
The Presence of M. Gorky

After sketching some of the parameters of Gorky's historical singularity, the introduction to this book ended by suggesting that the time might be ripe for separating the writing from the writer, and the writer from the legend that went by his name, acted in that name, and for four decades led an evolving life of its own.

A trial separation of that sort is more than legitimate, it is overdue. But it entails unusual difficulties. One reason is indicated by Adamovich when he writes: "What is important in Gorky is the wellspring, the deep source of the writing. Behind his every line you feel the man, with whose advent something changed in the world." To be sure, Adamovich wrote this in 1936, when Gorky's presence on the cultural scene was still enormous; today the permanence of the change he represented and helped bring about is by no means clear. And still the difficulties persist, for the simple reason that Gorky's texts themselves resist the separation.

A striking constant of Gorky's prose is his presence *in* (as well as anterior to) his texts, and its effect is to confer a tinge of memoir on them all, whatever their genre. Often, particularly in the short stories, he figures explicitly as witness. On occasion he is a participant as well, though when he is, his presence serves usually as a precipitating factor, and what he does reveals little of significance about him—hence V. S. Pritchett's contention that "what [Gorky] lived and saw, not what he constructed, contains his importance."[1]

Gorky himself confessed to having little skill in fashioning structures, and little patience with what he was quick to dismiss as "verbal intoxication." His contemporary Alexei Remizov noted that "where there was any complexity at all, Gorky closed his eyes and would not hear. . . . [He] was repelled by Joyce, and Proust, and all the complexity of verbal art."[2] For him, experience was the crux. He once defined a writer as "essentially a

man more saturated than others with experience, with knowledge of life—
[one] who has come to possess, in response to the pressure of that experience, an ability to cloak his impressions in the form of images."[3] "Anyone
who has seen and experienced a great deal," he declared to the young
Vsevolod Ivanov in 1921, "has an obligation to write."[4]

Pursuing that obligation over the decades made "Gorky" part of a
single ongoing creative act—made the creator, in other words, part of the
creation and the implied author a quasi-character, to be glimpsed with
some frequency and intuited constantly, without ever being made the object of sustained contemplation.

Something analogous took place on the stage of public life, where Gorky
was constantly to be found organizing, opining, and advocating, playing
different roles and taking radically different positions with different people,
all the while adamantly refusing to acknowledge (let alone engage with) his
contradictions. Confronting them might well have fueled great writing; certainly it would have taken his talent into new regions and greater depths.
But he preferred to let his contradictions appear (or not) seriatim. His
friend Leonid Andreyev saw this: "All his life looking with one eye (albeit
by turns, never with both at the same time), Gorky ended by establishing
one-eyedness as an article of faith."[5]

So it is that, whatever one may be tempted to say about Gorky in any of
his roles or aspects, the record will always contain something that shows it to
be inadequate and thus relativizes it. The effect is to make his capacity to surprise seem inexhaustible. That effect, observable at all stages of his career,
becomes particularly acute in the early 1920s when, as Arkadii Vaksberg
notes, one can regularly find Gorky thinking one thing, saying another, while
doing a third. Absolutely nothing he said or wrote can be taken in isolation
from what he was saying or writing about the same thing to others. "He was
able to take quite different positions on the very same matters, to the baffle-
ment of objective historians and the unbounded joy of non-objective ones,
for each had the opportunity to find in him what he wanted to find."[6]

The conclusion is inescapable that the Gorky phenomenon—the elu-
sive presence at the core of the biography, the writing (fiction and nonfic-

tion alike), and all the public acts and pronouncements (not to mention all the accounts and judgments by others)—is problematic in the way that the greatest narrative art is problematic. Precisely because this "Gorky" is so rife with lacunae and contradictions, he ultimately demands that we approach him as we would a fictional character, analyzing his actions through the same sorts of inference we bring to the understanding and interpreting of characters in novels. (It is surely indicative that some of the most detailed and objective Russian studies of him published since the end of communism have been labeled "documentary novel," "artistic research," and the like.)

Excessive though it may seem to estheticize Gorky in this way, it is, I believe, not only just but inescapable. V. S. Pritchett has claimed that "he was really a life rather than a novelist," and more than one contemporary observed that he was an artist in the fashioning of his life (no less, and perhaps more, than in the fashioning of his work). That life can be seen by turns as romantic drama, political drama, social and domestic drama, and finally as tragedy, its import and essential pathos only deepened by its having been played out on the stage of history. So one has every right to say of Maxim Gorky what Baudelaire said of Balzac—that he himself was, in the end, "the most heroic, the most singular, . . . [and] the most poetic of all the characters" he ever created. We can forget none of this when we address any aspect of the unlikely and astonishing phenomenon that goes by his name. No one but he could have invented such a character and such a story.

Often a second- or third-rate writer, Gorky could produce works of undoubted greatness, too, and move even detractors to admit as much. But always there was a still larger claim beyond the admission. Thus Merezhkovsky, writing about Gorky's autobiographical *Childhood* in 1916, two years after its publication, ranks it not simply among the best but among the "eternal" Russian books. All the same, he insists, there is no comparing Gorky with Tolstoy and Dostoevsky as artists. "They can be judged for what they say, Gorky cannot: *more important than anything he says is what he is.*" But it is precisely what he is that restores him to their company: "The very possibility of such a phenomenon as he, . . . as a lived thing, is no less significant than the whole artistic creation of Tolstoy and Dostoevsky.[7]

Boris Pasternak was to concur a decade later, finding Gorky "a great titan" and "an oceanic individual." He hailed "the depth and virtual ubiquity of [his] soul." It was not enough, Pasternak maintained, to regard him as a great writer: "A reader's natural gratitude," he wrote to Gorky in 1928, "is subsumed into a broader appreciation for you as, thanks to your exceptional nature, a unique historical personification."[8] This ascription of larger-than-life features, together with the use of a vocabulary reserved for figures in literature on the scale of Hamlet, Don Quixote, or Oblomov, is all the more telling when voiced by a writer so alien in so many ways to Gorky. Examples could easily be multiplied. Marina Tsvetayeva and Osip Mandelstam, too, found Gorky to be the embodiment of an era.

With a prescience that can only be called uncanny, even sober Anton Chekhov seems to have sensed the possibility of such a view as early as 1903 (when Gorky's career was still in an early phase and all three of Russia's twentieth-century revolutions were still in the future). "In my opinion," he wrote to a correspondent, "a time will come when people will forget Gorky's works, but he himself will hardly be forgotten even in a thousand years.[9]

For present purposes the relative plausibility of Chekhov's prediction is less important than its implicit reminder of how, at this point in history, the complex phenomenon that goes by the name of Maxim Gorky—no less than the best of the writing signed with that name—clamors for rediscovery.

Notes

Introduction: The Singularity of M. Gorky

1. See E. V. Ivanova, "*'Očerki i rasskazy'* v otzyvax sovremennikov," in AN SSSR, In-t mirovoj literatury im. A.M. Gor'kogo, *Gor'kij i ego epoxa*, vyp. 2 (Moscow: "Nauka," 1989), 132.

2. Gejr X'etso [Geir Kjetsaa], *Maksim Gor'kij: Sud'ba pisatelja* (Moscow: "Nasledie," 1997), 136.

3. N. Berberova, *Kursiv moj; avtobiografija* (Moscow: "Soglasie," 1996), 211. In English: *The Italics are Mine,* Philippe Radley, trans. (New York: Harcourt, Brace and World, 1969).

4. Valentina Xodasevič, *Portrety slovami* (Moscow, 1987), 111.

5. Viktor Šklovskij, *Udači i poraženija Maksima Gor'kogo* (Tiflis: "Zakkniga," 1926), 6-7, 39.

6. K. Čukovskij, *Dnevnik, 1901–1929* (Moscow: Sovetskij pisatel', 1991), 110, 133. Cf. Kornei Chukovsky, *Diary, 1901–1969,* Victor Erlich, ed., Michael Henry Heim, trans. (New Haven: Yale University Press, 2005), 50, 61.

7. Vyač. Vs. Ivanov, "Počemu Stalin ubil Gor'kogo?" *Voprosy literatury,* 1993, no. 1: 104–5. Translated as "Why Did Stalin Kill Gorky?" *Russian Studies in Literature: A Journal of Translations* 30, no. 4 (Fall 1994): 5–40.

8. Berberova, *Kursiv moj,* 229.

9. See his *Untimely Thoughts,* Herman Ermolayev, ed. and trans. (New York: Paul S. Eriksson, 1968).

10. M. Gor'kij, *Polnoe sobranie sočinenij. Pis'ma v dvadcati četyrex tomax,* 6 (Moscow: "Nauka," 2000), 196 (hereafter abbreviated as *Pis'ma*). This was a widespread view among the Russian intelligentsia of the time. Mikhail Gershenzon identified and attacked it in the 1909 volume *Vekhi*. A member of the Russian intelligentsia, he wrote, "is a person who has literally lived *outside himself* since youth, recognizing as the only worthy object of his interest and sympathy something outside of his own personality: the people, society, or the state. . . . For three-quarters of a century now [our public opinion] has stubbornly adhered to the same overriding principle, that it is egotistical and indecent to think about one's own personality, and that the only real man is the one who thinks about public affairs, is interested in society's problems, and works for the common good." (*Vekhi, Landmarks,* Marshall S. Shatz and Judith E. Zimmerman, trans. and ed. [Armonk: M. E. Sharpe, 1994], 51.)

11. *Pis'ma,* 9 (2002), 205.

12. Letter of October 27, 1928, to O. F. Ivnina-Lošakova; quoted in L. Spiridonova, *M. Gor'kij: Novyj vzgljad* (Moscow: IMLI-RAN, 2004), 47–48.

13. D. S. Mirsky, *Contemporary Russian Literature, 1881–1925* (London: G. Routledge, 1926), 118.

14. Čukovskij, *Dnevnik, 1901–1929,* 122.

15. K. Čukovskij, *Dnevnik, 1930–1969* (Moscow: Sovremennyj pisatel', 1994), 131.

16. "Maksim Gor'kij," *Enciklopedija dlja detej,* 9 (Moscow: Avantat, 1999), 144.

17. Quoted in N. N. Primočkina, "Merežkovskie i Gor'kij v gody revoljucii," in R. Devis and V.A. Keldyš, eds., *S dvux beregov: Russkaia literature XX veka v Rossii i za rubežom* (Moscow: IMLI-RAN, 2002), 748.

18. The formulation is Arkadii Vaksberg's, in his *Gibel' burevestnika* (Moscow: Terra Sport, 1999), 176.

19. Rossijskaja Akademija nauk, In-t mirovoj literatury im. A. M. Gor'kogo, *Vokrug smerti Gor'kogo. Dokumenty, fakty, versii. Serija M. Gor'kij, Materialy i issledovanija,* vyp. 6 (Moscow: IMLI-RAN, 2001).

20. Čukovskij, *Dnevnik, 1930–1969,* 46. Cf. Chukovsky, *Diary, 1901–1969,* 262.

21. M. Agurskij, "M. Gor'kij i Yu. N. Danzas," *Minuvšee. Istoričeskij al'manax,* no. 5 (Paris: Atheneum, 1988), 376.

22. Vitalij Šentalinskij, *Raby svobody. V literaturnyx arxivax KGB* (Moscow: Parus, 1995), 316.

Part One. Gorky: Memoirs

Chapter 1. Lev Tolstoy

1. *M. Gor'kij i ego epoxa. Materialy i issledovanija,* vyp. 4 (Moscow: "Nauka," 1995), 236.

2. B. M. Ejxenbaum, "O L've Tolstom," in his *Skvoz' literaturu* (Leningrad: "Academia," 1924), 63.

3. Lidija Ginzburg, *Zapisnye knižki. Vopominanija. Esse* (Sankt-Peterburg: "Iskusstvo-SPB," 2002), 133.

4. Alfred Kazin, "Maxim Gorky and the Master Friends," in his *The Inmost Leaf* (New York: Harcourt Brace, 1955), 28–29.

5. Isaiah Berlin, "Tolstoy and Enlightenment," in his *Russian Thinkers* (London: Hogarth Press, 1978), 243. (For a subtle analysis of their relationship, viewed in terms of the literary and cultural situation in Russia at the turn of the century, see Boris Eikhenbaum's article "Gorky as a Russian Writer" in this volume.)

6. *Pis'ma,* 2 (1997), 13–14.

7. Letter of 9 February 1900. L. N. Tolstoj, *Polnoe sobranie sočinenij* (Jubilee Edition) (Moscow: Xudožestvennaja literatura, 1933), 72: 303.

8. Letter to M. M. Kocjubinskij, 8 (21) November 1910; in *Pis'ma,* 8 (2001), 181.

9. Letter to A. V. Amfiteatrov, 4 (17) November 1910, ibid., 176–77.

10. Kazin, "Maxim Gorky and the Master Friends," 32.

11. L. N. Tolstoj, *Polnoe sobranie sočinenij* (Jubilee Edition), 57 (Moscow: Xudožestennaja literatura, 1952), 176–77.

12. See Hugh McLean, "A Clash of Utopias: Tolstoy and Gorky," *Tolstoy Studies Journal* 14 (2002).

13. V. S. Baraxov, "Tolstoj—eto celyj mir," in his *Iskusstvo literaturnogo portreta* (Moscow: "Nauka," 1976), 94.

14. M. L. Slonimskij, *Literaturnyj sovremennik*, 1941, no. 6: 107; quoted in M. Gor'kij, *Polnoe sobranie sočinenij* (Moscow: "Nauka," 1968–76), 16: 581 (henceforth abbreviated as *PSS*).

15. Ibid.

16. Šklovskij, *Udači i poraženija Maksima Gor'kogo*, 209.

17. This argument is made by Dan Levin, who calls the book "a short lyric novel" and finds it built around "an interplay of thoughts and passions and beliefs that comprise the characters and relations" of the four men in question. See his *Stormy Petrel: The Life and Work of Maxim Gorky* (New York: Appleton-Century, 1965), 227

18. Tolstoj, *Polnoe sobranie sočineij* (Jubilee Edition), 63 (1934), 112.

19. *PSS*, 16: 260–312.

20. In the original book publication of this memoir and in some others, the line reads, "He'd have flown off anyway" (*On by i tak udral*); in later editions the verb *udaril* is substituted, meaning "he'd have pounced," though the syntax is now strained to the point of strangeness. In either case Tolstoy is regretting the fact that he shouted. The first version makes better sense, but I have opted for the later version since it expresses Tolstoy's unsentimental acceptance of predation among animals.

21. Viktor Šklovskij, "O Peskove-Gor'kom," in his *Gamburgskij sčet: Stat'i, vospominanija, èssè* (Moscow: Sovetskij pisatel', 1990), 318.

22. Čukovskij, *Dnevnik, 1901–1929*, 110. Cf. Chukovsky, *Diary, 1901–1969*, 49–50.

23. N. Valentinov [pseud. of Nikolaj Vladislavovič Vol'skij], "Vstreči s Maksimom Gor'kim," *Novyj žurnal*, kn. 78 (1965): 137–38.

24. M. Gor'kij, *Xudožestvennye proizvedenija. Stat'i. Zametki* (Arxiv A. M. Gor'kogo, 12) (Moscow: "Nauka," 1969), 214.

25. Ibid., 214–15.

Chapter 2. Anton Chekhov

1. *Pis'ma*, 1 (Moscow: "Nauka," 1997), 283.

2. Ibid., 321.

3. *PSS*, 6: 476.

4. Čukovskij, *Dnevnik, 1901–1929*, 110.

5. Alfred Kazin, "Maxim Gorky and the Master Friends," in his *The Inmost Leaf* (New York: Harcourt Brace, 1955), 35.

Chapter 3. L. A. Sulerzhitsky

1. "Pis'ma k čitateljam 'L. A. Suleržickij,'" *PSS*, 16: 471–81. I have slightly abridged the article, principally by dropping the didactic frame.

Chapter 4. Leonid Andreyev

1. In his *And Even Now*.

2. Pavel Basinskij, *Gor'kij* (Moscow: Molodaja gvardija, 2005), 253.

3. Ibid., 254. Basinskij points out that Gorky, though nonreligious, lived like any true Christian with no fear of death whatsoever. "Here, surely," he comments, "is the main paradox of his world view. Gorky is a believer without God, an immortal without faith in an afterlife. His faith lay within the bounds of human reason. And to the extent that human reason, as he believed, is boundless, everything that lies outside its boundaries for the time being is without significance."

4. Their opposing views on these matters produced an extraordinary correspondence, a counterpart in many ways to the classic correspondence between Flaubert and George Sand. See Peter Yershov, ed., *Letters of Gorky and Andreyev, 1899–1912* (New York: Columbia University Press, 1958). In Russian their correspondence can be found, along with much other material bearing on the Gorky-Andreyev relationship, in *Gor'kij i Leonid Andreev: neizdannaja perepiska [Literaturnoe nasledstvo,* 72 [Moscow: "Nauka," 1965]).

5. *PSS*, 16: 313–57. Gorky's memoir appeared in a memorial volume for Andreyev published at the beginning of 1922 and, in expanded form, in the second edition of that volume later the same year.

Chapter 5. A. A. Blok

1. *PSS*, 17: 221–28. First published in the ill-fated journal *Beseda* in the first two issues (1923), Gorky subsequently included it in his *Fragments from My Diary. Reminiscences.*

Part Two. Gorky: *Fragments from My Diary*

1. Quoted in I. A. Revjakina, "Kniga M. Gor'kogo 'Zametki iz dnevnika. Vospominanija' v kritike russkogo zarubež'ja 20–30-x godov," *Social'nye i gumanitarnye nauki, Otečestvennaja i zarubežnaja literatura,* Serija 7, Literaturovedenie, 1999–2 (Moscow, 1999), 162.

2. *PSS*, 17: 568.

3. A. Voronskij, "Vstreči i besedy s Maksimom Gor'kim," in his *Iskusstvo videt' mir* (Moscow: Sovetskij Pisatel', 1987), 64.

4. A contemporary critic, K. Loks, wrote of Gorky's turning away from literature as conventionally construed, with the result that "the more the line is blurred between a short

story in the old sense of the word and a real document or observation, the more sharply and authentically does the narration develop." Quoted in B. Ejxenbaum, *O literature* (Moscow: Sovetskij pisatel', 1987), 526.

5. M. Gor'kij, *Xudožestvennye proizvedenija. Stat'i. Zametki* (Arxiv A. M. Gor'kogo, 12), (Moscow: "Nauka," 1969), 31.

6. *PSS,* 18: 401–2.

7. *PSS,* 17: 7–15. The other sketches translated here all come from this volume.

8. See Andrew Barrett and Barry P. Scherr, eds. and trans., *Maksim Gorky: Selected Letters* (New York: Oxford University Press, 1997); Peter Yershov, ed., *Letters of Gorky and Andreev, 1899–1912* (New York: Columbia University Press, 1958). See also *Correspondance Romain Rolland, Maxime Gorki* (Paris: A. Michel, c. 1991); *M. Gor'kij i R. Rollan: Perepiska (1916–1936)* (Moscow: "Nasledie," 1995); *A. M. Gor'kij i M. I. Budberg: Perepiska, 1920–1936* (Moscow: IMLI-RAN, 2001).

9. Gor'kij, *Xudožestvennye proizvedenija. Stat'i. Zametki,* 5–6.

10. Ibid., 193. Unless otherwise indicated, further references are to this volume; pages numbers will be indicated in brackets in the text.

11. M. Gor'kij, *Polnoe sobranie sočinenij: Varianty k xudožestvennym proizvedenijam,* 6 (Moscow: "Nauka," 1978), 478.

Part Three. Others on Gorky

Chapter 15. Khodasevich: "Gorky"

1. For a full account of the journal's importance and fate, see I. Vajnberg, "Žizn' i gibel' berlinskogo žurnala Gor'kogo 'Beseda'," *Novoe literaturnoe obozrenie,* 1996, no. 21: 361–75.

2. Letter of 2 February 1928, in Ol'ga Kaznina and G. S. Smith, "D. S. Mirsky to Maksim Gor'ky: Sixteen Letters (1928–1934)," *Oxford Slavonic Papers* 26 (1993): 93. For a colorful description of the Gorky household, see Nina Berberova, *Moura: The Dangerous Life of the Baroness Budberg* (New York: New York Review Books, 2005), 100–109. See also Valentina Xodasevič, *Portrety slovami: očerki* (Moscow: Sovetskij pisatel', 1987), 125–26; and Arkadij Vaksberg, *Gibel' burevestnika* (Moscow: Terra Sport, 1999), 72 and passim.

3. Vladislav Xodasevič, *Nekropol': Vospominanija. Literatura i vlast'. Pis'ma B.A. Sadovskomu* (Moscow: SS, 1996), 149–75; first published in *Sovremennye zapiski* [Paris], 63 (1937).

4. "Gor'kij<2>," ibid., 207–208; first published in *Sovremennye zapiski* (Paris), 70 (1940).

Chapter 16. Zamiatin: "M. Gorky"

1. For a collection of the essays, see *A Soviet Heretic / Yevgeny Zamyatin,* Mirra Ginsberg, trans. and ed. (Chicago: University of Chicago Press, 1970). For the fiction, see

Yevgeny Zamyatin, *The Dragon: Fifteen Stories,* Mirra Ginsburg, trans. and ed. (Chicago: University of Chicago Press, 1976).

2. E. Zamjatin, *Lica* (New York: Izd-vo imeni Čexova, 1955), 81–98.

3. *Les Bas-fonds,* directed by Jean Renoir and starring Jean Gabin and Louis Jouvet, came out in 1936.

Chapter 17. Eikhenbaum: "Gorky as a Russian Writer"

1. "Pisatel'skij oblik M. Gor'kogo," in B. Ejxenbaum, *O literature* (Moscow: Sovet-skij Pisatel', 1987), 437–42.

Chapter 18. Adamovich: "Maxim Gorky"

1. "Maksim Gor'kij," *Sovremennye zapiski* (Paris) 61 (1936): 389–93.

Afterword: The Presence of M. Gorky

1. V. S. Pritchett, "The Young Gorky," in his *The Living Novel and Later Apprecia-tions* (New York: Random House, 1964), 433.

2. In a letter of 1927 to A. I. Tsvetayeva, sister of the poet, Gorky wrote: "I do not un-derstand verbal intoxication generally, not in anyone." (E. B. Pasternak and E. V. Paster-nak, "Boris Pasternak v perepiske s Maksimom Gor'kim," AN SSSR, *Izvestija, Otdelenie literatury i jazyka* 45, no. 3 [1986]: 224.) Remizov, "Aleksej Maksimovič Gor'kij, 1868–1936," in *Maksim Gor'kij: Pro et Contra* (St. Petersburg: Izd-vo russkogo xristian-skogo gumanitarnogo instituta, 1997), 219–20.

3. M. Gor'kij, *Istorija russkoj literatury* (Arxiv A. M. Gor'kogo, 1) (Moscow: Gosu-darstvennoe Izd-vo "Xudožestvennaja literatura," 1939), 3–4.

4. Vs. Ivanov, "Vstreči s Gor'kim," in *Maksim Gor'kij v vospominanijax sovremen-nikov* (Moscow: "Xudožestrvennaja literatura," 1981), 2: 70.

5. Quoted in Pavel Basinskij, *Gor'kij* (Moscow: Molodaja gvardija, 2005), 266. Cf. Zamiatin's notes for a lecture on contemporary Russian prose, from the early 1920s: "I will be speaking to you about two very dissimilar writers. The first is young, wild, stubborn, rebellious, and prizes above all else freedom, liberty, anarchy . . . He is an eternal, unre-lenting rebel . . . The second knows everything; for him, everything is decided, there are no questions. The second is a man of programs and laws. The first is an anarchist, the sec-ond a Marxist . . . The first is given entirely to feeling, the second to reason. And both these writers together bear a single name: Maxim Gorky. . . . In Gorky's work one can clearly trace . . . the struggle of two diametrically opposed principles—a struggle for indi-viduality and a struggle against individuality, for the collective." (N. N. Primočkina, "M. Gor'kij i E. Zamjatin," *Russkaja literatura,* 1987, no. 4: 133.)

6. Arkadij Vaksberg, *Gibel' burevestnika* (Moscow: Terra Sport, 1999), 158.

7. Dmitrij Merežkovskij, "Ne svjataja Rus' (Religija Gor'kogo)," in his *Akropol'* (Moscow: Izd-vo "Knižnaja palata," 1991), 305. The article was first published in the newspaper *Russkoe slovo* for 11 September 1916. Emphasis added.

8. "Boris Pasternak v perepiske s Maksimom Gor'kim," 265.

9. Letter to A. I. Sumbatov (Yuzhin), 26 February 1903. The context offers no clue as to Chekhov's basis for this assertion.